Beginning WebGL
for HTML5

Brian Danchilla

Apress·

ISBN-13 (pbk): 978-1-4302-3996-3

ISBN-13 (electronic): 978-1-4302-3997-0

President and Publisher: Paul Manning
Lead Editor: Ben Renow-Clarke
Technical Reviewer: Massimo Nardone
Editorial Board: Steve Anglin, Ewan Buckingham, Gary Cornell, Louise Corrigan, Morgan Ertel, Jonathan Gennick, Jonathan Hassell, Robert Hutchinson, Michelle Lowman, James Markham, Matthew Moodie, Jeff Olson, Jeffrey Pepper, Douglas Pundick, Ben Renow-Clarke, Dominic Shakeshaft, Gwenan Spearing, Matt Wade, Tom Welsh
Coordinating Editor: Jennifer Blackwell, Anamika Panchoo
Copy Editor: Nancy Sixsmith
Compositor: SPi Global
Indexer: SPi Global
Artist: SPi Global
Cover Designer: Anna Ishchenko

Distributed to the book trade worldwide by Springer Science + Business Media New York, 233 Spring Street, 6th Floor, New York, NY 10013. Phone 1-800-SPRINGER, fax (201) 348–4505, e-mail orders-ny@springer-sbm.com, or visit www.springeronline.com.

For information on translations, please e-mail rights@apress.com, or visit www.apress.com.

Apress and friends of ED books may be purchased in bulk for academic, corporate, or promotional use. eBook versions and licenses are also available for most titles. For more information, reference our Special Bulk Sales–eBook Licensing web page at www.apress.com/bulk-sales.

Any source code or other supplementary materials referenced by the author in this text is available to readers at www.apress.com. For detailed information about how to locate your book's source code, go to www.apress.com/source-code.

For Tressa, as fierce as she is delicate.

Contents at a Glance

Contents

About the Author

Brian Danchilla is a freelance developer and author. He is ZEND PHP Certified and cowrote the book *Pro PHP Programming*. Brian is a contributing author to the book *HTML5 Games Most Wanted*, and was a technical reviewer for *Foundation HTML5 Animation for JavaScript* and *PHP: The Good Parts*. Brian is a seasoned web developer, Java, and OpenGL programmer and has a BA degree as a double major in computer science and mathematics. After several years working within the computer industry, he is now enjoying the flexibility of freelance work. Brian has a strong desire and ability to learn new technologies and APIs and is an avid technical reader. When not programming, Brian likes to play guitar, cook, and travel. He resides in Saskatoon, SK, Canada with his fiancée Tressa.

About the Technical Reviewer

Massimo Nardone holds a Master of Science degree in Computing Science from the University of Salerno, Italy. He works currently as a PCI QSA and Senior Lead IT Security/Cloud Architect for IBM Finland. With more than 19 years of work experience in Cloud Computing, IT Infrastructure, Mobile, Security and WWW technology areas for both national and international projects, Massimo has worked as a Project Manager, Software Engineer, Research Engineer, Chief Security Architect, and Software Specialist. He worked as visiting lecturer and supervisor for exercises at the Networking Laboratory of the Helsinki University of Technology (Helsinki University of Technology TKK became a part of Aalto University) for the course of "Security of Communication Protocols." He holds four international patents (PKI, SIP, SAML and Proxy areas). His beloved baby girl, Neve, was born some days ago and he wants to welcome her from the bottom of his heart.

Acknowledgments

I would like to thank my family: mom, dad, Robert, Karen, Tressa. Longtime friends: Vince, Nick, and Tim. It was not always a smooth journey during this book project and I am very grateful for your support along the way.

Thank you to everyone on the Apress team who was involved with this book. I would especially like to thank Ben Renow-Clarke for getting this book title off the ground, Louise Corrigan for valuable editing advice, Anamika Panchoo for her coordinating skills, and the technical reviewing of Massimo Nardone.

Thank you to my university professor David Mould for introducing me to OpenGL, and my high school art teacher Mrs. Robinson for helping develop my artistic side.

I am thankful for having a good set of headphones and a great music collection that enabled me to zone in and work. Thanks to late, late night *Super Mario Galaxy 2* sessions for inspiration and coffee, lots of coffee.

Several years ago, I first read computer graphics books and thoroughly enjoyed the experience. Now I am blessed to have been able to write my own book about an exciting new technology, WebGL.

Introduction

WebGL (Web-based Graphics Language) is a wonderful and exciting new technology that lets you create powerful 3D graphics within a web browser. The way that this is achieved is by using a JavaScript API that interacts with the Graphics Processing Unit (GPU). This book will quickly get you on your way to demystify shaders and render realistic scenes. To ensure enjoyable development, we will show how to use debugging tools and survey libraries which can maximize productivity.

Audience

Beginning WebGL for HTML5 is aimed at graphics enthusiasts with a basic knowledge of computer graphics techniques. A knowledge of OpenGL, especially a version that uses the programmable pipeline, such as OpenGL ES is beneficial, but not essential. We will go through all the relevant material. A JavaScript background will certainly help.

When writing a book of this nature, we unfortunately cannot cover all the prerequisite material. Baseline assumptions about the reader need to be made. The assumptions that I have made are that the reader has a basic knowledge of 2D and 3D computer graphics concepts such as pixels, colors, primitives, and transforms. Appendix B quickly refreshes these concepts. It is also assumed that the reader is familiar (though need not be an expert) with HTML, CSS, and JavaScript. Although much of the book makes use of plain "vanilla" JavaScript, we will use some jQuery. Appendix A discusses newer HTML5 concepts and a quick jQuery crash course that will be essential for properly understanding the text. Appendix D provides a complete reference for further reading on topics that are presented throughout the book.

What You Will Learn

This book presents theory when necessary and examples whenever possible. You will get a good overview of what you can do with WebGL. What you will learn includes the following:

- Understanding the model view matrix and setting up a scene
- Rendering and manipulating primitives
- Understanding shaders and loving their power and flexibility
- Exploring techniques to create realistic scenes
- Using basic physics to simulate interaction
- Using mathematics models to render particle systems, terrain, and fractals
- Getting productive with existing models, shaders, and libraries

- Using the Three.js framework
- Learning about GLGE and philoGL frameworks and a survey of other frameworks available
- Debugging and performance tips
- Understanding other shader uses, such as image processing and nonphotorealistic rendering
- Using an alternate framebuffer to implement picking and shadowmaps
- Learning about current browser and mobile support and the future of WebGL

Book Structure

It is recommended that you start by reading the first two chapters before moving on to other areas of the book. Even though the book does follow a fairly natural progression, you may choose to read the book in order or skip around as desired. For example, the debugging section of Chapter 9 is not strictly essential, but is very useful information to know as soon as possible.

Chapter 1: Setting the Scene

We go through all the steps to render an image with WebGL, including testing for browser support and setting up the WebGL environment, using vertex buffer objects (VBOs), and basic shaders. We start with creating a one color static 2D image, and by the end of the chapter have a moving 3D mesh with multiple colors.

Chapter 2: Shaders 101

Shaders are covered in depth. We show an overview of graphics pipelines (fixed and programmable), give a background of the GL Shading Language (GLSL), and explain the roles of vertex and fragment shaders. Next we go over the primitive types and language details of GLSL and how our WebGL application will interact with our shaders. Finally, we show several examples of GLSL usage.

Chapter 3: Textures and Lighting

We show how to apply texture and simple lighting. We explain texture objects and how to set up and configure them and combine texture lookups with a lighting model in our shader.

Chapter 4: Increasing Realism

A more realistic lighting model—Phong illumination—is explained and implemented. We discuss the difference between flat and smooth shading and vertex and fragment calculations. We show how to add fog and blend objects; and discuss shadows, global illumination, and reflection and refraction.

Chapter 5: Physics

This chapter shows how to model gravity, elasticity, and friction. We detect and react to collisions, model projectiles and explore both the conservation of momentum and potential and kinetic energy.

Chapter 6: Fractals, Height Maps, and Particle Systems

In this chapter we show how to paint directly with the GPU, discuss fractals, and model the Mandlebrot and Julia sets. We also show how to produce a height map from a texture and generate terrain. We also explore particle systems.

Chapter 7: Three.js Framework

The Three.js WebGL framework is introduced. We provide a background and sample usage of the library, including how to fall back to the 2D rendering context if necessary, API calls to easily create cameras, objects, and lighting. We compare earlier book examples to the equivalent Three.js API calls and introduce tQuery, a library that combines Three.js and jQuery selectors.

Chapter 8: Productivity Tools

We discuss the benefits of using frameworks and the merit of learning core WebGL first. Several available frameworks are discussed and the GLGE and philoGL frameworks are given examples. We show how to load existing meshes and find other resources. We list available physics libraries and end the chapter with an example using the physi.js library.

Chapter 9: Debugging and Performance

An important chapter to help identify and fix erroneous code and improve performance by following known WebGL best practices.

Chapter 10: Effects, Tips, and Tricks

Image processing and nonphotorealistic shaders are discussed and implemented. We show how to use offscreen framebuffers that enable us to pick objects from the canvas and implement shadow maps.

Afterword: The Future of WebGL

In the afterword, we will speculate on the bright future of WebGL, the current adoption of it within the browser, and mobile devices and what features will be added next.

Appendix A: Essential HTML5 and JavaScript

We cover some of the changes between HTML 4 and 5, such as shorter tags, added semantic document structure, the `<canvas>` element, and basic JavaScript and jQuery usage.

Appendix B: Graphics Refresher

This appendix is a graphics refresher covering coordinate systems, elementary transformations and other essential topics.

Appendix C: WebGL Specification Odds and Ends

Contains part of the WebGL specification, available at http://www.khronos.org/registry/webgl/specs/latest/, which were not covered in the book, but are nonetheless important.

Appendix D: Additional Resources

A list of references for further reading about topics presented in the book such as HTML5, WebGL, WebGLSL, JavaScript, jQuery, server stacks, frameworks, demos, and much more.

WebGL Origins

The origin of WebGL starts 20 years ago, when version 1.0 of OpenGL was released as a nonproprietary alternative to Silicon Graphics' Iris GL. Up until 2004, OpenGL used a fixed functionality pipeline (which is explained in Chapter 2). Version 2.0 of OpenGL was released that year and introduced the GL Shading Language (GLSL) which lets you program the vertex and fragment shading portions of the pipeline. The current version of OpenGL is 4.2, however WebGL is based off of OpenGL Embedded Systems (ES) 2.0, which was released in 2007 and is a trimmer version of OpenGL 2.0.

Because OpenGL ES is built for use in embedded devices like mobile phones, which have lower processing power and fewer capabilities than a desktop computer, it is more restrictive and has a smaller API than OpenGL. For example, with OpenGL you can draw vertices using both a glBegin...glEnd section or VBOs. OpenGL ES only uses VBOs, which are the most performance-friendly option. Most things that can be done in OpenGL can be done in OpenGL ES.

In 2006, Vladimar Vukićević worked on a Canvas 3D prototype that used OpenGL for the web. In 2009, the Khronos group created the WebGL working group and developed a central specification that helps to ensure that implementations across browsers are close to one another. The 3D context was modified to WebGL, and version 1.0 of the specification was completed in spring 2011. Development of the WebGL specification is under active development, and the latest revision can be found at http://www.khronos.org/registry/webgl/specs/latest/.

How Does WebGL work?

WebGL is a JavaScript API binding from the CPU to the GPU of a computer's graphics card. The API context is obtained from the HTML5 <canvas> element, which means that no browser plugin is required. The shader program uses GLSL, which is a C++ like language, and is compiled at runtime.

Without a framework, setting up a WebGL scene does require quite a bit of work: handling the WebGL context, setting buffers, interacting with the shaders, loading textures, and so on. The payoff of using WebGL is that it is much faster than the 2D canvas context and offers the ability to produce a degree of realism and configurability that is not possible outside of using WebGL.

Uses

Some uses of WebGL are viewing and manipulating models and designs, virtual tours, mapping, gaming, art, data visualization, creating videos, manipulating and processing of data and images.

Demonstrations

There are many demos of WebGL, including these:

- `http://www.chromeexperiments.com/webgl`

- `https://code.google.com/p/webglsamples/`

- `http://aleksandarrodic.com/p/jellyfish/`

- Google Body (now `http://www.zygotebody.com`), parts of Google Maps, and Google Earth

- `http://www.ro.me/tech/`

- `http://alteredqualia.com/`

Supported Environments

Does your browser support WebGL? It is important to know that WebGL is not currently supported by all browsers, computers and/or operating systems (OS). Browser support is the easiest requirement to meet and can be done simply by upgrading to a newer version of your browser or switching to a different browser that does support WebGL if necessary. The minimum requirements are as follows:

- Firefox 4+

- Safari 5.1+ (OS X only)

- Chrome 9+

- Opera 12alpha+

- Internet Explorer (IE)—no native support

Although IE currently has no built in support, plugins are available; for example, JebGL (available at `http://code.google.com/p/jebgl/`), Chrome Frame (available at `http://www.google.com/chromeframe`), and IEWebGL (`http://iewebgl.com/`). JebGL converts WebGL to a Java applet for deficient browsers; Chrome Frame allows WebGL usage on IE, but requires that the user have it installed on the client side. Similarly, IEWebGL is an IE plugin.

In addition to a current browser, you need a supported OS and newer graphics card. There are also several graphics card and OS combinations that have known security vulnerabilities or are highly prone to a severe system crash and so are blacklisted by browsers by default.

Chrome supports WebGL on the following operating systems (according to Google Chrome Help (`http://www.google.com/support/chrome/bin/answer.py?answer=1220892`):

- Windows Vista and Windows 7 (recommended) with no driver older than 2009-01

- Mac OS 10.5 and Mac OS 10.6 (recommended)

- Linux

Often, updating your graphics driver to the latest version will enable WebGL usage. Recall that OpenGL ES 2.0 is based on OpenGL 2.0, so this is the version of OpenGL that your graphics card should support for WebGL usage. There is also a project called ANGLE (Almost Native Graphics Layer Engine) that ironically uses Microsoft Direct X to enhance a graphics driver to support OpenGL ES 2.0 API calls through conversions to Direct X 9 API calls. The result is that graphics cards that only support OpenGL 1.5 (OpenGL ES 1.0) can still run WebGL. Of course, support for WebGL should improve drastically over the next couple of years.

Testing for WebGL Support

To check for browser support of WebGL. there are several websites such as http://get.webgl.org/, which displays a spinning cube on success; and http://doesmybrowsersupportwebgl.com/, which gives a large "Yay" or "Nay" and specific details if the webgl context is supported. We can also programmatically check for WebGL support using modernizr (http://www.modernizr.com).

Companion Site

Along with the Apress webpage at http://www.apress.com/9781430239963, this book has a companion website at http://www.beginningwebgl.com. This site demonstrates the examples found in the book, and offers an area to make comments and add suggestions directly to the author. Your constructive feedback is both welcome and appreciated.

Downloading the code

The code for the examples shown in this book is available on the Apress website, http://www.apress.com. A link can be found on the book's information page, http://www.apress.com/9781430239963, under the Source Code/Downloads tab. This tab is located underneath the Related Titles section of the page. Updated code will also be hosted on github at https://github.com/bdanchilla/beginningwebgl.

Contacting the Author

If you have any questions or comments—or even spot a mistake you think I should know about—you can contact the author directly at bdanchilla@gmail.com or on the contact form at http://www.beginningwebgl.com/contact.

CHAPTER 1

■ ■ ■

Setting the Scene

In this chapter we will go through all the steps of creating a scene rendered with WebGL. We will show you how to

- obtain a WebGL context
- create different primitive types in WebGL
- understand and create vertex buffer objects (VBOs) and attributes
- do static two-dimensional rendering
- create a program and shaders
- set up the view matrices
- add animation and movement
- render a three-dimensional model

A Blank Canvas

Let's start by creating a HTML5 document with a single `<canvas>` element (see Listing 1-1).

Listing 1-1. A basic blank canvas

```
<!doctype html>
<html>
    <head>
        <title>A blank canvas</title>
        <style>
                body{ background-color: grey; }
                canvas{ background-color: white; }
        </style>
    </head>
    <body>
        <canvas id="my-canvas" width="400" height="300">
                Your browser does not support the HTML5 canvas element.
        </canvas>
    </body>
</html>
```

The HTML5 document in Listing 1-1 uses the shorter `<!doctype html>` and `<html>` declaration available in HTML5. In the `<head>` section, we set the browser title bar contents and then add some basic styling that will change the `<body>` background to gray and the `<canvas>` background to white. This is not necessary but helps us to easily see the canvas boundary. The content of the body is a single canvas element. If viewing the document with an old browser that does not support the HTML 5 canvas element, the message *"Your browser does not support the HTML5 canvas element."* will be displayed. Otherwise, we see the image in Figure 1-1.

Figure 1-1. *A blank canvas*

▓ **Note**   If you need a refresher on HTML5, please see Appendix A. Additional reference links are provided in Appendix D.

Getting Context

When we draw inside of a canvas element, we have more than one option of how we produce our image. Each option corresponds to a different application programming interface (API) with different available functionality and implementation details and is known as a particular context of the canvas. At the moment there are two canvas contexts: `"2D"` and `"webgl"`. The canvas element does not really care which context we use, but it needs to explicitly know so that it can provide us with an appropriate object that exposes the desired API.

To obtain a context, we call the canvas method `getContext`. This method takes a context name as a first parameter and an optional second argument. The WebGL context name will eventually be `"webgl"`, but for now, most browsers use the context name `"experimental-webgl"`. The optional second argument can contain buffer settings and may vary by browser implementation. A full list of the optional `WebGLContextAttributes` and how to set them is shown in Appendix C.

Listing 1-2. Establishing a WebGL context

```
<!doctype html>
<html>
```

```
<head>
        <title>WebGL Context</title>
        <style>
                body{ background-color: grey; }
                canvas{ background-color: white; }
        </style>
        <script>
                window.onload = setupWebGL;
                var gl = null;

                function setupWebGL()
                {
                        var canvas = document.getElementById("my-canvas");
                        try{
                                gl = canvas.getContext("experimental-webgl");
                        }catch(e){
                        }

                        if(gl)
                        {
                                //set the clear color to red
                                gl.clearColor(1.0, 0.0, 0.0, 1.0);
                                gl.clear(gl.COLOR_BUFFER_BIT);
                        }else{
                                alert( "Error: Your browser does not appear to support
                        WebGL.");
                        }
                }
        </script>
</head>
<body>
        <canvas id="my-canvas" width="400" height="300">
                Your browser does not support the HTML5 canvas element.
        </canvas>
</body>
</html>
```

In Listing 1-2, we define a JavaScript setup function that is called once the window's Document Object Model (DOM) has loaded:

```
window.onload = setupWebGL;
```

We initiate a variable to store the WebGL context with var `gl = null`. We use
`gl = canvas.getContext("experimental-webgl");` to try to get the experimental-webgl context from our canvas element, catching any exceptions that may be thrown.

■ **Note**   The name "gl" is conventionally used in WebGL to refer to the context object. This is because OpenGL and OpenGL ES constants begin with GL_ such as GL_DEPTH_TEST; and functions begin with gl, such as glClearColor.

WebGL does not use these prefixes, but when using the name "gl" for the context object, the code looks very similar: gl.DEPTH_TEST and gl.clearColor

This similarity makes it easier for programmers who are already familiar with OpenGL to learn WebGL.

On success, gl is a reference to the WebGL context. However, if a browser does not support WebGL, or if a canvas element has already been initialized with an incompatible context type, the getContext call will return null. In Listing 1-2, we test for gl to be non-null; if this is the case, we then set the clear color (the default value to set the color buffer) to red. If your browser supports WebGL, the browser output should be the same as Figure 1-1, but with a red canvas now instead of white. If not, we output an alert as shown in Figure 1-2. You can simulate this by misspelling the context, to "zzexperimental-webgl" for instance.

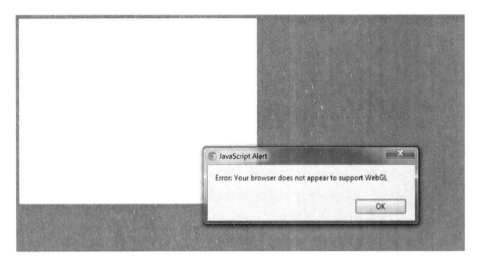

Figure 1-2. Error alert if WebGL is not supported

Being able to detect when the WebGL context is not supported is beneficial because it gives us the opportunity to program an appropriate alternative such as redirecting the user to http://get.webgl.org or falling back to a supported context such as "2D". We show how to do the latter approach with Three.js in Chapter 7.

■ **Note** There is usually more than one way of doing things in JavaScript. For instance, to load the setupWebGL function in code Listing 1-2, we could have written the onload event in our HTML instead:

```
<body onload="setupWebGL();">
```

If we were using jQuery, we would use the document ready function:

```
$(document).ready(function(){ setupWebGL(); });
```

We may make use of these differing forms throughout the book.

With jQuery, we can also shorten our canvas element retrieval to: var canvas = $("#my-canvas").get(0);

WebGL Components

In this section we will give an overview of the drawing buffers, primitive types, and vertex storage mechanisms that WebGL provides.

The Drawing Buffers

WebGL has a color buffer, depth buffer, and stencil buffer. A *buffer* is a block of memory that can be written to and read from, and temporarily stores data. The color buffer holds color information—red, green, and blue values—and optionally an alpha value that stores the amount of transparency/opacity. The depth buffer stores information on a pixel's depth component (z-value). As the map from 3D world space to 2D screen space can result in several points being projected to the same (x,y) canvas value, the z-values are compared and only one point, usually the nearest, is kept and rendered. For those seeking a quick refresher, Appendix B discusses coordinate systems.

The stencil buffer is used to outline areas to render or not render. When an area of an image is marked off to not render, it is known as masking that area. The entire image, including the masked portions, is known as a stencil. The stencil buffer can also be used in combination with the depth buffer to optimize performance by not attempting to render portions of a scene that are determined to be not viewable. By default, the color buffer's alpha channel is enabled and so is the depth buffer, but the stencil buffer is disabled. As previously mentioned, these can be modified by specifying the second optional parameter when obtaining the WebGL context as shown in Appendix C.

Primitive Types

Primitives are the graphical building blocks that all models in a particular graphics language are built with. In WebGL, there are three primitive types: points, lines and triangles and seven ways to render them: `POINTS`, `LINES`, `LINE_STRIP`, `LINE_LOOP`, `TRIANGLES`, `TRIANGLE_STRIP`, and `TRIANGLE_FAN` (see Figure 1-3).

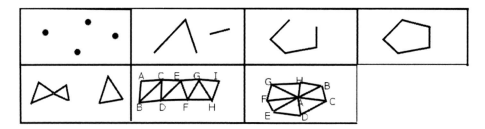

Figure 1-3. *WebGL Primitive Types (top row, l—r: POINTS, LINES, LINE_STRIP, and LINE_LOOP; bottom row, l—r: TRIANGLES, TRIANGLE_STRIP, and TRIANGLE_FAN)*

`POINTS` are vertices (spatial coordinates) rendered one at a time. `LINES` are formed along pairs of vertices. In Figure 1-3 two of the lines share a common vertex, but as each line is defined separately, it would still require six vertices to render these three lines. A `LINE_STRIP` is a collection of vertices in which, except for the first line, the starting point of each line is the end point of the previous line. With a `LINE_STRIP`, we reuse some vertices on multiple lines, so it would take just five vertices to draw the four lines in Figure 1-3. A `LINE_LOOP` is similar to a `LINE_STRIP` except that it is a closed off loop with the last vertex connecting back to the very first. As we are again reusing vertices among lines, we can produce five lines this time with just five vertices.

`TRIANGLES` are vertex trios. Like `LINES`, any shared vertices are purely coincidental and the example in Figure 1-3 requires nine vertices, three for each of the three triangles. A `TRIANGLE_STRIP` uses the last two vertices along with the next vertex to form triangles. In Figure 1-3 the triangles are formed by vertices ABC, (BC)D, (CD)E, (DE) F, (EF)G, (FG)H, and (GH)I. This lets us render seven triangles with just nine vertices as we reuse some vertices in multiple triangles. Finally, a `TRIANGLE_FAN` uses the first vertex specified as part of each triangle. In the preceding example this is vertex A, allowing us to render seven triangles with just eight vertices. Vertex A is used a total of seven times, while every other vertex is used twice.

■ **Note**   Unlike OpenGL and some other graphics languages, a quad is not a primitive type. Some WebGL frameworks provide it as a "basic" type and also offer geometric solids built in, but at the core level these are all rendered from triangles.

Vertex Data

Unlike old versions of OpenGL or "the '2D' canvas context", you can't directly set the color or location of a vertex directly into a scene. This is because WebGL does not have fixed functionality but uses programmable shaders instead. All data associated with a vertex needs to be streamed (passed along) from the JavaScript API to the Graphics Processing Unit (GPU). With WebGL, you have to create vertex buffer objects (VBOs) that will hold vertex attributes such as position, color, normal, and texture coordinates.

These vertex buffers are then sent to a shader program that can use and manipulate the passed-in data in any way you see fit. Using shaders instead of having fixed functionality is central to WebGL and will be covered in depth in the next chapter.

We will now turn our attention to what vertex attributes and uniform values are and show how to transport data with VBOs.

Vertex Buffer Objects (VBOs)

Each VBO stores data about a particular attribute of your vertices. This could be position, color, a normal vector, texture coordinates, or something else. A buffer can also have multiple attributes interleaved (as we will discuss in Chapter 9).

Looking at the WebGL API calls (which can be found at http://www.khronos.org/files/webgl/webgl-reference-card-1_0.pdf or at http://www.khronos.org/registry/webgl/specs/latest/), to create a buffer, you call `WebGLBuffer createBuffer()` and store the returned object, like so:

```
var myBuffer = gl.createBuffer();
```

Next you bind the buffer using `void bindBuffer(GLenum target, WebGLBuffer buffer)` like this:

```
gl.bindBuffer(gl.ELEMENT_ARRAY_BUFFER, myBuffer);
```

The target parameter is either `gl.ARRAY_BUFFER` or `gl.ELEMENT_ARRAY_BUFFER`. The target `ELEMENT_ARRAY_BUFFER` is used when the buffer contains vertex indices, and `ARRAY_BUFFER` is used for vertex attributes such as position and color.

Once a buffer is bound and the type is set, we can place data into it with this function:

```
void bufferData(GLenum target, ArrayBuffer data, GLenum usage)
```

The usage parameter of the bufferData call can be one of `STATIC_DRAW`, `DYNAMIC_DRAW`, or `STREAM_DRAW`. `STATIC_DRAW` will set the data once and never change throughout the application's use of it, which will be many times. `DYNAMIC_DRAW` will also use the data many times in the application but will respecify the contents to be used each time. `STREAM_DRAW` is similar to `STATIC_DRAW` in never changing the data, but it will be used at most a few times by the application. Using this function looks like the following:

```
var data = [     1.0, 0.0, 0.0,
                 0.0, 1.0, 0.0,
                 0.0, 1.0, 1.0
          ];
gl.bufferData(gl.ARRAY_BUFFER, data, gl.STATIC_DRAW);
```

Altogether the procedure of creating, binding and storing data inside of a buffer looks like:

```
var data = [     1.0, 0.0, 0.0,
                 0.0, 1.0, 0.0,
                 0.0, 1.0, 1.0
          ];
```

```
var myBuffer = gl.createBuffer();
gl.bindBuffer(gl.ARRAY_BUFFER, myBuffer);
gl.bufferData(gl.ARRAY_BUFFER, data, STATIC_DRAW);
```

Notice that in the `gl.bufferData` line, we do not explicitly specify the buffer to place the data into. WebGL implicitly uses the currently bound buffer.

When you are done with a buffer you can delete it with a call to this:

```
void deleteBuffer(WebGLBuffer buffer);
```

As the chapter progresses, we will show how to setup a shader program and pass VBO data into it.

Attributes and Uniforms

As mentioned, vertices have attributes which can be passed to shaders. We can also pass uniform values to the shader which will be constant for each vertex. Shader attributes and uniforms can get complex and will be covered in more depth in the next chapter but touched upon here. As the shader is a compiled external program, we need to be able to reference the location of all variables within the program. Once we obtain the location of a variable, we can send data to the shader from our web application. To get the location of an attribute or uniform within the WebGL program, we use these API calls:

```
GLint getAttribLocation(WebGLProgram program, DOMString name)
WebGLUniformLocation getUniformLocation(WebGLProgram program, DOMString name)
```

The `GLint` and `WebGLUniformLocation` return values are references to the location of the attribute or uniform within the shader program. The first parameter is our `WebGLProgram` object and the second parameter is the attribute name as found in the vertex or fragment shader source. If we have an attribute in a shader by the name of `"aVertexPosition"`, we obtain its position within our JavaScript like this:

```
var vertexPositionAttribute = gl.getAttribLocation(glProgram, "aVertexPosition");
```

If we are sending an array of data to an attribute, we have to enable array data with a call to this:

```
void enableVertexAttribArray(GLuint index)
```

Here, the index is the attribute location that we previously obtained and stored. The return value is void because the function returns no value.

With our previously defined attribute location, this call looks like the following:

```
gl.enableVertexAttribArray(vertexPositionAttribute);
```

Now that we have the location of an attribute and have told our shader that we will be using an array of values, we assign the currently bound ARRAY_BUFFER target to this vertex attribute as we have demonstrated in the previous section:

```
gl.bindBuffer(gl.ARRAY_BUFFER, myBuffer);
```

Finally, we let our shader know how to interpret our data. We need to remember that the shader knows nothing about the incoming data. Just because we name an array to help us understand what data it contains, such as myColorData, the shader just sees data without any context. The API call to explain our data format is as follows:

```
void vertexAttribPointer(GLuint index, GLint size, GLenum type, GLboolean normalized, GLsizei
stride, GLintptr offset)
```

`size` is the number of components per attribute. For example, with RGB colors, it would be 3; and with an alpha channel, RGBA, it would be 4. If we have location data with (x,y,z) attributes, it would be 3; and if we had a fourth parameter w, (x,y,z,w), it would be 4. Texture parameters (s,t) would be 2. type is the datatype, `stride` and `offset` can be set to the default of 0 for now and will be reexamined in Chapter 9 when we discuss interleaved arrays.

7

Altogether, the process of assigning values to a shader attribute looks like the following:

```
vertexPositionAttribute = gl.getAttribLocation(glProgram, "aVertexPosition");
gl.enableVertexAttribArray(vertexPositionAttribute);
gl.bindBuffer(gl.ARRAY_BUFFER, myBuffer);
gl.vertexAttribPointer(vertexPositionAttribute, 3, gl.FLOAT, false, 0, 0);
```

Now that we have gone over some of the relevant theory and methods, we can render our first example.

Rendering in Two Dimensions

In our first example, we will output two white triangles that look similar to a bowtie (see Figure 1-4). In order to get our feet wet and not overwhelm the reader, I have narrowed the focus of this example to have very minimalistic shaders and also not perform any transforms or setup of the view. Listing 1-3 builds upon the code of Listing 1-2. New code is shown in bold.

Listing 1-3. Partial code for rendering two triangles

```
<!doctype html>
<html>
        <head>
                <title>A Triangle</title>
                <style>
                        body{ background-color: grey; }
                        canvas{ background-color: white; }
                </style>
                <script id="shader-vs" type="x-shader/x-vertex">
                        attribute vec3 aVertexPosition;
                        void main(void) {
                                gl_Position = vec4(aVertexPosition, 1.0);
                        }
                </script>
                <script id="shader-fs" type="x-shader/x-fragment">
                        void main(void) {
                                gl_FragColor = vec4(1.0, 1.0, 1.0, 1.0);
                        }
                </script>
                <script>
                        var     gl = null,
                                canvas = null,
                                glProgram = null,
                                fragmentShader = null,
                                vertexShader = null;

                        var     vertexPositionAttribute = null,
                                trianglesVerticeBuffer = null;

                        function initWebGL()
                        {
                                canvas = document.getElementById("my-canvas");
                                try{

                                        gl =    canvas.getContext("webgl") ||
                                                canvas.getContext("experimental-webgl");
                                }catch(e){
                                }
```

```
                              if(gl)
                              {
                                      setupWebGL();
                                      initShaders();
                                      setupBuffers();
                                      drawScene();
                              }else{
                                      alert(  "Error: Your browser does not appear to" +
                                              "support WebGL.");
                              }
                      }

                      function setupWebGL()
                      {
                              //set the clear color to a shade of green
                              gl.clearColor(0.1, 0.5, 0.1, 1.0);
                              gl.clear(gl.COLOR_BUFFER_BIT);
                      }

                      function initShaders(){}
                      function setupBuffers(){}
                      function drawScene(){}
              </script>
      </head>
      <body onload="initWebGL()">
              <canvas id="my-canvas" width="400" height="300">
              Your browser does not support the HTML5 canvas element.
              </canvas>
      </body>
</html>
```

If you run the code at this point, you will still see a green rectangle because we defined shaders but have not hooked them into our application yet. The first new parts of Listing 1-3 are our vertex and fragment shaders. As mentioned earlier, shaders can get complex and are covered in detail in Chapter 2. Right now, you simply need to know that the vertex shader will set the final position of a vertex while the fragment shader (also known as a pixel shader) will set the final color of each pixel.

The following vertex shader takes each (x,y,z) vertex point that we will pass in to it and sets the final position to the homogeneous coordinate (x,y,z,1.0).

```
<script id="shader-vs" type="x-shader/x-vertex">
        attribute vec3 aVertexPosition;
        void main(void) {
                gl_Position = vec4(aVertexPosition, 1.0);
        }
</script>
```

The fragment shader will simply set each fragment that it receives to the color white (1.0, 1.0, 1.0, 1.0). The fourth component is the alpha value.

```
<script id="shader-fs" type="x-shader/x-fragment">
        void main(void) {
                gl_FragColor = vec4(1.0, 1.0, 1.0, 1.0);
        }
</script>
```

Eventually, we will pass in vertex points that correspond to the two triangles that we are rendering, but right now nothing is passed in and so we still see only the green clear color. In Listing 1-3 we have also added new variables that will store our WebGL shading language program, fragment and vertex shaders, vertex position attribute that will be passed to the vertex shader, and the vertex buffer object that will store our triangle vertices as shown in this code:

```
var     gl = null,
        canvas = null,
        glProgram = null,
        fragmentShader = null,
        vertexShader = null;

var     vertexPositionAttribute = null,
        trianglesVerticeBuffer = null;
```

▒ **Note**   Our modified line in Listing 1-3 to get the WebGL context is future compatible. It will check for the "webgl" context first. If this is not supported, it will try the "experimental-webgl" context next, as shown in the following code:

gl = canvas.getContext("webgl") || canvas.getContext("experimental-webgl");

Once we successfully obtain a WebGL context, we call four functions:

```
setupWebGL();
initShaders();
setupBuffers();
drawScene();
```

We currently have these functions defined as follows:

```
function setupWebGL()
{
        //set the clear color to a shade of green
        gl.clearColor(0.1, 0.5, 0.1, 1.0);
        gl.clear(gl.COLOR_BUFFER_BIT);
}

function initShaders(){}
function setupBuffers(){}
function drawScene(){}
```

The first function sets the clear color to green, and the other three at this point are stub functions so that the program runs without error. The next bit of functionality that we will implement is the creation of the shader program and shaders. This involves using several functions to set up each shader and the program.

For each shader, we call the API function createShader to create a WebGLShader object, in which the type parameter is either VERTEX_SHADER or FRAGMENT_SHADER for the vertex and fragment shaders, respectively:

```
WebGLShader createShader(GLenum type)
```

These calls look like this:

```
var vertexShader = gl.createShader(gl.VERTEX_SHADER);
var fragmentShader = gl.createShader(gl.FRAGMENT_SHADER);
```

Next we attach the source to each shader with API calls to:

```
void shaderSource(WebGLShader shader, DOMString source)
```

In practice, this can look like:

```
var     vs_source = document.getElementById('shader-vs').html(),
        fs_source = document.getElementById('shader-fs').html();
gl.shaderSource(vertexShader, vs_source);
gl.shaderSource(fragmentShader, fs_source);
```

Last, we compile each shader with the API call:

```
void compileShader(WebGLShader shader)
```

It looks like this:

```
gl.compileShader(vertexShader);
gl.compileShader(fragmentShader);
```

At this point we have compiled shaders but need a program to attach them into. We will create a WebGLProgram object with the API call:

```
WebGLProgram createProgram()
```

Next we attach each shader to our program with calls to:

```
void attachShader(WebGLProgram program, WebGLShader shader)
```

In an application, these two calls would look like:

```
var glProgram = gl.createProgram();
gl.attachShader(glProgram, vertexShader);
gl.attachShader(glProgram, fragmentShader);
```

After this we link the program and tell WebGL to use it with API calls to:

```
void linkProgram(WebGLProgram program) and
void useProgram(WebGLProgram program).
```

Our code for this would be the following:

```
gl.linkProgram(glProgram);
gl.useProgram(glProgram);
```

When we are finished with a shader or program, we can delete them with API calls to:

```
void deleteShader(WebGLShader shader) and
```

```
void deleteProgram(WebGLProgram program) respectively.
```

This will look like:

```
gl.deleteShader(vertexShader);
gl.deleteShader(vertexShader);
gl.deleteProgram(glProgram);
```

In Listing 1-4, we show the initialization of our shaders and program. We still are not displaying triangles at this point because we have not defined the vertices or passed them on to the shader.

Listing 1-4. Initializing our shaders and program

```
function initShaders()
{
        //get shader source
```

11

```
            var      fs_source = document.getElementById('shader-fs').html(),
                     vs_source = document.getElementById('shader-vs').html();

            //compile shaders
            vertexShader = makeShader(vs_source, gl.VERTEX_SHADER);
            fragmentShader = makeShader(fs_source, gl.FRAGMENT_SHADER);
            //create program
            glProgram = gl.createProgram();

            //attach and link shaders to the program
            gl.attachShader(glProgram, vertexShader);
            gl.attachShader(glProgram, fragmentShader);
            gl.linkProgram(glProgram);

            if (!gl.getProgramParameter(glProgram, gl.LINK_STATUS)) {
                    alert("Unable to initialize the shader program.");
            }

            //use program
            gl.useProgram(glProgram);
}

function makeShader(src, type)
{
            //compile the vertex shader
            var shader = gl.createShader(type);
            gl.shaderSource(shader, src);
            gl.compileShader(shader);

            if (!gl.getShaderParameter(shader, gl.COMPILE_STATUS)) {
                    alert("Error compiling shader: " + gl.getShaderInfoLog(shader));
            }
            return shader;
}
```

The preceding code contains all the steps that are involved in the usage of a shader program which we have just gone through. We first retrieve our shader sources from the DOM of our HTML document and compile each. We have added a utility function makeShader, which takes a source string and shader type that can be VERTEX_ SHADER or FRAGMENT_SHADER. This function then sets the shader source, compiles it, and returns the compiled shader. After obtaining compiled shaders, we create a program, attach our shaders to it, link them, and then tell our WebGL context to use this shader program. An extra step that we have added in Listing 1-4 is to check for errors after compiling each shader and linking them together.

Now we have shaders and a program, but we still do not have any primitives defined in our program. Recall that primitives in WebGL are composed of points, lines, or triangles. Our next step is to define and place the triangle vertex positions into a VBO that will then be passed in as data to our vertex shader. This is shown in Listing 1-5.

Listing 1-5. Setting up our vertex buffer and vertex position attribute

```
function setupBuffers()
{
            var triangleVertices = [
                    //left triangle
                    -0.5, 0.5, 0.0,
                     0.0, 0.0, 0.0,
                    -0.5, -0.5, 0.0,
```

```
                //right triangle
                0.5, 0.5, 0.0,
                0.0, 0.0, 0.0,
                0.5, -0.5, 0.0
    ];

    trianglesVerticeBuffer = gl.createBuffer();
    gl.bindBuffer(gl.ARRAY_BUFFER, trianglesVerticeBuffer);
    gl.bufferData(gl.ARRAY_BUFFER, new Float32Array(triangleVertices), gl.STATIC_DRAW);
}
```

In the setupBuffers method, we define an array of six vertices—three for each triangle. Then we call gl.createBuffer() to create a new VBO. We then bind our data to this buffer. We now need to tell our application which buffer to pass to the aVertexPosition attribute of our shader and then write to the draw buffer.

There are three ways to write to the draw buffer. These API function calls are the following:

```
void clear(GLbitfield mask)
void drawArrays(GLenum mode, GLint first, GLsizei count)
void drawElements(GLenum mode, GLsizei count, GLenum type, GLintptr offset)
```

The clear method mask parameter determines which buffer(s) are cleared. The drawArrays function is called on each enabled VBO array. The drawElements function is called on a VBO of indices that, as you may recall, is of type ELEMENT_ARRAY_BUFFER.

In this example, we will use the drawArrays method to render our two triangles:

```
function drawScene()
{
        vertexPositionAttribute = gl.getAttribLocation(glProgram, "aVertexPosition");
        gl.enableVertexAttribArray(vertexPositionAttribute);

        gl.bindBuffer(gl.ARRAY_BUFFER, trianglesVerticeBuffer);
        gl.vertexAttribPointer(vertexPositionAttribute, 3, gl.FLOAT, false, 0, 0);
        gl.drawArrays(gl.TRIANGLES, 0, 6);
}
```

In the drawScene method, we assign the vertex shader attribute aVertexPosition's location to a variable—vertexPositionAttribute. We enable array data for the attribute and bind our array to the current buffer. Then we point our trianglesVerticeBuffer data to the value stored in our vertexPositionAttribute variable. We tell the vertexAttribPointer that our data has three components (x,y,z) per vertex. Finally, we call drawArrays with a primitive type of gl.TRIANGLES, the starting vertex and the total number of vertices to render. You can see the output of this example with various primitive types in Figure 1-4.

Figure 1-4. The output of our first program: (left) two white triangles; (center) lines; (right) points

To render lines instead of triangles, you just need to change the `drawArrays` call to:

```
gl.drawArrays(gl.LINES, 0, 6);
```

Note that because two of the lines connect at the central vertex, it appears that only two lines are rendered. However if you view the lines piecewise, you can see the three individual lines by running separately three times:

```
gl.drawArrays(gl.LINES, 0, 2);
gl.drawArrays(gl.LINES, 2, 2);
gl.drawArrays(gl.LINES, 4, 2);
```

This will show you the line between the first two points, then the next two points, and finally the last pair of points. To render just the vertex points, you can adjust the `drawArrays` call to:

```
gl.drawArrays(gl.POINTS, 0, 6);
```

You will only see five vertex points because the center point is used twice. To increase the size of the points you can add the following line to your vertex shader:

```
gl_PointSize = 5.0;
```

The complete code of our first example is shown in Listing 1-6.

Listing 1-6. Code to show two triangles on a white background

```
<!doctype html>
<html>
        <head>
                <title>Two Triangles</title>
                <style>
                        body{ background-color: grey; }
                        canvas{ background-color: white; }
                </style>
                <script id="shader-vs" type="x-shader/x-vertex">
                        attribute vec3 aVertexPosition;
                        void main(void) {
                                gl_Position = vec4(aVertexPosition, 1.0);
                        }
                </script>
                <script id="shader-fs" type="x-shader/x-fragment">
                        void main(void) {
                                gl_FragColor = vec4(1.0, 1.0, 1.0, 1.0);
                        }
                </script>
                <script>
                        var     gl = null,
                                canvas = null,
                                glProgram = null,
                                fragmentShader = null,
                                vertexShader = null;

                        var     vertexPositionAttribute = null,
                                trianglesVerticeBuffer = null;

                        function initWebGL()
                        {
                                canvas = document.getElementById("my-canvas");
```

```
        try{
                gl = canvas.getContext("webgl") ||
                        canvas.getContext("experimental-webgl");

        }catch(e){
        }
        if(gl)
        {
                setupWebGL();
                initShaders();
                setupBuffers();
                drawScene();
        }else{
                alert( "Error: Your browser does not appear to" +
                        "support WebGL.");
        }
}

function setupWebGL()
{
        //set the clear color to a shade of green
        gl.clearColor(0.1, 0.5, 0.1, 1.0);
        gl.clear(gl.COLOR_BUFFER_BIT);
}

function initShaders()
{
        //get shader source
var     fs_source = document.getElementById('shader-fs').innerHTML,
        vs_source = document.getElementById('shader-vs').innerHTML;

        //compile shaders
        vertexShader = makeShader(vs_source, gl.VERTEX_SHADER);
        fragmentShader = makeShader(fs_source, gl.FRAGMENT_SHADER);

        //create program
        glProgram = gl.createProgram();

        //attach and link shaders to the program
        gl.attachShader(glProgram, vertexShader);
        gl.attachShader(glProgram, fragmentShader);
        gl.linkProgram(glProgram);

        if (!gl.getProgramParameter(glProgram, gl.LINK_STATUS)) {
          alert("Unable to initialize the shader program.");
        }

        //use program
        gl.useProgram(glProgram);
}

function makeShader(src, type)
{
        //compile the vertex shader
        var shader = gl.createShader(type);
```

```
                        gl.shaderSource(shader, src);
                        gl.compileShader(shader);

                        if (!gl.getShaderParameter(shader, gl.COMPILE_STATUS)) {
                            alert("Error compiling shader: " +
                                        gl.getShaderInfoLog(shader));
                        }
                            return shader;
                    }

                function setupBuffers()
                {
                        var triangleVertices = [
                            //left triangle
                            -0.5, 0.5, 0.0,
                             0.0, 0.0, 0.0,
                            -0.5, -0.5, 0.0,

                            //right triangle
                            0.5, 0.5, 0.0,
                             0.0, 0.0, 0.0,
                            0.5, -0.5, 0.0
                        ];

                        trianglesVerticeBuffer = gl.createBuffer();
                        gl.bindBuffer(gl.ARRAY_BUFFER, trianglesVerticeBuffer);
                        gl.bufferData(gl.ARRAY_BUFFER, new
                                Float32Array(triangleVertices), gl.STATIC_DRAW);
                }

                function drawScene()
                {
                        vertexPositionAttribute = gl.getAttribLocation(glProgram,
                                                "aVertexPosition");
                        gl.enableVertexAttribArray(vertexPositionAttribute);

                        gl.bindBuffer(gl.ARRAY_BUFFER, trianglesVerticeBuffer);
                        gl.vertexAttribPointer(vertexPositionAttribute, 3,
                                                gl.FLOAT, false, 0, 0);

                        gl.drawArrays(gl.TRIANGLES, 0, 6);
                }
            </script>
        </head>
        <body onload="initWebGL()">
                <canvas id="my-canvas" width="400" height="300">
                Your browser does not support the HTML5 canvas element.
                </canvas>
        </body>
</html>
```

The View: Part I

Just as we can't see all parts of the world in our everyday life, but instead have a limited field of vision, we can view only part of a 3D world at once with WebGL. The view in WebGL refers to what region of our scene that we are observing—the viewing volume, along with the virtual camera—our viewing location and angle relative to what we are observing, and perspective rules—whether an object will appear smaller when farther away or not.

In the previous example of Listing 1-6, we did not alter our view at all. We defined (x,y,z) coordinates that were rendered by our shader to the canvas as final (x,y) coordinates. In that example, the z-coordinate was not a factor to our final view (as long as it was within our clipspace, as we will discuss next). However, in most instances, we will need to explicitly define our view and how to map coordinates from 3D to 2D space.

Clip Coordinates

In Listing 1-6, our triangle coordinates all fell between -0.5 and 0.5 in the x, y, and z directions. As an experiment, change the vertices of the last example to these:

```
var triangleVertices = [
        //left triangle
        -1.5, 1.5, 0.0,
        0.0, 0.0, 0.0,
        -1.5, -1.5, 0.0,

        //right triangle
        1.5, 1.5, 0.0,
        1.0, 1.0, 0.0,
        1.5, -1.5, 0.0
];
```

You might expect to see two triangles of differing appeareance to those on the left of Figure 1-4. But in fact, you will only get one white triangle as shown in Figure 1-5 as output.

Figure 1-5. Only one triangle is visible after modifying our vertices

What is the reason for this? Well, by default WebGL has a clip volume centered at the origin (0,0,0) and extending +/- 1 along each of the x,y, and z axes. The clip volume defines the (x,y,z) points that will be rendered by the fragment shader. Any fragment (pixel) within the clipping volume is rendered, and points outside of it are discarded (clipped). The vertex shader transforms points to a final gl_Position. Then a clip test is done on each fragment, with those falling within the clip volume continuing on to the fragment shader.

In the vertex shader of Listing 1-6, we use the input position as the output position. When we modified the vertex points to those values that produce Figure 1-5, the left triangle has one point (0,0,0) within the clipping volume while the other two lie outside. Fragments of the left triangle will get clipped if they are past +/- 1. On the right triangle, no point lies within the clipping volume (well, just the single point [1.0, 1.0, 0.0]), so we don't see any fragment of the triangle.

Why Manipulate Coordinates?

One reason to manipulate 3D coordinates is because it allows us to deal with more intuitive values. We are not limited to stay within the clip volume range. Instead we could have a viewing volume of any dimension and scale the vertex positions when we pass them on to our shader. It usually makes more sense dealing with coordinates such as (30, 5, 10) then (0.36, 0.06, 0.12). Manipulating coordinates allows us to use friendlier numbers and transform them to values that are still within the clipping volume.

The main reason to manipulate coordinates is because we deal with different coordinate spaces. We have coordinates relative to a particular model, relative to the world and relative to the virtual camera. We need to be able to represent our scene and objects in a meaningful manner that transforms a model from its original size and location to a relative size and location within our scene and then take this scene and only view a particular portion of it with our virtual camera.

As an example, suppose you have a 3D model of a shipping crate (box) that is perfectly cubic and centered around the origin. Perhaps you would like to model a scene of a shipping yard with hundreds of shipping containers. In the scene, these containers can vary in size, position, and orientation. They could be cubic or rectangular. Except for a box of the exact same dimensions as the original model, centered around the origin of your scene, you would want to manipulate this model.

To accomplish this, our first step is to move from model to world coordinates. This will involve basic transformations of scaling, rotating, and translating. If you have many boxes, these transformations would be distinct among each box instance. After you have placed all your boxes around your world, our next step is to adjust our view. The view is like a camera pointed at the world. The camera can be positioned and rotated to point a certain direction in our scene.

We set our projection type, which determines whether elements further away look smaller then same-sized objects that are nearer to the camera (perspective projection) or appear to be the same size no matter their distance (orthogonal projection). Lastly, the viewport defines what part of a screen (the <canvas>) is rendered to and the dimensions of this area.

This multistep process that involves transforming a model's local coordinates to "world" coordinates, then to "view" coordinates, is commonly known as the Model-View-Projection (MVP) matrix transformation. We will now show how to set up the viewport before returning to the MVP setup.

The Viewport

The viewport defines where the origin (lower-left) point (x,y) to render on the canvas should be located, and what width and height of the canvas to render onto. We set the viewport with the API call:

```
void viewport(GLint x, GLint y, GLsizei width, GLsizei height);
```

Setting the origin to (0, 0) and the width and height equal to the canvas dimensions will fill the entire canvas. This is done with the following code:

```
gl.viewport(0, 0, canvas.width, canvas.height);
```

You can see the result in Figure 1-6.

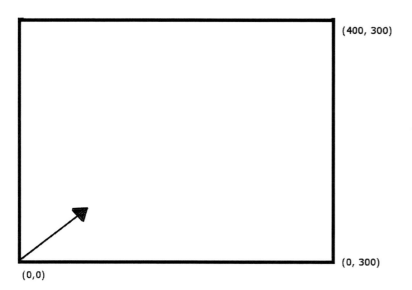

(400, 300)

(0, 300)

(0,0)

Figure 1-6. *Viewport coordinates that fill our entire 400×300 canvas element*

Alternatively, you could decide to render to only part of the canvas. Some reasons to do this might be to tile the same rendering multiple times in the viewport or display a unique image in each region of the viewport. This technique is used in the image processing examples of Chapter 10. Using only a quarter of the rendering area is shown in Listing 1-7.

Listing 1-7. Rendering to part of the canvas

```
//top right quadrant
gl.viewport(canvas.width/2.0, canvas.height/2.0, canvas.width/2.0, canvas.height/2.0);

//top left quadrant
gl.viewport(0, canvas.height/2.0, canvas.width/2.0, canvas.height/2.0);

//bottom left quadrant
gl.viewport(0, 0, canvas.width/2.0, canvas.height/2.0);

//bottom right quadrant
gl.viewport(canvas.width/2.0, 0, canvas.width/2.0, canvas.height/2.0);
```

Adjusting Listing 1-6 to use the top left quadrant viewport in the setupWebGL method:

```
function setupWebGL()
{
        //set the clear color to a shade of green
        gl.clearColor(0.1, 0.5, 0.1, 1.0);
        gl.clear(gl.COLOR_BUFFER_BIT);
        //gl.viewport(0, 0, canvas.width, canvas.height);
        gl.viewport(0, canvas.height/2.0, canvas.width/2.0, canvas.height/2.0);
}
```

This will produce the output shown in Figure 1-7.

Figure 1-7. Setting our triangle example to a top-left quadrant viewport

---

■ **Note**   Although WebGL will initialize the viewport to the full canvas, it will not adjust the viewport if the canvas is resized because automatically adjusting the viewport can interfere with applications that manually set it. For this reason, it is best to always explicitly set the viewport before rendering with the current canvas dimensions: `gl.viewport(0, 0, canvas.width, canvas.height);`. Alternatively, you can listen for canvas size changes by setting an `onresize` event handler and only adjust the viewport when necessary.

To keep the examples as simple as possible, we will now show how to define color per vertex and set up an animation loop. Then we will return to working with the view, as we explain how to set up the MVP matrix.

Adding Color

In our next example, we will add a color attribute to our vertices. Starting from the code shown in Listing 1-6, we will modify our shaders (where new code is shown in bold) to be as follows:

```
<script id="shader-vs" type="x-shader/x-vertex">
    attribute vec3 aVertexPosition;
    attribute vec3 aVertexColor;

    varying highp vec4 vColor;
    void main(void) {
        gl_Position = vec4(aVertexPosition, 1.0);
        vColor = vec4(aVertexColor, 1.0);
    }
</script>
<script id="shader-fs" type="x-shader/x-fragment">
    varying highp vec4 vColor;
    void main(void) {
        gl_FragColor = vColor;
    }
</script>
```

Even though the fragment shader controls the final color, we can't pass vertex attribute data directly to it. So we create a new attribute, aVertexColor, in the vertex shader and pass the input data to the fragment shader by assigning it to a varying variable:

```
varying highp vec4 vColor;
```

The qualifier highp sets the floating point precision to high. The focus of this chapter is general application setup and not shaders, but these concepts and keywords will be expanded upon in Chapter 2. We declare vColor in both the vertex and fragment shader as the output value of the vertex shader becomes the input to the fragment shader. Then we add a variable to our application to store the color attribute and the color data buffer:

```
var     vertexPositionAttribute = null,
        trianglesVerticeBuffer = null,
        vertexColorAttribute = null,
        trianglesColorBuffer = null;
```

In our setupBuffers method, we will add the following code:

```
var triangleVerticeColors = [
        //red left triangle
        1.0, 0.0, 0.0,
        1.0, 1.0, 1.0,
        1.0, 0.0, 0.0,

        //blue right triangle
        0.0, 0.0, 1.0,
        1.0, 1.0, 1.0,
        0.0, 0.0, 1.0
];

trianglesColorBuffer = gl.createBuffer();
gl.bindBuffer(gl.ARRAY_BUFFER, trianglesColorBuffer);
gl.bufferData(gl.ARRAY_BUFFER, new Float32Array(triangleVerticeColors), gl.STATIC_DRAW);
```

Notice that the center vertex of each triangle is white. In Figure 1-8, the color is interpolated between vertices. Finally we need to connect the color buffer to the shader attribute in our drawScene method:

```
function drawScene()
{
        vertexPositionAttribute = gl.getAttribLocation(glProgram, "aVertexPosition");
        gl.enableVertexAttribArray(vertexPositionAttribute);
        gl.bindBuffer(gl.ARRAY_BUFFER, trianglesVerticeBuffer);
        gl.vertexAttribPointer(vertexPositionAttribute, 3, gl.FLOAT, false, 0, 0);

        vertexColorAttribute = gl.getAttribLocation(glProgram, "aVertexColor");
        gl.enableVertexAttribArray(vertexColorAttribute);
        gl.bindBuffer(gl.ARRAY_BUFFER, trianglesColorBuffer);
        gl.vertexAttribPointer(vertexColorAttribute, 3, gl.FLOAT, false, 0, 0);

        gl.drawArrays(gl.TRIANGLES, 0, 6);
}
```

The full code listing for this example and all other code listings in the book is available online at the Apress website http://www.apress.com/9781430239963 and on the companion website at http://beginningwebgl. com/code. The file of this example is 01/ch1_colored-triangles.html. You can see the output of this in Figure 1-8.

Figure 1-8. *Per vertex color attributes*

Animation and Model Movement

Let's now add some movement to our triangles. To do this we first need to set up an animation loop.

Using requestAnimationFrame

For animation, the newer browser method `window.requestAnimationFrame` is better than the older methods `window.setTimeout`(which calls a function once after a fixed delay) and `window.setInterval`(which repeatedly calls a function with a fixed delay between calls). These two functions can be used to adjust the framerate when rendering. The reason that the new method, `window.requestAnimationFrame`, is better than the older methods is because it is more accurate and also will not animate a scene when you are in a different browser tab. The second benefit means that using `requestAnimationFrame` will help prevent battery life from being wasted on mobile devices.

However, support for `requestAnimationFrame` is still browser-dependent. As such, we should test for it, reverting to the `window.setTimeout` fallback if it is not available. This is done by using a shim (it transparently intercepts an API call and redirects the underlying calls to a supported method) or polyfill (code designed to provide additional technology that is not natively provided) to wrap the function, such as the one by Opera engineer Erik Möller and modified by Paul Irish at his blog http://paulirish.com/2011/requestanimationframe-for-smart-animating/. The polyfill is also fairly actively edited at https://gist.github.com/1579671.

Download a recent version of the file (Google "requestAnimationFrame polyfill") and place it inside of a separate file that we will call `raf_polyfill.js`:

```
<script src="raf_polyfill.js"></script>
```

This file should be placed in the same directory as your webroot or else you will need to adjust the path accordingly.

We now just need to place our `setupWebGL` and `drawScene` functions within an animation loop, as shown in Listing 1-8.

Listing 1-8. Animation loop

```
initShaders();
setupBuffers();
 (function animLoop(){
        setupWebGL();
        setupDynamicBuffers();
        drawScene();
        requestAnimFrame(animLoop, canvas);
 })();
```

The first parameter of `requestAnimFrame` is the callback function, and the second argument is the element to act upon. Because `requestAnimFrame` calls `animLoop`, the function will continue calling itself again and again as long as the application is running. We also have added a new function, `setupDynamicBuffers`, which is shown fully in Listing 1-9 in the next section. We have repeated animation calls now, but our scene will still appear static. This is because we have not changed any of our vertices or the view between animation frames.

Creating Movement

There are two ways to create movement—either you move an object in a scene or you move the view of the scene. We will not be adjusting the view in this example, but instead will be adjusting the coordinates of the model. The reason why we are moving the model instead of the view is simple; we do not yet know how to adjust our view.

Our first change is to modify the vertices VBO type from `STATIC_DRAW` to `DYNAMIC_DRAW`:

```
gl.bufferData(gl.ARRAY_BUFFER, new Float32Array(triangleVertices), gl.DYNAMIC_DRAW);
```

A simple way to alter the x values of our triangles and keep them in the clipspace range (`-1, 1`) is to set the x value equal to the cosine or sine of an angle. If you need a trigonometric refresher, please refer to the diagrams in Appendix B and the links provided in Appendix D.

In Listing 1-9, we extract the vertice buffer creation code out of `setupBuffers` and into a new function `setupDynamicBuffers`, which will be called every time through the animation loop. The `setupDynamicBuffers` method shown in bold is new code.

Listing 1-9. Splitting up our buffers into static and dynamic data calls

```
function setupBuffers()
{
        var triangleVerticeColors = [
                //left triangle
                 1.0, 0.0, 0.0,
                 1.0, 1.0, 1.0,
                 1.0, 0.0, 0.0,

                //right triangle
                0.0, 0.0, 1.0,
                 1.0, 1.0, 1.0,
                0.0, 0.0, 1.0,
        ];

        trianglesColorBuffer = gl.createBuffer();
        gl.bindBuffer(gl.ARRAY_BUFFER, trianglesColorBuffer);
        gl.bufferData(gl.ARRAY_BUFFER, new Float32Array(triangleVerticeColors), gl.STATIC_DRAW);
}
```

```
function setupDynamicBuffers()
{
        //limit translation amount to -0.5 to 0.5
        var x_translation = Math.sin(angle)/2.0;

        var triangleVertices = [
                //left triangle
                -0.5 + x_translation, 0.5, 0.0,
                 0.0 + x_translation, 0.0, 0.0,
                -0.5 + x_translation, -0.5, 0.0,

                //right triangle
                0.5 + x_translation, 0.5, 0.0,
                 0.0 + x_translation, 0.0, 0.0,
                0.5 + x_translation, -0.5, 0.0
        ];
        angle += 0.01;

        trianglesVerticeBuffer = gl.createBuffer();
        gl.bindBuffer(gl.ARRAY_BUFFER, trianglesVerticeBuffer);
        gl.bufferData(gl.ARRAY_BUFFER, new Float32Array(triangleVertices), gl.DYNAMIC_DRAW);
}
```

If you run the application now, you will see the triangles move from side to side, stopping at the edges. Notice that the animation slows toward the edges, as a natural consequence of using the sine function. The full code of this example is found online in the file 01/2d_movement.html.

The View: Part II

In this section, we will show how to generate the MVP matrix to transform our original vertices into values that fall within the clip space range.

As a precursor to see why we need to modify our coordinates by the MVP matrix, look at what happens next when we try to naively make the scene 3D in appearance by having differing z-values. Adjust the right triangle coordinates of the 2d_movement.html file to:

```
//right triangle
0.5 + x_translation, 0.5, 0.0,
 0.0 + x_translation, 0.0, -0.5,
0.5 + x_translation, -0.5, 0.5,
```

Rerun the program and see that nothing has changed. As long as the z-values are between -1 and 1, the clip volume, it will appear the same no matter what the actual z-value.

So then how do we get a scene that looks 3D and has perspective? We have to multiply our original coordinates by the MVP matrices. We do this by setting a model-view matrix and a projection matrix in our application and passing them as uniforms to our shader, in which they will be multiplied by our original position to find a final position in the fragment shader.

Model-View Matrix

The model-view matrix combines two transformations—the model-to-world coordinate transformation and the world-to-view coordinate transformation—into one matrix. Recall that the model-to-world transformation takes a model within its local coordinates and transforms it into its spot within the world, as shown in Figure 1-9.

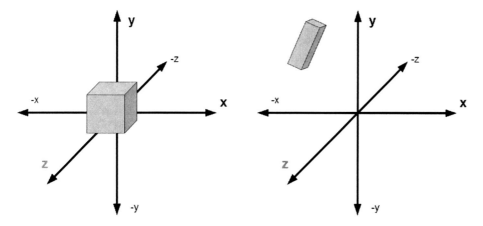

Figure 1-9. Model coordinates on the left transformed to world coordinates on the right

The world coordinate to view coordinate transform positions the camera view in the scene, as shown in Figure 1-10.

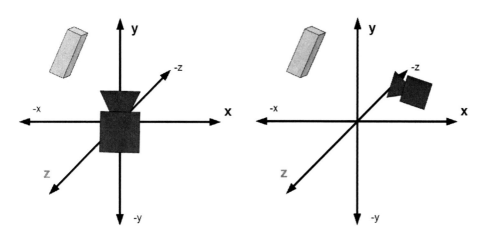

Figure 1-10. World coordinates transformed to camera view

Projection Matrix

The projection matrix can be orthogonal or perspective. In a perspective matrix, objects farther away that are the same dimension as nearer objects will appear smaller, making the view seem realistic. With perspective, all lines reach a central vanishing point that gives the illusion of depth. In an orthogonal (parallel) projection matrix, objects of the same dimensions will always appear to be the same size. The orthogonal projection is also known as a parallel projection because lines do not converge but remain parallel (see Figure 1-11).

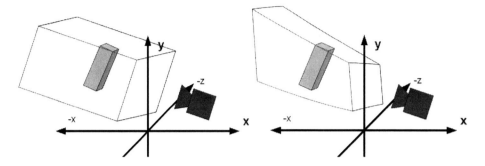

Figure 1-11. *Camera coordinates transformed to screen view; left is orthogonal (parallel) and right is perspective*

Choosing a Matrix Library

It is a good idea to use an existing matrix library instead of creating your own. Existing matrix libraries are usually well-tested, -documented and -thought out. The operations within are fairly elementary and rigid. In other words, you would not be providing anything unique, and you do not want to spend time reinventing the wheel. (There are many libraries to choose from and references are listed in Appendix D. I prefer `gl-matrix.js`, written by Brandon Jones and Colin MacKenzie IV, available at https://github.com/toji/gl-matrix and will use it throughout the book).

Three-Dimensional Rendering

We will now extend upon our two-dimensional example to add depth and make it appear three-dimensional.

2D Models in a 3D World

Working from our previous example (`2d_movement.html`) as a basis, we will implement MVP matrices. First, we need to download and include the gl-matrix library:

```
<script src="gl-matrix-min.js"></script>
```

We also need to declare two new variables to store our model-view and projection matrices:

```
var     mvMatrix = mat4.create(),
        pMatrix = mat4.create();
```

Our `setupWebGL` function is updated to be:

```
function setupWebGL()
{
        //set the clear color to a shade of green
        gl.clearColor(0.1, 0.5, 0.1, 1.0);
        gl.clear(gl.COLOR_BUFFER_BIT);

        gl.viewport(0, 0, canvas.width, canvas.height);
        mat4.perspective(45, canvas.width / canvas.height, 0.1, 100.0, pMatrix);
        mat4.identity(mvMatrix);
        mat4.translate(mvMatrix, [0, 0, -2.0]);
}
```

mat4.perspective is a helper function of the gl-matrix library, which takes field of view, aspect ratio, and near and far bounds as arguments. There is also a mat4.ortho call in the library, which can produce an orthogonal projection. When we create our mvMatrix, we simply adjust the z-coordinate because the camera lies at the origin by default (0,0,0), so we move back in order to see our triangles that also lie on the z-axis.

Next we need to find the location of these uniforms within our shader and also be able to update the values. The matrices are uniforms because they are applied with the same values for every vertex. We add two new helper methods, getMatrixUniforms and setMatrixUniforms. We call getMatrixUniforms outside of our animation loop as the location within the shader will always stay the same, while we call setMatrixUniforms each animation loop as it could be different between one animation frame and the next:

```
function getMatrixUniforms(){
    glProgram.pMatrixUniform = gl.getUniformLocation(glProgram, "uPMatrix");
    glProgram.mvMatrixUniform = gl.getUniformLocation(glProgram, "uMVMatrix");
}

function setMatrixUniforms() {
    gl.uniformMatrix4fv(glProgram.pMatrixUniform, false, pMatrix);
    gl.uniformMatrix4fv(glProgram.mvMatrixUniform, false, mvMatrix);
}
        ...
        ...

    initShaders();
    setupBuffers();
    getMatrixUniforms();
    (function animLoop(){
            setupWebGL();
            setupDynamicBuffers();
            setMatrixUniforms();
            drawScene();
            requestAnimationFrame(animLoop, canvas);
    })();
```

We also need to update our vertex shader to have these new uniform values:

```
<script id="shader-vs" type="x-shader/x-vertex">
        attribute vec3 aVertexPosition;
        attribute vec3 aVertexColor;

        uniform mat4 uMVMatrix;
        uniform mat4 uPMatrix;

        varying highp vec4 vColor;
        void main(void) {
                gl_Position = uPMatrix * uMVMatrix * vec4(aVertexPosition, 1.0);
                vColor = vec4(aVertexColor, 1.0);
        }
</script>
```

The final position is calculated as the projection matrix multiplied by the model-view matrix and then finally the original vertex position. Let's adjust the depth coordinates of our two triangles:

```
var triangleVertices = [
        //left triangle
        -0.5 + x_translation, 0.5, -0.5,
         0.0 + x_translation, 0.0, -0.5,
        -0.5 + x_translation, -0.5, -0.5,
```

```
        //right triangle
        0.5 + x_translation, 0.5, 0.5,
        0.0 + x_translation, 0.0, 0.5,
        0.5 + x_translation, -0.5, 0.5,
];
```

The full code of this example is in the file 01/3d_movement.html. You can see the output of this in Figure 1-12.

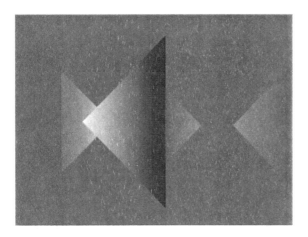

Figure 1-12. *Composite image of animation. The triangles now have different depths*

An Example with Depth

For the last example in this chapter, we will render a 3D solid of a triangular prism. It can often help to sketch up the vertices of such a figure and label the vertices, as shown in Figures 1-13 and 1-14.

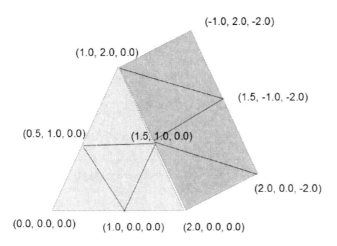

Figure 1-13. *A prism sketch with some of the key points labeled*

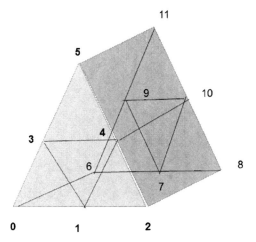

Figure 1-14. The vertex numbers of the prism labeled

Using an Index Buffer

A quick count of Figures 1-13 and 1-14 shows that there will be 18 distinct triangles (including two on the bottom face) and 12 distinct vertices needed. Rather than explicitly set all the vertices for the triangles that would take 54 (x,y,z) values (18 triangles with 3 vertices per triangle), we can just declare our 12 vertices and then declare the 54 indices to use as shown in the bold part of Listing 1-10.

Listing 1-10. Using vertice indices to reuse vertices for multiple triangles

```
function setupBuffers()
{
        var triangleVerticeColors = [
                    //front face
                    0.0, 0.0, 1.0,
                    1.0, 1.0, 1.0,
                    0.0, 0.0, 1.0,
                    0.0, 0.0, 1.0,
                    0.0, 0.0, 1.0,
                    1.0, 1.0, 1.0,

                    //rear face
                    0.0, 1.0, 1.0,
                    1.0, 1.0, 1.0,
                    0.0, 1.0, 1.0,
                    0.0, 1.0, 1.0,
                    0.0, 1.0, 1.0,
                    1.0, 1.0, 1.0
        ];

        trianglesColorBuffer = gl.createBuffer();
        gl.bindBuffer(gl.ARRAY_BUFFER, trianglesColorBuffer);
        gl.bufferData(gl.ARRAY_BUFFER, new Float32Array(triangleVerticeColors), gl.STATIC_DRAW);

        //12 vertices
        var triangleVertices = [
```

```
            //front face
            //bottom left to right, to top
            0.0, 0.0, 0.0,
            1.0, 0.0, 0.0,
            2.0, 0.0, 0.0,
            0.5, 1.0, 0.0,
            1.5, 1.0, 0.0,
            1.0, 2.0, 0.0,

            //rear face
            0.0, 0.0, -2.0,
            1.0, 0.0, -2.0,
            2.0, 0.0, -2.0,
            0.5, 1.0, -2.0,
            1.5, 1.0, -2.0,
            1.0, 2.0, -2.0
    ];

    trianglesVerticeBuffer = gl.createBuffer();
    gl.bindBuffer(gl.ARRAY_BUFFER, trianglesVerticeBuffer);
    gl.bufferData(gl.ARRAY_BUFFER, new Float32Array(triangleVertices), gl.STATIC_DRAW);

    //setup vertice buffers
    //18 triangles
    var triangleVertexIndices = [
            //front face
            0,1,3,
            1,3,4,
            1,2,4,
            3,4,5,

            //rear face
            6,7,9,
            7,9,10,
            7,8,10,
            9,10,11,

            //left side
            0,3,6,
            3,6,9,
            3,5,9,
            5,9,11,

            //right side
            2,4,8,
            4,8,10,
            4,5,10,
            5,10,11,

            //bottom faces
            0,6,8,
            8,2,0
    ];
    triangleVerticesIndexBuffer = gl.createBuffer();
    triangleVerticesIndexBuffer.number_vertex_points = triangleVertexIndices.length;
```

```
        gl.bindBuffer(gl.ELEMENT_ARRAY_BUFFER, triangleVerticesIndexBuffer);
        gl.bufferData(gl.ELEMENT_ARRAY_BUFFER, new Uint16Array(triangleVertexIndices),
gl.STATIC_DRAW);
}
```

Notice that we are no longer dynamically setting the vertices. We will produce movement by altering the mvMatrix instead—alterations can be translations, rotations, and/or scaling. Also note that the indice buffer type is gl.ELEMENT_ARRAY_BUFFER.

To produce movement we initialize a variable, angle, to store an angle and then increment it each frame to rotate our mvMatrix a little more each animation frame:

```
mat4.identity(mvMatrix);
mat4.translate(mvMatrix, [-1.0, -1.0, -7.0]);
mat4.rotate(mvMatrix, angle, [0.0, 1.0, 0.0]);
angle += 0.01;
```

When we draw our scene, we use gl.drawElements instead of gl.drawArrays:

```
gl.bindBuffer(gl.ELEMENT_ARRAY_BUFFER, triangleVerticesIndexBuffer);
gl.drawElements(gl.TRIANGLES, triangleVerticesIndexBuffer.number_vertex_points, gl.UNSIGNED_
SHORT, 0);
```

The primitive type in this example is still gl.TRIANGLES, and we have the value of triangleVerticesIndexBuffer.number_vertex_points, which is 54, to draw. The result of this example is shown in Figure 1-15, and the full code is in the file 01/3D_triangles.html.

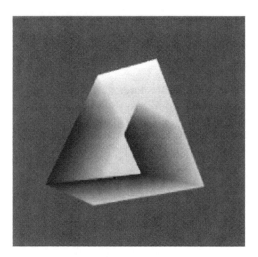

Figure 1-15. *Not enabling the depth test can produce strange results*

Depth Testing

Unless we check the depth of our primitives, some faces that should be hidden from view might not be. This can produce unexpected results, as we saw in Figure 1-15. Enabling depth testing is easy and involves calling this:

```
gl.enable(gl.DEPTH_TEST);
```

We will also clear the depth buffer in our `setupWebGL` function:

```
gl.clear(gl.COLOR_BUFFER_BIT|gl.DEPTH_BUFFER_BIT);
```

In Figure 1-16, you can see a more expected result.

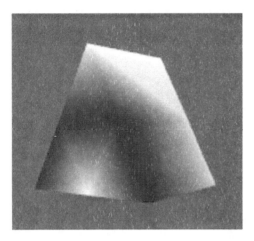

Figure 1-16. *After enabling the depth test, everything looks as it should*

In this chapter we have shown how to color a 3D mesh. In Chapter 3, we will come back to this last example and apply texture and lighting to it.

Summary

In this chapter, we have made great strides going from a blank canvas to a moving 3D object. Even though this was the first chapter, in a lot of ways it was a tough one because we needed to introduce so many new concepts at once. So congratulations on making it this far and now we can build upon our new skills in the forthcoming chapters. In the next chapter, we will dive into the details of the OpenGL Shading Language (GLSL) and start exploring the capabilities of vertex and fragment shaders. We're just getting started with what WebGL can do!

CHAPTER 2

■ ■ ■

Shaders 101

In this chapter, we will be covering the GL Shading Language (GLSL) in depth. Topics that we will cover include

- an overview of the WebGL graphics pipeline
- the difference between fixed functionality and modern-day programmable shaders
- the role of vertex shaders and fragment shaders within the GLSL
- how to create and use shaders within a WebGL application
- a detailed overview of the GLSL including its primitive types and built-in functions
- examples of procedural fragment shaders

Graphics Pipelines

A *graphics pipeline* consists of the steps that an image goes through from initial definition to final screen rendering. This pipeline is composed of several steps done in a predefined order. Components of the pipeline can be either fixed in functionality or programmable.

Fixed Functionality or Programmable Shaders

The more traditional graphics pipeline has a fixed implementation. The initial image definition would be the set of vertex location points and information associated with these points such as color, a normal vector, and texture coordinates. With fixed functionality, operations are done in a set order. You can disable some elements such as lighting or texturing, but not modify how the underlying lighting or texturing calculations are done. The graphics pipeline of OpenGL before version 2.0 used fixed functionality only.

Fixed functionality, as its name suggests, is quite rigid. It allows for quicker and easier generation of images because lighting formulas and shading are already built into the system. However, it limits what we can accomplish because we cannot override these settings. OpenGL Fixed functionality had separate pipeline steps for vertex transformations and lighting. This is now all done within the vertex shader (VS) and fragment shader (FS). Similarly, texture application, color summation, fog, and alpha testing were all discrete steps. Now these components are done within the FS.

A high-level view of how the WebGL API, programmable and nonprogrammable components of the pipeline interact is shown in Figure 2-1.

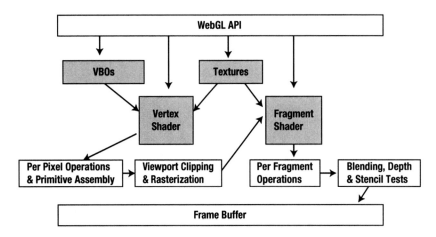

Figure 2-1. *Simplified diagram of the WebGL programmable pipeline. Steps with a shaded background are editable*

A programmable pipeline can display a greater range of effects because you can define parts of the pipeline (not all of it) and override the calculations used for computing color, position, texture coordinates or the lighting model. The programmable pipeline components use a vertex program and a fragment program which are known collectively as shaders. These shaders are run on the powerful Graphics Processing Units (GPU) found in modern computers. OpenGL versions 2.0 to 3.0 allowed the use of either fixed functionality or shaders. The slimmed down API of OpenGL ES and WebGL only supports shaders and not fixed functionality.

Why Shaders?

If shaders are much more work to set up, why do we bother using them? What are their benefits?

Well, with shaders you can create effects that add increased realism to a scene. You can create nonphotorealistic images that look cartoonish. You can also create convolution filters and masks in shaders; and do additional antialiasing, blending, shadow creation, and advanced texture manipulation within the shader, and pretty much anything else you can think of and implement.

You can also program the Graphics Processing Unit (GPU) to do side calculations. The power of the GPU can be used to offset browser calculations and is much faster and better for general computing.

The WebGL Graphics Pipeline

In WebGL, the rendering process is the following:

- Take vertex array data and place it into vertex buffer objects (VBOs).

- Stream the VBO data to the VS and send indice information using a call to either drawArrays with implicit index ordering or with drawElements and an index array.

- The VS runs, minimally setting the screen position of each vertex and optionally performing additional calculations, which are then passed on to the FS.

- Output data from the VS continues down the fixed portion of the pipeline.

- The GPU produces primitives using vertices and indices.

- The rasterizer discards any primitive part that lies outside of the viewport. Parts within the viewport are then broken up into pixel-sized fragments.

- Vertice values are then interpolated across each fragment.

- Fragments with these interpolated values are passed on to the FS.

- The FS minimally sets the color value, but can also do texture and lighting operations.

- Fragments can be discarded or passed on to the framebuffer, which stores a 2D image and optionally also uses a depth and stencil buffer. In this case, depth testing and stencil testing can discard some fragments from being rendered in the final image. This image is either passed on to the drawing buffer and shown to the user or alternatively saved to an offscreen buffer for later usage such as to save as texture data.

A high-level view of the WebGL rendering process is shown in Figure 2-2.

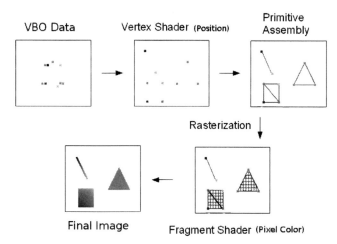

Figure 2-2. *WebGL rendering process overview*

In Figure 2-2, we start with vertex positions that are in model coordinate space. The VS then transforms the vertices to a final position. Appropriate primitive types are formed, the image clipped, rasterized, and passed on to the FS. The FS interpolates values and sends the result optionally through the depth and stencil buffers and finally the framebuffer.

GL Shading Language

Learning the GL Shading Language (GLSL) is essential to learning WebGL. I like to reference the Khronos WebGL wiki, which aptly states:

"Nothing happens in WebGL without shaders."

Background

The shading language used in WebGL is actually the OpenGL ES Shading Language (also known as GLSL ES or ESSL) and is based on the OpenGL Shading Language (GLSL) version 1.20. The complete specification of OpenGL ESSL can be downloaded from http://www.khronos.org/registry/gles/specs/2.0/GLSL_ES_ Specification_1.0.17.pdf.

GLSL is based on C++ and is actually two separate but closely related languages for vertex and fragment processors. The compiled source on each processor is known as a VS or FS, respectively. The VS and FS are linked together to form a single program that is run on the GPU.

The VS acts on one vertex at a time, and each vertex can have various attributes associated with it. The FS acts on a part of the rasterized image and can interpolate vertex data. It cannot change the position of the fragment or view the data of neighboring fragments. The VS can send data on to the FS. The ultimate goal of the shader program is to update the frame (drawing) buffer or a texture buffer.

WebGL uses the JavaScript scripting language to bind our shaders to the GLSL application programming interface (API). It can be a little confusing to realize that we are embedding the GLSL, which has a C++ like syntax, inside of a `<script>` tag. We do this with either of the following:

- Embedding the VS and FS sources within the same web file in a `<script>` tag of type `"x-shader/x-vertex"` or `"x-shader/x-fragment"`, respectively

- Placing the VS and FS in external files and loading them with Ajax

---

▪ **Note** By default, the `<script>` tag sets the `type` attribute to `javascript` or `text/javascript`. The types `"x-shader/x-vertex"` and `"x-shader/x-fragment"` are actually not recognized by the browser and ignored. The content is still loaded within the Document Object Model (DOM) for later retrieval but is otherwise not used.

We will come back to the GLSL later in the chapter. For now, let us discuss the roles of the shaders.

Shader Roles

The VS and FS have distinct roles that work together to render a finished image. Essentially, the VS acts on every vertex and is responsible for setting the final vertex location while the FS acts upon each pixel and sets the final color.

Vertex Shader (VS)

The VS is responsible for all vertex coordinate transformations. This includes model view and projection matrix view calculations. It also calculates normal vector and texture coordinate generation and transformations. The VS can perform per-vertex lighting calculations and pass these values on to the FS for a per-pixel computation.

In summary, the VS is responsible for

- final vertex position

and optionally

- per vertex normal, texture, lighting, and color

- passing values on to the FS

Minimally, a VS needs to set the gl_Position, which as we will discuss later in the chapter, is a built-in VS variable (see Listing 2-1).

Listing 2-1. Simple vertex shader, which passes the input vertex positions to the fragment shader

```
<script id="shader-vs" type="x-shader/x-vertex">
    attribute vec3 aVertexPosition;
```

```
    void main(void) {
        gl_Position = aVertexPosition;
    }
</script>
```

Fragment Shader (FS)

The FS operates on a pixel, which is a rasterized portion of a primitive(s). It computes final per-pixel color can perform texture lookups, and can also be used to produce effects such as fog. You can think of the VS and FS as a team. The VS passes values to the FS, but the FS gets final say and could choose to not use these values. The FS also does not render portions of an image that are obscured by another object or fall outside of the viewport by choosing to discard them.

In summary, the FS is responsible for

- setting the final color of each pixel

and optionally

- performing texture lookups
- discarding fragments

Minimally, the FS needs to set the fragment color, as shown in Listing 2-2.

Listing 2-2. A fragment shader that sets every fragment to blue

```
<script id="shader-fs" type="x-shader/x-fragment">
    void main(void) {
        gl_FragColor = vec4(0.0, 0.0, 1.0, 1.0);
    }
</script>
```

Basic Usage

We have gone over the steps of creating a shader program in Chapter 1 and also shown the API signatures of each method that we used. Here we will briefly recap how to set up and clean up a shader program in WebGL.

Setting Up a Shader Program

Within a WebGL application, the program is a WebGLProgram object, and each shader is a WebGLShader object. We define variables to hold our shaders and program:

```
var vertexShader   = null,
  fragmentShader = null,
  shaderProgram  = null;
```

Here are the steps to use shaders within a WebGL program:

1. Create the shaders:

    ```
    vertexShader = gl.createShader(GL.VERTEX_SHADER);
    fragmentShader = gl.createShader(GL.FRAGMENT_SHADER);
    ```

2. Set the source code of each shader:

```
<script id="shader-vs" type="x-shader/x-vertex">
    ...
</script>

<script id="shader-fs" type="x-shader/x-fragment">
    ...
</script>

var vertex_source = document.getElementById('shader-vs').innerHTML
var fragment_source = document.getElementById('shader-fs').innerHTML,

gl.shaderSource(vertexShader, vertex_source);
gl.shaderSource(fragmentShader, fragment_source);
```

3. Compile each shader and check for errors:

```
gl.compileShader(vertexShader);
if (!gl.getShaderParameter(vertexShader, gl.COMPILE_STATUS)) {
    alert( "Error compiling vertex shader: " +
                        gl.getShaderInfoLog(vertexShader));
    }

gl.compileShader(fragmentShader);
if (!gl.getShaderParameter(fragmentShader, gl.COMPILE_STATUS)) {
    alert( "Error compiling fragment shader: " +
                        gl.getShaderInfoLog(fragmentShader));
    }
```

4. Create a program:

```
shaderProgram = gl.createProgram();
```

5. Attach our shaders to the program:

```
gl.attachShader(shaderProgram, vertexShader);
gl.attachShader(shaderProgram, fragmentShader);
```

6. Link the program and check for errors:

```
gl.linkProgram(shaderProgram);

if (!gl.getProgramParameter(shaderProgram, gl.LINK_STATUS)) {
    alert("Unable to initialize the shader program.");
}
```

7. Tell WebGL to use our program:

```
gl.useProgram(shaderProgram);
```

Clean Up

To remove the shaders from our program, we perform the opposite procedure:

1. Detach the shaders from the program:

```
gl.detachShader(shaderProgram, vertexShader);
gl.detachShader(shaderProgram, fragmentShader);
```

2. Delete each shader:

```
gl.deleteShader(vertexShader);
gl.deleteShader(fragmentShader);
```

3. Delete the program:

```
gl.deleteProgram(shaderProgram);
```

The preceding quickly recaps the steps to create and use a shader program in WebGL. If we need to, we can create multiple shader programs within an application and switch between them by calling useProgram with the appropriate shader: gl.useProgram(shaderProgram). As discussed in Chapter 9, it is an expensive operation, so switching should be used as much as possible.

We will now show you how to load shaders from external sources instead of embedded within the same document as our main program.

Loading Shaders with Ajax

We have shown how to include our shader programs within the same file that holds our WebGL application. To keep our application file shorter and more modular, we can use Ajax to load in our shaders from separate external files.

▓ **Note** Due to WebGL security restrictions and the same origin policy, to include an external shader, we need to be running a web server. Setting up a local web server is beyond the scope of this book, but does not need to be difficult. Some great LAMP, MAMP, and WAMP (Linux/Mac/Windows, Apache, MySQL and PHP/Perl/Python) stacks are listed in Appendix D. There is also an increasing number of cloud platforms available that offer free accounts.

Loading external sources is optional, and if you cannot get a local server setup or prefer embedded shaders, by all means stick with that approach.

XMLHttpRequestObject

To load Ajax content from an external file we can use regular JavaScript to directly use the XMLHttpRequestObject (XHR). The XHR is used to send a request from the client to the server and receive a response without requiring reloading the page or interrupting a user's browsing experience.

Briefly, we can think of the XMLHttpRequestObject by the components in its name:

- *XML*: The document format sent; can also be JSON, HTML or plain text

- *HTTP*: The protocol used; can also be HTTPS

- *Request*: The action; can also refer to responses

In addition, the requests may be asynchronous calls that do not block other calls, or synchronous calls that do. With an asynchronous call, other requests can take place in parallel while with a synchronous call; all other requests need to wait for completion of the current request before starting processing. Synchronous calls take place in serial order. Usually asynchronous calls are done on websites for improved loading times. However, there are times when a synchronous call is needed to ensure the proper order of events. In Listing 2-3, setting the third parameter of the open method to false tells the XMLHttpRequestObject not to do an asynchronous call.

In Listing 2-3 we create a new instance of the XMLHttpRequestObject, set up the details of the document that we want to retrieve with the open method, actually send out the request with the send method, and then observe the readyState and status properties. We will not go into great detail about the XMLHttpRequestObject, but additional resources are listed in Appendix D.

Listing 2-3. Loading shaders with the XMLHttpRequestObject

```
//get shader sources with XMLHttpRequestObject
var      fs_source = null,
         vs_source = null;

var xhr = new XMLHttpRequest();
//synchronous request requires a false third parameter
xhr.open('GET', './shader.vs', false);
//overriding the mime type is required
xhr.overrideMimeType('text/xml');
xhr.send(null);

if (xhr.readyState == xhr.DONE) {
        if(xhr.status === 200)
        {
                vs_source = xhr.responseXML.documentElement.firstChild.data;
        } else {
                console. error("Error: " + xhr.statusText);
        }
}
xhr.open('GET', './shader.fs', false);
xhr.send(null);

if (xhr.readyState == xhr.DONE) {
        if(xhr.status === 200)
        {
                fs_source = xhr.responseXML.documentElement.firstChild.data;
        } else {
                console. error("Error: " + xhr.statusText);
        }
}
```

In Listing 2-3 we are sending synchronous requests. Alternatively, we could use asynchronous calls and callback functions to signal that we are ready to move on with our program. In Listing 2-3 we also have to override the mime type to XML because the browser may not otherwise recognize the content of our shaders as a XML document. When the readyState is equal to XMLHttpRequestObject.DONE, then we check the status. A status of 200 means success and we can grab the data we need from the responseXML object: responseXML. documentElement.firstChild.data. If the status is not 200, we output an error message to the console.

Starting with a copy of the 01/3D_triangles_depth_test.html file that was the last example of Chapter 1, remove the inline shader scripts at the top of the file and swap out these lines with those found in Listing 2-3:

```
//get shader source
var fs_source = document.getElementById('shader-fs').innerHTML,
vs_source = document.getElementById('shader-vs').innerHTML;
```

When you run the modified application, you will see that it works exactly the same as before. This can be found in the 02/vanilla_ajax.html file.

■ **Note**   Remember that you must be running a web server to use this approach. In Figure 2-3, I naively try running my file directly in the browser. You can see in the Chrome developer tools console the error that this causes. Developer and debugging tools are very useful and are covered in depth in Chapter 9.

Figure 2-3. *Error caused by trying to load an external file without a web server*

Using jQuery

If we use a higher-level JavaScript API such as the very popular jQuery, there are a couple of advantages. First, it is easier because some of the low-level code is obscured for us. Second, it is more cross-browser compatible. A quick background of jQuery can be found in Appendix A. The equivalent jQuery functionality of Listing 2-3 is shown in Listing 2-4:

Listing 2-4. Loading shaders with jQuery

```
//get shader sources with jQuery Ajax
$.ajax({
  async: false,
  url: './shader.vs',
  success: function (data) {
    vs_source = data.firstChild.textContent;
  },
  dataType: 'xml'
});
$.ajax({
  async: false,
  url: './shader.fs',
  success: function (data) {
    fs_source = data.firstChild.textContent;
  },
  dataType: 'xml'
});
```

Because jQuery extracts away the underlying XHR calls and the $.ajax method explicitly states the parameters that it is using, Listing 2-4 is both more concise and easier to understand than Listing 2-3.

Remember to also include a link to the jQuery library. The latest version of the jQuery library hosted on the jQuery CDN is available for development usage from http://code.jquery.com/jquery-latest.js and for production usage, the minified form can be found at http://code.jquery.com/jquery-latest.min.js. The full source code for this example is available on the books companion sites and is available in the file 02/jquery_ajax.html. There is an issue associated with including the full shader source, including script tags, externally and then parsing. The issue and solution are discussed in Chapter 9.

GLSL Specification in More Detail

Earlier, I mentioned that the GLSL is similar to C++. It uses a subset of ASCII characters and carriage return and/or line feeds to terminate each line. The language is case sensitive and it is interesting to note that unlike C/C++, there are no character or string types used. As such, there are also no characters used for quoting. Variable and function names must start with an alphabet character or underscore, but cannot start with `gl_` or be a reserved language word. Each shader program can have only one `main` method, which is the same as C/C++.

Primitive Types

The available basic types that are inherited from C++ are shown in Table 2-1.

Table 2-1. *C++ Inherited Types and Descriptions*

C++ types	Description
void	Used to specify a function with no return value and/or no parameters
bool	Boolean true or false
int	Signed integers. Example: 1, 7, 13
float	Floating point number. Example: 1.3, 7.0, 13.445

GLSL defines new primitive types that are shown in Table 2-2.

Table 2-2. *GLSL Types and Descriptions*

GLSL types	Description
vec2, vec3, vec4, ivec2, ivec3, vec4, bvec2, bvec3, bvec4	Vector of size 1×2, 1x3, or 1x4; and of type float, integer, or bool, respectively
mat2, mat3, mat4	Floating point matrix of size 2x2, 3x3, or 4x4
sampler2D, samplerCube	Handles to 2D or cube mapped textures

We can also create structures that can hold more complex composite types. For instance:

```
struct myStruct{
      vec3 something;
      mat4 somethingElse;
}
```

Qualifiers

GLSL has several optional qualifiers for variables. These fall into the categories of *storage, parameter, precision* and *invariant* qualifiers.

Storage Qualifiers

Storage qualifiers describe both the variable scope and relation to the WebGL program.

A variable might be declared with `attribute` storage as `attribute vec3 aColor;`.

Table 2-3. *Storage Qualifiers*

Qualifier	Description
[none]	The default for a variable is to have no storage qualifier. Local variables and function input parameters have no storage qualifiers.
const	Constant throughout the program. Read only.
uniform	Constant value across an entire primitive.
attribute	VS per vertex information from our WebGL application.
varying	VS write, FS read.

▒ **Note** Prefixes are not required, but are commonly used to help represent the storage type of variables to other programmers: v for varying, u for uniform, and a for attribute. For example:

```
attribute vec3 aVertexNormals;
uniform uSampler;
varying vOriginalPosition;
```

Parameter Qualifiers

Parameter qualifiers are used for function parameters (see Table 2-4).

A function in WebGL might look like this:

```
vec3 a = (0, 1, 0);
vec3 c;
void myFunction(a, out c){
    c = a * 2;
}
```

Table 2-4. *Parameter Qualifiers*

Qualifier	Description
[none]	The default, which is the same thing as specifying the in qualifier
In	Parameters passed into a function
Out	Parameters to be passed out of a function, but were not initialized
Inout	Initialized parameter that will also be passed out of a function

Precision Qualifiers

There are three different precision qualifiers for the GLSL: `highp`, `mediump`, and `lowp`. `highp` satisfies the minimum requirements for the vertex language. `mediump` satisfies the minimum precision for the FS. `lowp` is less than medium but still fully represents the values of a color channel.

Invariant Qualifier

Lastly, there is the `invariant` qualifier. It ensures that a variable can no longer be modified.

Qualifier Order

The order of qualifiers is important. For variables it is:

> *invariant, storage, precision for example:* `invariant uniform highp mat4 m;`

For parameters, the order is:

> *storage, parameter, precision For example:* `void myFunc(const in lowp c){ ; }`

Built-in Variables

The GLSL has a number of built-in variables that are shown in Table 2-5.

Table 2-5. *Built-in Shader Variables*

Variable	Type	Description	Used In	Input/Output
gl_Position	vec4	Vertex position	VS	output
gl_PointSize	float	Point size	VS	output
gl_FragCoord	vec4	Fragment position within the frame buffer	FS	input
gl_FrontFacing	bool	Whether the fragment is part of a front or back facing primitive	FS	input
gl_PointCoord	vec2	Fragment position within a point	FS	input
gl_FragColor	vec4	Final fragment color	FS	output
gl_FragData[n]	vec4	Fragment color for a color attachment, n	FS	output

Built-in Constants

There are also built-in constants in WebGL. They have implementation-dependent values, but the minimum requirement of each is listed here:

```
const mediump int gl_MaxVertexAttribs = 8;
const mediump int gl_MaxVertexUniformVectors = 128;
const mediump int gl_MaxVaryingVectors = 8;
const mediump int gl_MaxVertexTextureImageUnits = 0;
const mediump int gl_MaxCombinedTextureImageUnits = 8;
const mediump int gl_MaxTextureImageUnits = 8;
const mediump int gl_MaxFragmentUniformVectors = 16;
const mediump int gl_MaxDrawBuffers = 1;
```

Vector Components

For convenience, besides numeric array subscripts, vector components can be accessed by a single letter. These letters vary based on the vector type, as displayed in Table 2-6.

Table 2-6. *Vector Components*

Usage	Shorthand Notation
Coordinate positions and normals	{x,y,z,w}
Colors	{r,g,b,a}
Textures	{s,t,p,q}

The usual third component of a texture, r, is renamed p to be distinct from the red color component. With vector components you can do assignments and calculations such as:

```
vec4 green = vec4(0.0, 1.0, 0.0, 1.0);
vec4 blue = vec4(0.0, 0.0, 1.0, 1.0);
vec4 final_color;

final_color = vec4(green.rg, blue.ba); //use red, green from one vector and blue, alpha from
            another
final_color.rgb = green.rrr; //use only the red channel
final_color.rg = green.gr; //swap red, green
final_color.g = green.gr; //average green, blue
```

Vector and Matrix Operations

GLSL has built-in support for vector and matrix operations. When a scalar operates on a vector or matrix, or the operation is addition or subtraction, then calculation is done component-wise. When performing vector or matrix multiplication, then we follow regular linear algebra multiplication rules. Some example declarations:

```
vec3 u, v, w;
float f;
mat3 m;
```

We can also initialize scalar variables, vectors and matrices on declaration:

```
float f = 1.4;
vec4 color = vec4(1.0, 0.0, 0.0, 1.0); //red
vec4 a = vec2(1.0, 2.0);
vec2 b = vec2(3.0, 4.0);

mat2 m = mat2(a, b);
//column major order - columns are listed in sequence. So the above
//produces a matrix with values:
//    1.0       3.0
//    2.0       4.0
//
//and stored in memory as 1.0 2.0 3.0 4.0

mat2 m = mat2(1.0, 0.0, 0.0, 1.0);   //2x2 identity matrix
mat2 m = mat2(1.0);                  //also 2x2 identity matrix

v = u + f;
```

is the same as:

```
v.x = u.x + f;
v.y = u.y + f;
```

```
v.z = u.z + f;
w = u - v;
```

is the same as:

```
w.x = u.x - v.x;
w.y = u.y - v.y;
w.z = u.z - v.z;
```

The GLSL also has functions for performing dot products and cross products, which are dot and cross respectively.

```
w = dot(u, v);
```

is the same as:

```
w.x = u.x*v.x;
w.y = u.y*v.y;
w.z = u.z*v.z;
```

and:

```
w = cross(u, v);
```

is the same as:

```
w.x = u.y * v.z* - u.z * v.y;
w.y = u.z * v.x* - u.x * v.z;
w.z = u.x * v.y* - u.y * v.x;
```

Built-in Functions

The GLSL defines many built-in functions for common operations. We have just seen two: dot and cross. There are many more and should always be used over equivalent user-defined functions as the built-in versions will be optimized.

For all the functions to be listed, the input and output types can be float, vec2, vec3, or vec4. To avoid redundancy and for a cleaner appearance, we will use T to signify any one of these types. Just keep in mind that if an input parameter is of a certain type, all other inputs and outputs must be that type as well. For example:

```
T sin(T angle) can represent
float sin(float angle) or
vec2 sin(vec2 angle) but not
vec2 sin(float angle)
```

For the vec2, vec3, or vec4 instances of a function, the operation is done on each component. Also note that if the divisor of one of these functions is 0, the result will be undefined, but there will be no divide by zero error produced.

Angle and Trigonometry Functions

GLSL functionality to convert between degrees and radians and calculate trigonometric values are shown in Table 2-7. Recall that degrees = radians * 180/π, so one radian ≈ 57.3 degrees.

Table 2-7. *Trigonometric Functions in GLSL*

GLSL Function	Description
T radians(T degrees)	Convert degrees to radians; radians = degrees/57.3
T degrees(T angle)	Convert angle (in radians) to degrees; degrees = angle*57.3
T sin(T angle)	Sine function (Opposite/hypotenuse); angle in radians, output is in the range [–1, 1]
T cos(T angle)	Cosine function (Adjacent/hypotenuse); angle in radians, output is in the range [–1, 1]
T tan(T angle)	Tangent function (Opposite/adjacent); angle in radians, range is +/- infinity; undefined when angle is a multiple of $\pi/2$
T asin(T x)	Arcsine function; given input in [–1, 1] produces an angle in the range [$-\pi/2$, $\pi/2$]; undefined for |x| > 1.
T acos(T x)	Arccosine function; given input in [-1, 1] produces an angle in the range [0, π]; undefined for |x| > 1.
T atan(T y, T x)	Arctangent; undefined if both x and y are 0; Output is $[-\pi,\pi]$
T atan(T y_over_x)	Arctangent; output range is $[-\pi/2,\pi/2]$.

Exponential Functions

Functionality to handle exponential powers and their inverses, logarithms, along with powers of +/– ½, which are square root and inverse square root, are shown in Table 2-8.

Table 2-8. *Exponential Functions in GLSL*

GLSL Function	Math Function	Description
T pow(T x, T y)	x^y	Returns x raised to the power of y, x^y. Results are undefined for x < 0 or x=0 and y<=0
T exp(T x)	e^x	Natural exponentiation of x, e^x.
T exp2(T x)	2^x	2 to the power of x, 2^x.
T log(T x)	$y = \log_e x$	Natural logarithm x, $x = e^y$, $y = \log_e x$. Undefined if x <= 0.
T log2(T x)	$y = \log_2 x$	Logarithm of base 2, $x = 2^y$, $y = \log_2 x$. Undefined if x <= 0.
T sqrt(T x)	$\sqrt{x}$	Returns the positive square root of x, $x^{1/2}$ or $\sqrt{x}$. Undefined if x < 0.
T inversesqrt(T x)	$\frac{1}{\sqrt{x}}$	The reciprocal of the positive square root of x, $x^{-1/2}$ or $\frac{1}{\sqrt{x}}$. Undefined if x <= 0.

Common Functions

Some other commonly used math functions are shown in Table 2-9. These include operations that grab the whole or fractional part of a number or perform other numeric manipulation.

Table 2-9. *Common Functions in GLSL*

GLSL Function	Description
T abs(T x)	Returns -x if x<0; otherwise returns x.
T sign(T x)	Returns 1.0 if x > 0, 0.0 if x = 0, or –1.0 if x < 0.
T floor(T x)	Returns the nearest integer below or equal to x. floor(4.7) = 4.0 = floor(4.0)
T ceil(T x)	Returns the nearest integer above or equal to x. ceil(4.7) = 5.0 = ceil(5.0)
T fract(T x)	Returns the decimal part of a number. fract(x) = x - floor(x).
T mod(T x, T y)	Modulus operator. Returns x - y*floor(x/y) using the corresponding component of y.
T mod(T x, float y)	Modulus operator. Returns x - y*floor(x/y) using a single provided floating point value.
T min(T x, T y) T min(T x, float y)	Returns y if y<x; otherwise x. Component-wise or single float y version of function.
T max(T x, T y) T max(T x, float y)	Returns y if y>x; otherwise x. Component-wise or single float y version of function.
T clamp(T x, T minVal, T maxVal) T clamp(T x, float minVal, float maxVal)	Returns (min(max(x, minVal), maxVal)). Ensures that minVal <= x <= maxVal. Component-wise or single min and max value versions. Undefined if minVal > maxVal.
T mix(T x, T y, T a) T mix(T x, T y, float a)	Returns a linear blend of x and y corresponding to the equation x(1-a) + y*a. Component-wise or single min and max value versions.
T step(T edge, T x) T step(T float edge, T x)	Returns 0.0 if x < edge, 1.0 otherwise. Component-wise or single min and max value versions.
T smoothstep(T edge0, T edge1, T x) T smoothstep(float edge0, float edge1, T x)	Returns 0.0 if x < edge, 1.0 if x >= edge1 and uses smooth interpolation (Hermite) between 0 and 1 otherwise. Undefined if edge0 >= edge1.

Geometric Functions

The following GLSL functions in Table 2-10 are not calculated component-wise but follow vector-on-vector operation rules to compute geometric results.

Table 2-10. *Geometric Functions in GLSL*

GLSL Function	Description
float **length**(T x)	Returns the length of the vector.
float **distance**(T x, T y)	Returns the distance between vectors x and y, length(x - y).
float **dot**(T x, T y)	Returns the dot product of vectors x and y, $x_0{}^*y_0 + x_1{}^*y_1 + ...$
vec3 **cross**(vec3 x, vec3 y)	Returns the cross product of vectors x and y. This operation is available only for three-dimensional vectors.
T **normalize**(T x)	Returns a vector with the same direction as the input x, but with a new length of 1, $(x_0/\text{length}(x), x_1(\text{length}(x)), ...)$
T **faceforward** (T N, T I, T Nref)	Used to adjust a vertex normal to face the scene camera. N is a normal vector, I is the incidence vector(direction from the camera to a vertex), Nref is a reference vector. Determines the direction of a primitive face, by calculating dot (Nref, I). Returns N if the dot product is smaller than 0.0 and –N otherwise.
T **reflect**(T I, T N)	Returns the reflection direction. N is a normal vector, I is the incidence vector (direction from the camera to a vertex). Returns I - 2*dot(N, I)*N.
T **refract**(T I, T N, float eta)	Returns the refraction direction. N is a normal vector; I is the incidence vector (direction from the camera to a vertex), eta is the ratio of indices of refraction. I and N must be normalized to obtain correct results.

Matrix and Vector Functions

The following matrix function can use mat2, mat3, or mat4 so long as all inputs and the output are of the same type:

```
mat matrixCompMult (mat x, mat y)
```

Normally when two matrices are multiplied, (x*y), the computation of the result[i][j] = dot($x_{\text{row\_j}}$, $y_{\text{column\_i}}$). However, this function computes just the scalar product of each matrix element, result[i][j] = x[i][j] * y[i][j].

For component-wise value comparisons of vectors, we have the following functions that return a Boolean valued vector. In the following code, bvec can represent bvec2, bvec3, or bvec4. Similarly vec can be vec2, vec3, vec4, ivec2, ivec3, or ivec4 as long as both parameters are the same type.

```
bvec lessThan(vec x, vec y)
bvec lessThanEqual(vec x, vec y)
bvec greaterThan(vec x, vec y)
bvec greaterThanEqual(vecx, vec y)
```

This does component-wise comparision of x < y, x <= y, x > y or x >=y, respectively.

```
bvec equal(vec x, vec y)
bvec notEqual(vec x, vec y)
```

These functions can also take bvec parameters and return the component-wise comparision of x == y or x != y, respectively.

```
bool any(bvec x)
bool all(bvec x)
bvec not(bvec x)
```

The first function returns true if *any* component of x is true. The second returns true only if *all* components are true. The third function returns the complementary Boolean vector: input true components are set to false in the output vector and false components to true.

Texture Lookup Functions

Lastly, there are built-in functions for textures. Level of detail (Lod) suffixed functions are only available in the VS.

2D Texture Functions

```
vec4 texture2D (sampler2D sampler,vec2 coord )
vec4 texture2D (sampler2D sampler,vec2 coord, float bias)
vec4 texture2DProj (sampler2D sampler,vec3 coord )
vec4 texture2DProj (sampler2D sampler,vec3 coord, float bias)
vec4 texture2DProj (sampler2D sampler,vec4 coord)
vec4 texture2DProj (sampler2D sampler,vec4 coord, float bias)
vec4 texture2DLod (sampler2D sampler,vec2 coord, float lod)
vec4 texture2DProjLod (sampler2D sampler,vec3 coord, float lod)
vec4 texture2DProjLod (sampler2D sampler,vec4 coord, float lod)
```

coord is a texture coordinate that looks at the current texture bound to the sampler variable. A suffix containing Proj means the projective version of the function. In this case, the texture coordinates (coord.st) are divided by the last component of coord. If you use a coord of type vec4with the projective version, the third coordinate is simply ignored.

3D Texture Functions

```
vec4 textureCube (samplerCube sampler, vec3 coord )
vec4 textureCube (samplerCube sampler,vec3 coord, float bias )
vec4 textureCubeLod (samplerCube sampler,vec3 coord, float lod)
```

coord is a texture coordinate that looks at the current texture which is bound to the sampler. The direction of coord determines which face of the 3D cube to do a 2D texture lookup on.

Noise Functions

Unlike recent versions of the GLSL, the OpenGLES SL that WebGL uses does *not* have built-in noise functions for generating noise. Using noise can be very useful to add the appearance of randomness or grittiness to textures. We can also simulate clouds, fog, wood and marble, among other materials using noise. Though beyond the scope of this book, noise can be generated using algorithms such as Perlin noise in a shader program and stored in texture images for later use.

Interactive GLSL Environs

A good place to dive into the GLSL functions is an interactive editor that lets you adjust the VSs and FSs without needing to worry about the WebGL application code.

Several desktop programs to manipulate the GLSL exist, but are primarily geared toward OpenGL implementations and versions of the GLSL that are higher than WebGL supports. As such, they can still be useful but the reader should be warned that functionality that may work within these programs may not function properly when used as WebGL specific vertex and fragment shaders.

There are several websites that offer shader manipulation and also control the WebGL application, models, and program interaction for you. This lets you concentrate on the GLSL source. The number of useful programs and websites for WebGL shader development will increase with the maturity of the language and the community. At the moment, three good sites are:

- KickJS Shader Editor
  http://www.kickjs.org/example/shader_editor/shader_editor.html

- WebGL Playground
  http://webglplayground.net/

- SpiderGL MeShader
  http://spidergl.org/meshade/

You can see MeShade in action in Figure 2-4.

Figure 2-4. *Using the gargoyle mesh and editable shader source of MeShade*

Of the three sites lists, KickJS is the easiest to start using and has a nice real-time error console and adjustable settings.

Procedural Shaders

For the following examples, we will use an interactive shader environment to explore some *procedural shaders*, which produce effects through algorithms within the shaders instead of precomputed stored data passed in from our application. They are sometimes referred to as procedural texture shaders. We will cover stored textures in the next chapter.

Procedural shaders do not require memory to store an image and scale better than using normal textures. However, using procedural shaders requires an understanding of the algorithms used, which can be complex and also require much more computing power than a stored texture. The results of a procedural shader can also be rendered to a texture file for later static usage.

Procedural shaders can be written using both the VS and FS. In most of these examples, we will only use the VS to pass the final coordinates of each vertex on to the FS. The algorithms that will determine the final pixel color will be written within the FS.

Gradient Color

Our first example will produce a gradient color using the mix function and a component of the position or texture coordinate defined within our interactive environment. In Listing 2-5 we show the relevant FS code for the KickJS environment and in Listing 2-6 for the webglplayground.net editor (see Figure 2-5). As you can see, the only difference is the variable that we use for our mix amount.

Listing 2-5. Gradient FS at KickJS

```
varying vec2 uv;

void main(void)
{
 vec3 blue = vec3(0.0, 0.0, 1.0);
 vec3 green = vec3(0.0, 1.0, 0.0);
 gl_FragColor = vec4(mix(blue, green, uv.s), 1.0);
}
```

Listing 2-6. Gradient FS at webglplayground.net/

```
@glsl_fs1
varying vec2 pos;

void main() {
 vec3 blue = vec3(0.0, 0.0, 1.0);
 vec3 green = vec3(0.0, 1.0, 0.0);
 gl_FragColor = vec4(mix(blue, green, pos.y), 1.0);
}
```

Figure 2-5. *Gradient teapot on the left (KickJS); gradient plane on the right*

Stripes

Next we will show how to use the mod function to generate repetition and create stripes. In Listing 2-7 we take a texture parameter and multiply it by a variable, `repetition`, which determines the frequency of alternation. Then we test the output, setting the color value equally dependent on a threshold of 0.5. If this is set unevenly, toward 0.0 or 1.0, one color of stripes will be much wider than the other, resulting in more of a pinstriping appearance. In the center teapot of Figure 2-6, we use `uv.t` instead of `uv.s`, and in the right teapot we use (`uv.s * uv.t`).

Listing 2-7. Fragment shader code to generate black and white stripes

```
varying vec2 uv;
void main(void)
{
        float repetition = 15.0;
        vec3 black = vec3(0.0, 0.0, 0.0);
        vec3 white = vec3(1.0, 1.0, 1.0);
        bool color = (mod(uv.s * repetition, 1.0) > 0.5);

        if(color){
            gl_FragColor = vec4(black, 1.0);
        }else{
            gl_FragColor = vec4(white, 1.0);
        }
}
```

Figure 2-6. *Teapots with vertical, horizontal, and curved striping*

Notice the aliasing artifacts in Figure 2-6.

Discarding

We will explore the GLSL keyword, `discard`, which is used in the FS to *not* draw fragments. We will also use a few of the functions defined previously to produce grid point and lattice drawings. The nice thing with interactive shaders is that the models are rendered for us. We just worry about the VS and FS details. I have chosen the sphere mesh, but disabled lighting to simplify the shaders. The variable names are specific to the KickJS environment, but will work with any WebGL application as long as you rename the attributes and uniform variables to appropriate values.

Listing 2-8. The VS for use within the kickjs.org shader editor

```
attribute vec3 vertex;
attribute vec2 uv1;

uniform mat4 _mvProj;

varying vec2 uv;
varying vec3 vColor;

void main(void) {
        gl_Position = _mvProj * vec4(vertex, 1.0);
        uv = uv1;
        vColor = vec3(1.0,0.7,0.8);
}
```

Listing 2-9. The matching FS for use within the kickjs.org shader editor

```
varying vec3 highp vColor;
varying vec2 highp uv;

uniform sampler2D tex;

void main(void)
{
  gl_FragColor = texture2D(tex,uv)*vec4(vColor, 1.0);
}
```

The FS makes use of a texture that is stored in the sampler2D tex. We cover textures in the next chapter, but the shader editor loads it for us here. We just need to know that 2D textures have coordinates s and t, which lie in the range [0,1]. The default image produced is shown on the left of Figure 2-7.

We adjust the FS now to include the lines in Listing 2-10.

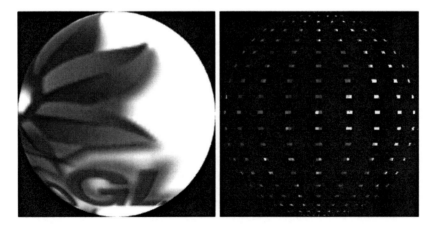

Figure 2-7. *Original image on the left, using discard on the right*

Listing 2-10. Using the discard function

```
const float scale = 20.0;
const vec2 latticeSize = vec2(0.1, 0.1);
vec2 fractional = fract(uv * scale);
bvec2 toDiscard = (greaterThan(fractional, latticeSize ));

if( any(toDiscard) )
{
    discard;
}
```

Adding the above code to the main function in Listing 2-9 produces the image on the right of Figure 2-7. In Listing 2-10, uv holds the texture coordinates passed in from the VS. These values will fall between 0.0 and 1.0. Multiplying by our scaling factor adjusts the range and determines how many sections we have. Next we use fract to get the fractional part of both scaled components. The greaterThan function will do a component-wise compare of fractional and latticeSize vector values and store the Boolean results in the toDiscard vector. Explicitly, it looks like this:

```
toDiscard = bvec2( fractional.x > latticeSize.x, fractional.y > latticeSize.y)
```

For a varying input uv value of (0.401, 0.32),

```
fractional = fract(8.02, 6.4) = (0.02, 0.4)
```

and

```
toDiscard = greaterThan( (0.02, 0.4), (0.1, 0.1) ) = (false, true)
```

We then check the Boolean vector of comparision results with the any function that returns true if any of the components of an input Boolean vector is true. With the previous example instance, toDiscard = (false, true), so the any function will return true.

When the function returns true we call the GLSL keyword discard, which tells the GPU not to render the fragment. In Listing 2-10, only parts of the image that are within a certain distance of regular grid points will be rendered.

You can decrease/increase the grid point size by decreasing/increasing one or both components of latticeSize. You can decrease/increase the total number of grid points by decreasing/increasing scale.

Now suppose we want to show latitude and longitude type lines along the sphere. That is easy; we simply use the all function instead of the any function used in Listing 2-10. This reduces what we discard because both the texture components must be greater than our lattice size to return true (see the left side of Figure 2-8). Finally, we

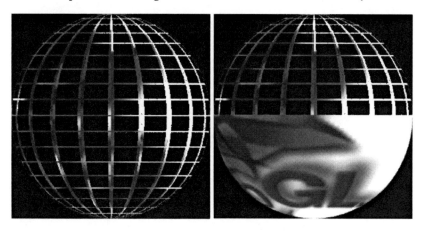

Figure 2-8. *A full lattice shown on the left, and half a lattice shown on the right*

can also specify that in addition to our lattice check that we also do not want to discard any part of the image that lies within a certain region. We can do this with an additional conditional test such as the following, which checks the t value of the texture:

```
if(uv.t < 0.5){ toDiscard.x = false; }
```

The output of adding this conditional test is shown on the right of Figure 2-8.

Summary

This chapter looked at the WebGL graphics pipeline, the role of shaders, and the GLSL in depth. We showed online interactive sites that let you easily play around with shaders without needing to create the mesh or viewport, and showed some procedural shading techniques. We will come back to procedural produced images in Chapter 6. We will build upon the knowledge gained in this chapter in more elaborate examples throughout the book, starting with the next chapter. In the next chapter, we will look at how to manipulate and apply texture to our meshes as well as discuss lighting models and surface normals.

CHAPTER 3

■ ■ ■

Textures and Lighting

In this chapter we will cover two topics that are fundamental to producing realistic scenes, texture and lighting. Specifically, we will

- discuss what textures are and how to apply them

- show what texture options are available and how to configure these

- use multiple textures in a shader

- present a basic lighting model

- create a directional light shader

By the end of the chapter, we will produce the textured and lit mesh on the right of Figure 3-1.

Figure 3-1. *Left - No texture or lighting; Right - both texture and lighting*

The left image in Figure 3-1 is a concrete example of why we need to use texture and lighting. In the last example of Chapter 1, a triangle mesh was visible as a 3D figure. The reason it appeared three-dimensional was only because the vertex colors were distinct and interpolated by our fragment shader. This provided depth cues for us. As you can see, when all the vertex points have the same color, and no lighting or texture is applied, the image looks like a flat two-dimensional polygon. It is actually still 3D; the reason that it appears flat is that there are no context clues to let us know that this is in fact a solid figure.

When we look at an image, we depend on clues such as variance on the faces of a solid in terms of lighting: darkness/illumination, reflection, shadows, and directional pattern changes from textures to inform us where one face ends and another begins. In the image on the right of Figure 3-1, we have added texture and lighting clues, and you can clearly tell that this is a solid.

Textures

Textures are images that are applied to surfaces within our program. Images used as textures may be bitmapped in origin or generated procedurally. Textures must be applied (mapped) to our image and in doing so are usually stretched, scaled, distorted, and/or repeated.

The width and height of a texture are usually the same and a power of 2, 2^n, such as 64, 128, 256, and 512. Each basic element of a texture is known as a *texel* which stands for **tex**ture **el**ement or **tex**ture pix**el**.

Texture Coordinates

In two dimensions, texture coordinates are referred to in (s,t) pairs instead of (x,y) pairs like vertex positions. Normally, texture coordinates are also limited to the range $(0,0)$ to $(1,1)$. For a texture size of 128x128 pixels, all points will be divided by 128 in order to lie within this range. The texture coordinate $(0.5, 0.25)$ for a 128x128 texture would refer to the texel $(64, 32)$.

Figure 3-2 shows the coordinates of a source image on the left and the equivalent texture coordinates on the right.

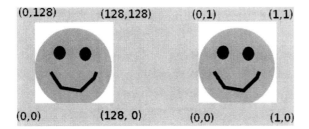

Figure 3-2. *Left - a square 128×128 pixel image with vertex coordinates; Right - the equivalent texture coordinates*

Texture coordinates are usually sent to the shader program as vertex attribute values, but (as we saw in the previous chapter) we can also manipulate them within our shader program.

Texture Objects

In WebGL, a texture is stored within a `WebGLTexture` object. To create and bind a `WebGLTexture` object, the API functions used are:

```
WebGLTexture createTexture();
void bindTexture(GLenum target, WebGLTexture texture);
```

The target for 2D textures will be TEXTURE_2D. Other target types are listed in Appendix C.
The code to create and bind a `WebGLTexture` will look like this:

```
var texture = gl.createTexture();
gl.bindTexture(gl.TEXTURE_2D, texture);
```

To check that a certain texture has loaded properly, you can use the API call:

```
GLboolean isTexture(WebGLTexture texture);
```

Code to check a texture will look like this:

```
if( !gl.isTexture(texture) )
{
        console.log("Error: Texture is invalid");
}
```

This is important to check because if no WebGLTexture is currently bound (by passing null or 0 to bindTexture), then further operation attempts on the texture will produce an INVALID_OPERATION error.

When you are done with a texture, you can delete it with a call to:

```
void deleteTexture(WebGLTexture texture);
```

It will look like this:

```
gl.deleteTexture(texture);
```

Now that we have initialized a WebGLTexture object, we are ready to load data into it.

texImage2D

The API call to load data into a texture is the texImage2D function. This function has five signature variations. The first four are of this form:

```
void texImage2D(  GLenum target, GLint level, GLenum internalformat,
                  GLenum format, GLenum type, [source]);
```

In this code, [source] may be one of ImageData, HTMLImageElement, HTMLCanvasElement, or HTMLVideoElement. The latter three may throw a DOMException.

The other form of the call is for specifying the data from a typed array:

```
void texImage2D(  GLenum target, GLint level, GLenum internalformat,
                  GLsizei width, GLsizei height, GLint border, GLenum format,
                  GLenum type, ArrayBufferView? pixels);
```

Example usage of this form of the function can be found in Chapter 6.

The level parameter refers to the level of detail used in mipmaps, which are discussed later in the chapter. This parameter is usually set to 0. The internalformat and format are usually RGBA. And the type is often UNSIGNED_BYTE. All the available formats and types are shown in Appendix C.

Loading Images into a Texture Object

The most common way to populate texture data is from an image file. We can also set the data or use other objects such as a HTMLCanvasElement or HTMLVideoElement.

We will declare a variable to hold our texture image data:

```
var textureImage = null;
```

We use an HTML Image object to load our texture image:

```
function loadTexture()
{
        textureImage = new Image();
        textureImage.onload = function() {
                setupTexture();
        }
```

```
        textureImage.src = "./textures/smiley-128px.jpg";
}
```

In the loadTexture method, we create a HTML Image object and set up the onload event. What this does is wait until the Image has been loaded through the textureImage.src assignment and then call the setupTexture method. The details of our texture setup are shown in Listing 3-1.

■ **Note**   We are storing the Image in the textureImage variable and not the texture variable which holds the WebGLTexture object.

Listing 3-1. Setting up the *WebGLTexture* object

```
function setupTexture()
{
        texture = gl.createTexture();
        gl.bindTexture(gl.TEXTURE_2D, texture);
        gl.pixelStorei(gl.UNPACK_FLIP_Y_WEBGL, true);
        gl.texImage2D(gl.TEXTURE_2D, 0, gl.RGBA, gl.RGBA, gl.UNSIGNED_BYTE, textureImage);
        gl.texParameteri(gl.TEXTURE_2D, gl.TEXTURE_MAG_FILTER, gl.NEAREST);
        gl.texParameteri(gl.TEXTURE_2D, gl.TEXTURE_MIN_FILTER, gl.NEAREST);

        if( !gl.isTexture(texture) )
        {
            console.log("Error: Texture is invalid");
        }
}
```

In the texture setup method of Listing 3-1 we create a WebGLTextureObject and then bind it. We then set the texture data by calling texImage2D with our loaded HTML Image object. The pixelStorei function tells WebGL how to store our data, and texParameteri sets options for how to handle texture filtering and wrapping. We will cover these two new functions in more detail later on in the chapter. Finally, we check that our texture object is valid and print an error message to the console if it is not.

■ **Note**   This is just one way to load image data. You can also use the image in an existing <img> tag:

```
<img src="./textures/smiley-128px.jpg" id="smiley-image" />
function loadTexture()
{
        textureImage = $("#smiley-image").get(0);
        setupTexture();
}
```

You can also use an image from an HTMLCanvasElement or HTMLVideoElement, or load raw data as your texture image.

Texture images must also follow the rules of Cross-Origin Resource Sharing (CORS). If your texture source(s) are in the same location as your JavaScript files, you don't need to worry about CORS. More information about the exact restrictions of CORS can be found at http://www.w3.org/TR/cors, and the stricter WebGL CORS restrictions can be found at http://www.khronos.org/registry/webgl/specs/latest/#4.2

Application and Shader Interaction

We need to send our loaded texture object from our application to the shader program. In our `setupTexture` function, we will add code to get the location of our `uSampler` uniform and set its value for use with our program.

```
glProgram.samplerUniform = gl.getUniformLocation(glProgram, "uSampler");
gl.uniform1i(glProgram.samplerUniform, 0);
```

The second parameter 0 refers to the `TEXTURE0` texture unit that is currently bound. `TEXTURE0` is the default texture unit.

For this example, we will define vertex points for a plane composed of two triangles with these data points:

```
var triangleVertices = [
    -0.5, -0.5, 0.0,
    0.5, -0.5, 0.0,
    0.5, 0.5, 0.0,

    0.5, 0.5, 0.0,
    -0.5, 0.5, 0.0,
    -0.5, -0.5, 0.0
];
```

These vertex points are sent to the shader using a normal *vertex buffer object* (VBO), just like we did in the Chapter 1 example of Listing 1-6.

Using a Texture in Our Shader

To use textures, we need to adjust our shaders to have access to the texture data. In this example, we are not using a separate texture coordinate attribute for each vertex. Instead, in our vertex shader we use the `x,y` coordinates of the position as our texture coordinate for each vertex. Each vertex coordinate passed in will be in the range [-0.5, 0.5], so we add 0.5 to both coordinates to map to the [0,1] range when we use them as texture coordinates. A varying variable stores the texture coordinate and is passed on to the fragment shader, as shown in Listing 3-2.

Listing 3-2. A Basic Vertex Shader to Compute and Pass Along a Texture Coordinate

```
<script type="x-shader/x-vertex">
    attribute vec3 aVertexPosition;
    varying highp vec2 vTextureCoord;

    void main(void) {
        gl_Position = vec4(aVertexPosition, 1.0);
        vTextureCoord = aVertexPosition.xy + 0.5;
    }
</script>
```

Texture data is accessible to our fragment shader through the use of a `uniform sampler2D` variable, as shown in Listing 3-3. In the `texture2D` function, the first parameter is our texture sampler and the second is the lookup location that was passed in from the vertex shader.

Listing 3-3. A Basic Fragment Shader that looks up texture values

```
<script id="shader-fs" type="x-shader/x-fragment">
    varying highp vec2 vTextureCoord;
    uniform sampler2D uSampler;
```

```
    void main(void) {
        gl_FragColor = texture2D(uSampler, vec2(vTextureCoord.s, vTextureCoord.t));
    }
</script>
```

The output of running our first program is shown in Figure 3-3. The left image is centered but looks skewed because the viewport is proportional to the canvas size. The right image has a viewport with height and width

Figure 3-3. Basic texturing: left - viewport proportional to the canvas dimensions; right - a square viewport

both set to the canvas.height and so is proportioned properly, but is no longer centered. The code of this example is available on the book companion sites in the 03/basic_texture.html file.

Texture Options

When we use textures, we do a lookup of stored data to find an appropriate return value to use. When the lookup value corresponds to exactly one texel, the return value is straightforward. However, when we are trying to find a texture value that overlaps texels, the value that we will get back is determined by the filter settings of our texture. How WebGL handles coordinates specified that lie outside of the [0,1] range of the texture or mapping to larger or smaller images than the texture size depends on the wrap settings. Enabling mipmaps can also impact the return value for a specific coordinate lookup. In addition, we can modify the storage format of our data.

Texture Filtering

When texels of noninteger position are requested (relative to the 0 to 1 range values multiplied by the actual texture size), such as, (64.35, 19.8) in a 128px texture, we need to perform texture filtering to obtain an appropriate value.

Filter parameters can either handle the stretching of a texture (TEXTURE_MAG_FILTER) or shrinking (TEXTURE_MIN_FILTER) to fit an image. For TEXTURE_MAG_FILTER we have two options, LINEAR and NEAREST, with LINEAR being an averaged value of nearby texels and producing fairly smooth interpolated results, and NEAREST being the closest texel so is fastest to compute but not as smooth. For TEXTURE_MIN_FILTER, we have more options. From quickest and roughest to slowest but smoothest are the following:

```
LINEAR, NEAREST,
NEAREST_MIPMAP_NEAREST, LINEAR_MIPMAP_NEAREST,
NEAREST_MIPMAP_LINEAR, LINEAR_MIPMAP_LINEAR
```

The last four options require having set mipmaps by calling gl.generateMipmap(gl.TEXTURE_2D) first. We will cover mipmaps later on in the chapter.

Texture filter parameters can be set by calling one of:

```
void texParameterf(GLenum target, GLenum param_name, GLfloat param);
void texParameteri(GLenum target, GLenum param_name, GLint param);
```

The result of shrinking a texture of a dog and varying the TEXTURE_MIN_FILTER setting can be seen in the difference of sharpness of the two resulting images in Figure 3-4.

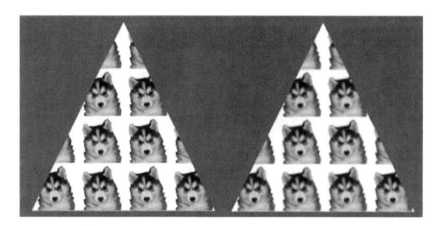

Figure 3-4. *Left - NEAREST filtering; Right - LINEAR_MIPMAP_LINEAR filtering*

The left image uses

```
gl.texParameteri(gl.TEXTURE_2D, gl.TEXTURE_MIN_FILTER, gl.NEAREST);
```

The right image uses

```
gl.texParameteri(gl.TEXTURE_2D, gl.TEXTURE_MIN_FILTER, gl.LINEAR_MIPMAP_LINEAR);
```

Texture Wrapping

Texture wrapping is the way we handle coordinates (s,t) that fall outside of our normal texture coordinate range of [0,1]. Wrapping parameter names, pname, can be either TEXTURE_WRAP_S or TEXTURE_WRAP_T.

The default wrapping mode is to REPEAT the texture (it uses only the fractional part of the texture coordinate). Two other options are CLAMP_TO_EDGE, which samples only coordinates that are within the range [0,1], and MIRRORED_REPEAT which is the same as REPEAT for coordinates with an even integer component (2.3 and 4.3 are both mapped to 0.3). For odd integer components, the fractional part of the coordinate is mapped to (1- *coordinate_fractional_value*), so 1.3 and 3.3 end up being both mapped to 0.7. Adjustments to the wrapping modes are shown in Figures 3-5 to Figure 3-7.

To find the current value of a texture parameter, you can use this function:

```
getTexParameter(GLenum target, GLenum pname)
```

Figure 3-5. *Left – original texture image; Center - texture application onto a triangle with default REPEAT; Right - multiplying the texture coordinate values in the shader to pronounce the repetition*

Figure 3-6. *Left - TEX_WRAP_S set to CLAMP_TO_EDGE; Center - TEX_WRAP_T set to CLAMP_TO_EDGE; Right - both S and T set to CLAMP_TO_EDGE*

Figure 3-7. *Left - TEX_WRAP_S set to MIRRORED_REPEAT; Center - TEX_WRAP_T set to MIRRORED_REPEAT; Right - both S and T set to MIRRORED_REPEAT*

Data Storage

We can adjust the way texture data is stored in WebGL through calls to this function:

```
void pixelStorei(GLenum pname, GLint param);
```

In Listing 3-1, we flipped the texture vertically using this:

```
gl.pixelStorei(gl.UNPACK_FLIP_Y_WEBGL, true);
```

The options we have for pname are UNPACK_FLIP_Y_WEBGL, UNPACK_PREMULTIPLY_ALPHA_WEBGL, and UNPACK_COLORSPACE_CONVERSION_WEBGL. For the first two options, any nonzero param value is interpreted as true.

UNPACK_FLIP_Y_WEBGL flips the source data along the vertical y-axis if set to true. This makes the last row of data to be the first row transferred. The reason to set this option to true is that data loaded from other HTML images have the y-axis naturally point in the opposite direction from WebGL. Without the call, the image will appear to be upside down.

If UNPACK_PREMULTIPLY_ALPHA_WEBGL is set to true, and the source data has an alpha channel, it will be multiplied against all the other channels during transfer: $(r,g,b,a) \Rightarrow (r*a, g*a, b*a, a)$.

Finally, UNPACK_COLORSPACE_CONVERSION_WEBGL converts the source data to the browser's default colorspace. For this option, param is set to either BROWSER_DEFAULT_WEBGL or NONE.

Mipmaps

To aid in accurate texture filtering, mipmaps are a precalculated optimized set of decreasingly sized versions of a texture. They are one place where the power of 2 comes in to play for textures. Each image in a mipmap is a smaller version of the last—starting with half the dimension size, then a quarter, an eighth, and so on.

For example, if the original texture was 256x256 pixels in dimension, we would have smaller textures in the mipmap of sizes 128x128, 64x64, 32x32, [...], 2x2, 1x1.

Because the size of each texture is only 25 percent (½ * ½) the size of the previous, the total size of a mipmap is only one-third larger than that of the original texture. Mipmaps improve accuracy when the surface that we are applying our texture to is smaller than our original texture.

To generate the mipmap for the currently bound texture, all you have to do is call this function:

```
void generateMipmap(GLenum target)
```

As we have shown in our code, the function looks like this:

```
gl.generateMipmap(gl.TEXTURE_2D);
```

▓ **Note** Calling generateMipmap with no WebGLTexture bound or a Non-Power-Of-Two (NPOT) texture will generate an INVALID_OPERATION error.

The texture image of our dog along with a decreasing series of texture sizes is shown in Figure 3-8. This image represents a mipmap.

Figure 3-8. *Mipmap representation of a dog texture*

Texturing a 3D Object

Now that we have a background of texturing and some 2D practice, we will texture a 3-D object. We will start with the last example from Chapter 1, found in the 01/3D_triangles_depth_test.html file. As you may recall, that example is of a rotating triangular prism. We will now texture it as a first step to producing the image on the right of Figure 3-1. We will use a separate attribute for texture coordinates. We shall see that 3D texturing can be more complex than 2D texturing. The texture we will load, textures/stone-128px.jpg, will display stone bricks.

Texture Coordinate Attribute

We need to calculate texture coordinates per vertex and send them on to our shader program. First, we add two new variables:

```
vertexTexCoordAttribute = null,
trianglesTexCoordBuffer = null,
```

Next we define texture coordinates for each vertex as shown in Listing 3-4.

Listing 3-4. Providing texture coordinates

```
var triangleTexCoords = [
        //front face
        0.0, 0.0,
        1.0, 0.0,
        2.0, 0.0,
        0.5, 1.0,
        1.5, 1.0,
        1.0, 2.0,

        //rear face
        0.0, 0.0,
        1.0, 0.0,
        2.0, 0.0,
        0.5, 1.0,
        1.5, 1.0,
        1.0, 2.0
];

trianglesTexCoordBuffer = gl.createBuffer();
gl.bindBuffer(gl.ARRAY_BUFFER, trianglesTexCoordBuffer);
gl.bufferData(gl.ARRAY_BUFFER, new Float32Array(triangleTexCoords), gl.STATIC_DRAW);
```

Here I have been lazy and just used the x and y values of the vertex points. Note that even though values lie past the [0.0, 1.0] range of texture coordinates, the coordinates we provide still work. This can be seen on the front face of the prism in Figure 3-9. The reason it still works is because, as mentioned above, the default WebGL wrap mode is gl.REPEAT and we are using a seamless tiled texture.

Finally, in our drawScene method, we need to use our buffer data:

```
vertexTexCoordAttribute = gl.getAttribLocation(glProgram, "aVertexTexCoord");
gl.enableVertexAttribArray(vertexTexCoordAttribute);
gl.bindBuffer(gl.ARRAY_BUFFER, trianglesTexCoordBuffer);
gl.vertexAttribPointer(vertexTexCoordAttribute, 2, gl.FLOAT, false, 0, 0);
```

Adjusting Our Shaders

In our vertex shader we now have an attribute that stores the texture coordinate data for each vertex. We also reintroduce the uPMatrix and uMVMatrix for setting up our 3D view. The vertex shader is shown in Listing 3-5 while the fragment shader stays the same as it was in Listing 3-3.

Listing 3-5. Vertex shader that has a separate texture coordinate attribute

```
<script type="x-shader/x-vertex">
        attribute vec3 aVertexPosition;
        attribute vec2 aVertexTextureCoord;

        uniform mat4 uMVMatrix;
        uniform mat4 uPMatrix;

        varying highp vec2 vTextureCoord;

        void main(void) {
            gl_Position = uPMatrix * uMVMatrix * vec4(aVertexPosition, 1.0);
            vTextureCoord = aVertexTextureCoord;
        }
</script>
```

The full code for the example at this point is in the file 03/texture-example1.html. The result of this first attempt to texture map the triangular prism is shown in Figure 3-9. Two of the faces look good, whereas the faces with differing z values have texture values that are clamped and linearly stretched across.

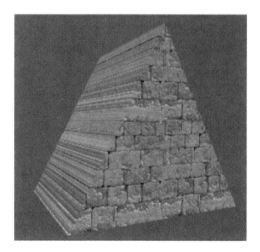

Figure 3-9. *Our first try at texture mapping the triangular prism*

What is happening here? Well let's look at the left-side vertices:

```
//left side
0,3,6,
3,6,9,
3,5,9,
5,9,11
```

Vertices $(0,3,6)$ correspond to texture coordinates:

```
0.0, 0.0,
0.5, 1.0,
0.0, 0.0
```

Two of the three vertices are identical. This flattens the normally triangular texture region into just a line. Let's look at the vertices $(3,6,9)$:

```
0.5, 1.0,
0.0, 0.0,
0.5, 1.0
```

Two of three are identical as well. This is obviously also true for vertices $(3,x,9)$, so vertices $(3,5,9)$ have only two unique texture coordinate pairs. Vertices $(5,9,11)$ has only two unique coordinate pairs as well.

Data Changes

How do we avoid the problem discussed here and illustrated in Figure 3-9? What if we picked (x,z) or (y,z) as our coordinates instead? Well that might fix the left and right sides, but then there is repetition in the z coordinate for our front and back sides. In general, this is an issue with using the same texture coordinate values for a vertex that is used on more than one face.

The solution here is to assign a texture coordinate and a vertex for every single vertex point, which is a lot of coordinates. We can avoid explicitly having to list all the points by procedurally generating the vertex and texture coordinates for each triangle.

We will get rid of our indice buffer, `triangleVerticesIndexBuffer`, but we can still make use of the indice information to generate our points as shown in Listing 3-6.

Listing 3-6. Generating 54 vertices using 12 distinct vertices and indice order arrays

```
function setupBuffers()
{
        //12 vertices
        var triangleVerticesOriginal = [
                //front face
                //bottom left to right, to top
                0.0, 0.0, 0.0,
                1.0, 0.0, 0.0,
                2.0, 0.0, 0.0,
                0.5, 1.0, 0.0,
                1.5, 1.0, 0.0,
                1.0, 2.0, 0.0,

                //rear face
                0.0, 0.0, -2.0,
                1.0, 0.0, -2.0,
                2.0, 0.0, -2.0,
                0.5, 1.0, -2.0,
                1.5, 1.0, -2.0,
                1.0, 2.0, -2.0
        ];
```

```
        //18 triangles
        var triangleVertexIndices = [
                0,1,3,                  //front face
                1,3,4,
                1,2,4,
                3,4,5,

                6,7,9,                  //rear face
                7,9,10,
                7,8,10,
                9,10,11,

                0,3,6,                  //left side
                3,6,9,
                3,5,9,
                5,9,11,

                2,4,8,                  //right side
                4,8,10,
                4,5,10,
                5,10,11,

                0,6,8,                  //bottom faces
                8,2,0
];

        //54 vertices
        var triangleVertices = [];
        var triangleTexCoords = [];

        for(var i=0; i<triangleVertexIndices.length; ++i)
        {
                var a = triangleVertexIndices[i];

                triangleVertices.push(triangleVerticesOriginal[a*3]);
                triangleVertices.push(triangleVerticesOriginal[a*3 + 1]);
                triangleVertices.push(triangleVerticesOriginal[a*3 + 2]);

                if(i >= 24)
                {
                        triangleTexCoords.push(triangleVerticesOriginal[a*3 + 2]);
                        triangleTexCoords.push(triangleVerticesOriginal[a*3 + 1]);
                }else{
                        triangleTexCoords.push(triangleVerticesOriginal[a*3]);
                        triangleTexCoords.push(triangleVerticesOriginal[a*3 + 1]);
                }
        }

        trianglesVerticeBuffer = gl.createBuffer();
        gl.bindBuffer(gl.ARRAY_BUFFER, trianglesVerticeBuffer);
        gl.bufferData(gl.ARRAY_BUFFER, new Float32Array(triangleVertices), gl.STATIC_DRAW);
        trianglesTexCoordBuffer = gl.createBuffer();
        gl.bindBuffer(gl.ARRAY_BUFFER, trianglesTexCoordBuffer);
        gl.bufferData(gl.ARRAY_BUFFER, new Float32Array(triangleTexCoords), gl.STATIC_DRAW);
}
```

> **Note** There are a few ways to combine arrays in JavaScript. The following flattens array b before adding it to a:

```
var a = [1,2,3];
var b = [4,5];
a.push.apply(a, b);
```

The contents of a will be [1,2,3,4,5] after this operation. Alternatively, a = a.concat(b) will also produce the same result.

Finally, we need to call drawArrays instead of drawElements in our drawScene function:

```
//gl.drawElements(gl.TRIANGLES, 18*3, gl.UNSIGNED_SHORT, 0);
gl.drawArrays(gl.TRIANGLES, 0, 18*3);
```

For our prism, we know that the last two sides that we render do not work well with xy coordinates as texture values. Instead, we use the xz coordinates. Alternatively, yz would work as well. Both of these coordinates are shown in Figure 3-10. The adjusted source code is in the file 03/texture-example1-fixed.html.

Figure 3-10. *Left - using xz coordinates for the sides; Right - using yz coordinates*

Toggling State

We will start our code in this next example by copying the 02/jquery_ajax.html file from the previous chapter. We are going to add some variables to toggle our program state through keyboard input. Keyboard actions could be used, for instance, to control movement in a game. Here, we will use them to toggle texture and lighting state in our shaders. This allows us to modify the program state without needing to modify the code and rerun the application. Personally, I find the ability to pause a scene and toggle the shader state useful for taking screenshots at the exact same scene location, but with varying effects.

We add new variables to keep track of our texture and lighting state:

```
var     paused = false,
        useTexture = false,
        useLighting = false;
```

To get keyboard input and toggle these values we will attach a handler to the document keyup event using jQuery. We check the event keyCode property value and toggle the appropriate variable as shown in Listing 3-7.

> ■ **Note**   There is no real authoritative keycode list. I recommend simply outputting the result of a key typed to the console with `console.log(evt.keyCode)`. For advanced `keyCode` values, you can perform a browser search.

Listing 3-7. Handling keyboard events with jQuery

```
$(document).keyup(function(evt){
    switch(evt.keyCode){
      case 80: //'p'
          paused =!paused;
          break;
      case 84: //'t'
          useTexture =!useTexture;
          break;
      case 76: //'l'
          useLighting =!useLighting;
          break;
      default:
          break;
    }
});
```

Now that we can toggle these state variables, we will check the paused variable to determine whether to redraw our scene or not. We will do nothing with the useTexture or useLighting variables for the time being.

```
(function animLoop(){
        if( !paused ){
                setupWebGL();
                setMatrixUniforms();
                drawScene();
        }
        requestAnimationFrame(animLoop, canvas);
})();
```

You can run the modified program in the browser and verify that the pause toggle works. Next we will add the option of being able to toggle the texture.

Toggling Textures On and Off

We will now add a uniform in our fragment shader and adjust it using our useTexture flag. Alternatively, we can define multiple shaders and switch them. We will do this latter approach in Chapter 10.

We will add a uniform uDoTexturing to our fragment shader and toggle it within our keyup event handler:

```
case 84: //'t'
      useTexture =!useTexture;
       if(useTexture)
      {
            gl.uniform1i(glProgram.uDoTexturing, 1);
      }else{
            gl.uniform1i(glProgram.uDoTexturing, 0);
      }
      break;
```

In our setupTexture method, we get the uniform location and initially set its value to 1:

```
glProgram.uDoTexturing = gl.getUniformLocation(glProgram, "uDoTexturing");
gl.uniform1i(glProgram.uDoTexturing, 1);
```

Finally, our fragment shader needs to be adjusted:

```
...
uniform int uDoTexturing;

void main(void) {
      if(uDoTexturing == 1){
            gl_FragColor = texture2D(uSampler, vec2(vTextureCoord.st) );

      }else{
            gl_FragColor = vec4(1.0, 0.1, 0.1, 1.0);
      }
}
```

Now we can toggle the texture by pressing the *t* key. The source code for these adjustments can be found in the 03/texture-example1-toggle.html file. We will not show the setting of a lighting uniform flag, but it can be done analogously to the texture flag.

Multiple Textures

In our next example, we will use multiple textures. You can use multitexturing to produce special effects such as light or height maps (which are explained in Chapter 6) or bumpmapping (simulating bumps and wrinkles). Here we will just take the WebGL logo as a texture and mix it with our stone texture.

Application Changes

In Listing 3-8, we assign constant values to the variables STONE_TEXTURE and WEBGL_LOGO_TEXTURE so that we can use them as our new array indices. Then we change our texture variable declarations to be arrays and adjust the loadTexture and setupTexture functions to handle multiple textures.

Listing 3-8. Preparing for multiple textures

```
      STONE_TEXTURE = 0,
      WEBGL_LOGO_TEXTURE = 1,
      texture = [],
      textureImage = [];
...

function loadTexture()
{
  textureImage[STONE_TEXTURE] = new Image();
  textureImage[STONE_TEXTURE].onload = function() {
        setupTexture(STONE_TEXTURE);
        gl.uniform1i(glProgram.samplerUniform, 0);
  }
  textureImage[STONE_TEXTURE].src = "./textures/stone-128px.jpg";

  textureImage[WEBGL_LOGO_TEXTURE] = new Image();
  textureImage[WEBGL_LOGO_TEXTURE].onload = function() {
```

```
                    setupTexture(WEBGL_LOGO_TEXTURE);
                    gl.uniform1i(glProgram.samplerUniform2, 1);
             }
           textureImage[WEBGL_LOGO_TEXTURE].src = "./textures/webgl_logo-512px.png";

   glProgram.uDoTexturing = gl.getUniformLocation(glProgram, "uDoTexturing");
   gl.uniform1i(glProgram.uDoTexturing, 1);
}
function setupTexture(i)
{
   gl.activeTexture(gl.TEXTURE0 + i);
   texture[i] = gl.createTexture();
   gl.bindTexture(gl.TEXTURE_2D, texture[i]);
   gl.pixelStorei(gl.UNPACK_FLIP_Y_WEBGL, true);
   gl.texImage2D(gl.TEXTURE_2D, 0, gl.RGBA, gl.RGBA, gl.UNSIGNED_BYTE, textureImage[i]);
   gl.texParameteri(gl.TEXTURE_2D, gl.TEXTURE_MAG_FILTER, gl.NEAREST);
   gl.texParameteri(gl.TEXTURE_2D, gl.TEXTURE_MIN_FILTER, gl.NEAREST);

   if( !gl.isTexture(texture[i]) )
   {
        console.error("Error: Texture is invalid");
   }
}
```

We now have a second sampler uniform, which we set with `gl.uniform1i(glProgram.samplerUniform2,` `WEBGL_LOGO_TEXTURE)`.We also have to tell WebGL which texture is active in the line `gl.activeTexture(gl.` `TEXTURE0 + i)`.

▓ **Note** I have used the notation gl.TEXTURE0 + i for convenience. This notation can alternately be written as follows:

gl.activeTexture(gl.TEXTURE1); //same as gl.activeTexture(gl.TEXTURE0 + 1);

gl.activeTexture(gl.TEXTURE2); //same as gl.activeTexture(gl.TEXTURE0 + 2);

Finally, we need to get the location of our new sampler:

```
function getMatrixUniforms(){
        glProgram.pMatrixUniform = gl.getUniformLocation(glProgram, "uPMatrix");
        glProgram.mvMatrixUniform = gl.getUniformLocation(glProgram, "uMVMatrix");
        glProgram.samplerUniform = gl.getUniformLocation(glProgram, "uSampler");
        glProgram.samplerUniform2 = gl.getUniformLocation(glProgram, "uSampler2");
}
```

We will use the same texture coordinates in this example for both textures.

Shader Program Changes

Our vertex shader is the same as in the case of a single texture. The fragment shader is changed to this:

```
<script id="shader-fs" type="x-shader/x-fragment">
    varying highp vec2 vTextureCoord;
```

```
    uniform sampler2D uSampler;
    uniform sampler2D uSampler2;
    uniform int uDoTexturing;

    void main(void) {
        if(uDoTexturing == 1){
                highp vec4 stoneColor = texture2D(uSampler, vec2(vTextureCoord.st));
                highp vec4 webglLogoColor = texture2D(uSampler2, vec2(vTextureCoord.st));

                gl_FragColor = mix(stoneColor, webglLogoColor, 0.5);
                //gl_FragColor = mix(stoneColor, webglLogoColor, webglLogoColor.a);
                //gl_FragColor = mix(stoneColor, webglLogoColor, 1.0 - webglLogoColor.a);
        }else{
                gl_FragColor = vec4(1.0, 0.1, 0.1, 1.0);
        }
    }
</script>
```

In the above fragment shader is a second sampler2D, uSampler2. We obtain the color of both the stone texture and the WebGL logo texture. Finally, we mix this value evenly. When you run the application, multitexture.html, you will see that it does not look quite right. Instead of transparent parts of the WebGL logo texture being see-through, they appear white in color (see the left side of Figure 3-11). This is not what we wish to display. If a pixel is transparent (the alpha value is 0.0), it should not show up. We will use the fragment shader to set the blend mode of the textures and hide the WebGL logo areas where there should be transparency.

The way that we do this is by using the alpha channel of the logo texture, webglLogoColor.a, as the amount to mix the textures. If the alpha value is 1.0 as in the logo region, the logo texture will be shown at full value while the stone texture will not be factored in at all. When the alpha value is 0.0, then only the stone texture will be used. This gives us the expected decal result (see the center of Figure 3-11). If we invert the mix ratio by using (1.0 - webglLogoColor.a), only the logo region is see-through; everything else is white like a stencil (see the right side of Figure 3-11).

Figure 3-11. *Left - Mixing two textures evenly; Center - mixing using the WebGL logo alpha value ; Right - mixing using one minus the alpha value*

▓ **Note**   In some versions of OpenGL, the function glTexEnvf had presets such as GL_DECAL that would mix textures in a specific manner. With shaders, we have the power to specify how textures should be mixed, and as such OpenGL ES 2.0 and WebGL no longer use or support this method.

Lighting

Lighting helps give visual cues to a scene so that it can appear even more recognizably three-dimensional and realistic. Lighting gives objects their visual shape. In order to see anything, we rely on light reflecting off of the surface of objects. The total reflected light can be made of several different light components.

Light Components

Ambient, diffuse, and specular light are all different components of lighting. *Ambient lighting* is the global illumination in an environment. It hits a surface at all angles and is reflected back at all angles. *Diffuse lighting* and *specular lighting* reflection depend on the angle of the light to a surface. The difference between diffuse and specular reflection is that once light hits a surface, diffuse reflection occurs in all directions, whereas specular reflection occurs in a single direction. This is shown in Figure 3-12.

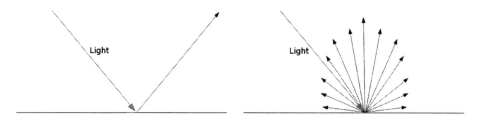

Figure 3-12. Left: specular reflection; right: diffuse reflection

Diffuse lighting is the major reflective component in reflection but is dull like matte materials, while specular reflection (also known as a specular highlight) is smaller and produces a shiny glossiness. Specular highlights also give a clue to the location of the light(s) in a scene.

Figure 3-13. Sphere (far left); diffuse reflection (left); specular reflection highlight (right); ambient component (far right)

Types of Lights

Some light types are *ambient* (directionless, even distribution), *directional* (sunlight) and *point* light (room light). Directional lights like the sun are so far away that we can consider all the light coming from one single source direction. Light types are shown in Figure 3-14.

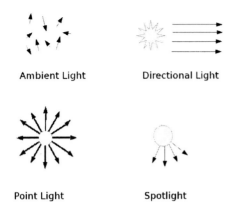

Ambient Light   Directional Light

Point Light   Spotlight

Figure 3-14. Different types of light

Normal Vectors

As reflective light (diffuse or specular) depends on the incoming angle from the light to the surface, we need to know the direction in which each surface is facing. We do this by calculating the normal vector to a surface that holds the perpendicular direction to that surface. For a given polygon, there are actually two normal vectors, each pointing in a different direction relating to the front or back of the surface, as shown on the right of Figure 3-15. We will want to be consistent with our choice of normal. Also, we are usually interested in vectors of unit length (normalized normal vectors). Once we calculate the normal of a vertice, we store it in a VBO and send it to our shader as a vertex attribute.

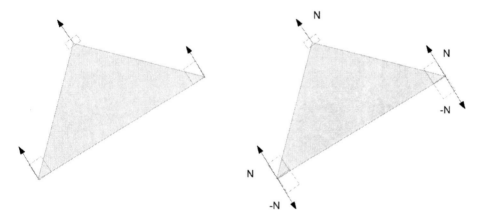

Figure 3-15. A triangle with vertex normal vectors (all identical in value) that are perpendicular to the triangle surface. Two of the three negative normals are visible on the right

Lighting Models

In WebGL we define our own lighting model. This differs from OpenGL where there are several built-in functions to help control lighting. In fact, as of this writing, a search for the term "light" within the WebGL specification will produce no results. The flip side is that we are not limited in any way in how we model our lighting. There are many existing lighting models that we can implement. We will cover the Phong illumination model in depth in the next chapter and build a simpler light model here.

Ambient and Directional Light

The first light components we will implement will have ambient and directional light and diffuse reflection, but no specular reflection. We add variables to hold our vertex normal data and a new matrix to convert normal vectors into the MVP space.

```
vertexNormalAttribute = null,
trianglesNormalBuffer = null;
...
normalMatrix = mat3.create();
```

In the `setupWebGL` method, we store the inverse matrix of the model view into our new normal matrix. This normal matrix will be used in our vertex shader to adjust each normal relative to our model view.

```
mat4.toInverseMat3(mvMatrix, normalMatrix);
mat3.transpose(normalMatrix);
```

▒ **Note**   The normal matrix is 3x3 in dimension and NOT 4x4. We take the upper 3x3 submatrix of the modelview matrix and compute the inverse transpose of it to find the normal matrix.

In Listing 3-9 we produce our normal vectors programatically, using the three vertices of each triangle to first compute two side vectors and then take the cross-product of these two new vectors. The cross-product produces the vector perpendicular to the triangle (the normal vector).

Listing 3-9. Calculating the normal vectors

```
var triangleNormals = [];
//18 triangles - normal will be the same for each vertex of triangle
for(var i=0; i<triangleVertexIndices.length; i+=3)
{
        var a = triangleVertexIndices[i];
        var b = triangleVertexIndices[i + 1];
        var c = triangleVertexIndices[i + 2];

        //normal is the cross-product
        var v1 = [
                triangleVerticesOriginal[a*3] - triangleVerticesOriginal[b*3],
                triangleVerticesOriginal[a*3 + 1] - triangleVerticesOriginal[b*3 + 1],
                triangleVerticesOriginal[a*3 + 2] - triangleVerticesOriginal[b*3 + 2],
        ];
        var v2 = [
                triangleVerticesOriginal[a*3] - triangleVerticesOriginal[c*3],
                triangleVerticesOriginal[a*3 + 1] - triangleVerticesOriginal[c*3 + 1],
                triangleVerticesOriginal[a*3 + 2] - triangleVerticesOriginal[c*3 + 2],
        ];
```

```
        var cross = [
                v1[1]*v2[2] - v1[2]*v2[1],
                v1[2]*v2[0] - v1[0]*v2[2],
                v1[0]*v2[1] - v1[1]*v2[0]
        ];
        //same value for each of the three vertices
        triangleNormals.push.apply(triangleNormals, cross);
        triangleNormals.push.apply(triangleNormals, cross);
        triangleNormals.push.apply(triangleNormals, cross);
}

trianglesNormalsBuffer = gl.createBuffer();
gl.bindBuffer(gl.ARRAY_BUFFER, trianglesNormalsBuffer);
gl.bufferData(gl.ARRAY_BUFFER, new Float32Array(triangleNormals), gl.STATIC_DRAW);
```

In the drawScene method, we get our normal attribute location:

```
vertexNormalAttribute = gl.getAttribLocation(glProgram, "aVertexNormal");
gl.enableVertexAttribArray(vertexNormalAttribute);
gl.bindBuffer(gl.ARRAY_BUFFER, trianglesNormalBuffer);
gl.vertexAttribPointer(vertexNormalAttribute, 3, gl.FLOAT, false, 0, 0);
```

We also get and set our normalMatrix:

```
function getMatrixUniforms(){
    glProgram.pMatrixUniform = gl.getUniformLocation(glProgram, "uPMatrix");
      glProgram.mvMatrixUniform = gl.getUniformLocation(glProgram, "uMVMatrix");
      glProgram.normalMatrixUniform = gl.getUniformLocation(glProgram, "uNormalMatrix");
}

function setMatrixUniforms() {
    gl.uniformMatrix4fv(glProgram.pMatrixUniform, false, pMatrix);
      gl.uniformMatrix4fv(glProgram.mvMatrixUniform, false, mvMatrix);
      gl.uniformMatrix3fv(glProgram.normalMatrixUniform, false, normalMatrix);
}
```

This takes care of our application code changes. Now we need to write our shaders. Let's start with the vertex shader in which new functionality is shown in bold:

```
<script type="x-shader/x-vertex">
    attribute vec3 aVertexPosition;
    attribute vec3 aVertexColor;
    attribute vec3 aVertexNormal;

    uniform mat3 uNormalMatrix;
    uniform mat4 uMVMatrix;
    uniform mat4 uPMatrix;

    varying highp vec4 vColor;
    varying highp vec3 vLight;

    void main(void) {
            gl_Position = uPMatrix * uMVMatrix * vec4(aVertexPosition, 1.0);
            vColor = vec4(aVertexColor, 1.0);

            //lighting
            vec3 ambientLight = vec3(0.1, 0.1, 0.1);
```

```
        vec3 diffuseLightColor = vec3(0.5, 0.5, 0.5);
        vec3 directionalLightPosition = normalize( vec3(10.0, 10.0, 5.0) );

        vec3 transformedNormal = uNormalMatrix * aVertexNormal;
        float diffuseLightAmount = max( dot( transformedNormal,
                                              directionalLightPosition), 0.0);
        vLight = ambientLight + (diffuseLightAmount * diffuseLightColor);
    }
</script>
```

There is an attribute for the normals in the vertex shader, a normal matrix, and a varying vector that will store our total amount of light to pass on to the fragment shader. We set the ambient light amount and diffuse light color. Next we set a position for our directional light and normalize it (we are interested only in the direction, not the actual position). We calculate the normal vector relative to the model view, which is done by multiplying by our normal matrix. To calculate the diffuse light amount, we take the dot product of the normal and the light direction. Finally we add the ambient and diffuse light components together.

Our fragment shader is much simpler. In it, we multiply our light vector by the color vector:

```
<script id="shader-fs" type="x-shader/x-fragment">
    varying highp vec4 vColor;
    varying highp vec3 vLight;

    void main(void) {
        gl_FragColor = vec4(vColor.xyz * vLight, vColor.a);
    }
</script>
```

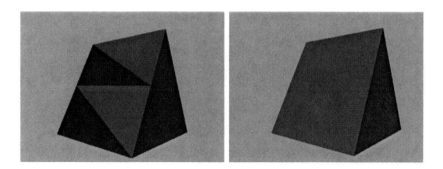

Figure 3-16. *Left - Basic lighting; Right - With consistent polygon winding*

Now if we run the application found in the file 03/ambient_and_directional_light.html, we get the figure on the left of Figure 3-16. The figure on the right is produced by making the winding order of our vertices consistent.

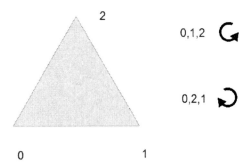

Figure 3-17. *Triangle winding can be clockwise (0,2,1) or counterclockwise (0,1,2)*

Triangular polygon winding refers to the direction that vertices are assembled. Every triangle can be assembled clockwise or counterclockwise. Which order you choose is irrelevant as long as you are consistent. The winding order affects the direction of normal calculations and also which side of the polygon is considered front and which is the back. See Figure 3-17.

For larger meshes, we would want to check the orientation of faces programmatically. The default winding order in WebGL is FRONT_FACE CCW. For our mesh we can refer to Figure 1-14 in the first chapter and inspect the winding visually to find that 6 vertices are clockwise and 12 are counterclockwise. Reversing the winding of the clockwise ones gives this:

```
//18 triangles
var triangleVertexIndices = [
      0,1,3,              //front face
      1,4,3, //flipped
      1,2,4,
      3,4,5,

      6,7,9,              //rear face
      7,10,9, //flipped
      7,8,10,
      9,10,11,

      0,6,3, //flipped    //left side
      3,6,9,
      3,9,5, //flipped
      5,9,11,

      2,8,4, //flipped    //right side
      4,8,10,
      4,10,5, //flipped
      5,10,11,

      0,6,8,              //bottom faces
      8,2,0
];
```

■ **Note**   TRIANGLE_STRIP primitives are composed of triangles with alternating winding order. WebGL takes this into account when you render using one.

A Point Light

Since we are not presently calculating specular reflections, all we need to do to adjust our directional light to a point light is calculate the direction from the point light location to each point in our scene in our vertex shader. Replace the previous vertex shader main method with the following (changes are in bold):

```
void main(void) {
      gl_Position = uPMatrix * uMVMatrix * vec4(aVertexPosition, 1.0);
       vColor = vec4(aVertexColor, 1.0);

      //lighting
       vec3 ambientLight = vec3(0.1, 0.1, 0.1);

       vec3 pointLightPosition = vec3(1.0,2.0,-1.0);
       vec3 pointLightDirection = normalize(
                   vec3(pointLightPosition.xyz - aVertexPosition.xyz));

       vec3 L = vec3(uPMatrix * uMVMatrix * vec4(pointLightDirection, 1.0));
       vec3 N = uNormalMatrix * aVertexNormal;
       float diffuseLightAmount = max( dot(normalize(N), normalize(L)), 0.0);

       vColor = ambientLight + (diffuseLightAmount * aVertexColor);
}
```

Figure 3-18. *Prism rendered with a point light*

The result of our point light is shown in the figure above results in smoother gradient lighting.

We have shown how to do basic per-vertex diffuse lighting on our triangular prism and have previously shown how to texture our prism. Now let's combine these two effects.

Texture and Lighting Together

The final example of the chapter will combine the point light and multitexture examples into an application with both textures and lighting. Continuing from the code in 03/point_light.html, we will re-add the texture loading code and texture coordinate buffer of the earlier multitexture example.

Our final vertex shader is a straightforward combination of 03/multitexture.vs and 03/point_light.vs shaderfiles:

```
<script type="x-shader/x-vertex">
    attribute vec3 aVertexPosition;
    attribute vec3 aVertexColor;
    attribute vec3 aVertexNormal;
    attribute vec2 aVertexTexCoord;

    uniform mat3 uNormalMatrix;
    uniform mat4 uMVMatrix;
    uniform mat4 uPMatrix;

    varying highp vec4 vColor;
    varying highp vec3 vLight;
    varying highp vcc2 vTextureCoord;

    void main(void) {
        gl_Position = uPMatrix * uMVMatrix * vec4(aVertexPosition, 1.0);
        vColor = vec4(aVertexColor, 1.0);
        vTextureCoord = aVertexTexCoord;

        //lighting
        vec3 ambientLight = vec3(0.3, 0.3, 0.3);

        vec3 pointLightPosition = vec3(1.0,2.0,-1.0);
        vec3 pointLightDirection = normalize(
                vec3(pointLightPosition.xyz - aVertexPosition.xyz));

        vec3 L = vec3(uPMatrix * uMVMatrix * vec4(pointLightDirection, 1.0));
        vec3 N = uNormalMatrix * aVertexNormal;
        float diffuseLightAmount = max( dot(normalize(N), normalize(L)), 0.0);

        vLight = ambientLight + vec3(.8,.8,.8) * diffuseLightAmount;
  }
</script>
```

Our final fragment shader is:

```
<script id="shader-fs" type="x-shader/x-fragment">
    varying highp vec4 vColor;
    varying highp vec3 vLight;
    varying highp vec2 vTextureCoord;

    uniform sampler2D uSampler;
    uniform sampler2D uSampler2;
    uniform int uDoTexturing;

    void main(void) {
        if(uDoTexturing == 1){
            highp vec4 stoneColor = texture2D(uSampler, vec2(vTextureCoord.st));
            highp vec4 webglLogoColor = texture2D(uSampler2, vec2(vTextureCoord.st));
            highp vec4 textureColor = mix(stoneColor, webglLogoColor, webglLogoColor.a);
            gl_FragColor = vec4(textureColor.xyz * vLight, textureColor.a);
        }else{
            gl_FragColor = vec4(vColor.xyz * vLight, vColor.a);
```

```
      }
   }
</script>
```

And the result is shown in Figure 3-19.

Figure 3-19. *Our triangular prism with texturing and a point light*

Summary

In this chapter we covered the essentials of texture and lighting within WebGL. This included specifying texture coordinates, creating mipmaps, and how to adjust filter and wrapping settings. We showed the components of light and how to programmatically create surface normal vectors. By the end of the chapter we had worked up to modeling a directional light with multitexturing.

Our lighting model is far from perfect, though. In the next chapter we will add specular highlights, look at the Phong lighting model and how to interpolate normal vector values. In addition, we will investigate blending, fog, and shadows.

CHAPTER 4

■ ■ ■

Increasing Realism

In this chapter we will present ways to improve the realism of our scenes. As proper lighting is so fundamental to our visual perception, much of this chapter will build upon the end of the last chapter and focus on improvements to our lighting model. Specifically, we will

- discuss the difference between flat and smooth shading

- explain the Phong illumination model and then implement it as a shader program

- show how to add fog

- discuss techniques to generate shadows and add global illumination

- blend objects and calculate reflection and refraction

As a mental exercise, take notice of your current surroundings. If you are indoors, take a look at the room that you are in. Is the lighting soft or hard? If you can see the sun through a window, how does sunlight compare to artificial light? Which objects are shiny and which are dull? Do any objects reflect other objects on their surface? Identify materials that are more reflective. Are any objects transparent or semitransparent?

If you are outside, what does the atmosphere look like? Is it clear or hazy? Is it windy—are objects being blown around? What does the shadow of a fast-moving car look like? What does your shadow look like?

Asking these types of questions and taking a deeper look at commonplace objects and environments will help you to appreciate what types of complex interaction take place in nature and give insight into what needs to be emulated and improved upon in our renderings to reproduce a realistic appearance.

The final image that we will work toward in this chapter is shown in Figure 4-1.

Figure 4-1. The final scene that we will be building toward in this chapter

Setup

In this chapter, we will display a more visually interesting example than a single mesh floating in space. Instead we will set up a scene with a few spherical meshes that rotate above a plane representing the ground. In order to do this, we will first create a few reusable utility objects.

In Chapters 1 and 3 we used the matrix objects and functions of the `gl-matrix.js` library. This library also provides vector objects and functions.

A Vector Object

We will perform some common vector operations on our mesh data. We have operations built into our shaders for easy vector (x,y,z) notation, but not in JavaScript. The `gl-matrix.js` library uses numeric indices such as `[0, 1, 2]`:

```
var n = vec3.create(0.0, 1.0, 0.0);
console.log(n[1]); //the 2nd element
```

■ **Note**   More usage examples of gl-matrix.js can be found online at https://github.com/toji/gl-matrix/blob/master/README.md

---

To use `x, y, z` component notation, we can use a full-featured vector and matrix library like the one included in `Three.js`. Although I am an advocate of code reuse, in this chapter we just need a few minimal operations such as the cross-product, length, and normalize functions. Here we can create a small vector object of our own like the one shown in Listing 4-1 (which is based on functionality found in the `Three.js` library).

Listing 4-1. A partial vector object containing only the functionality that we require in this chapter

```
//vector3.js
Vector3 = function ( x, y, z ) {
      this.x = x || 0;
      this.y = y || 0;
      this.z = z || 0;
};

Vector3.prototype = {
      divide: function ( s ) {
            if ( s ) {
                  this.x /= s;
                  this.y /= s;
                  this.z /= s;
            }
            return this;
      },

      cross: function ( v ) {
            var x = this.x, y = this.y, z = this.z;
            if ( v instanceof Vector3 ) {
                  this.x = y * v.z - z * v.y;
                  this.y = z * v.x - x * v.z;
                  this.z = x * v.y - y * v.x;
```

```
        }
        return this;
    },

    length: function () {
        return Math.sqrt( this.x * this.x + this.y * this.y + this.z * this.z );
    },

    normalize: function () {
        var length = this.length();
        return this.divide( length );
    },
};
```

Notice above that we set default values in our constructor of (0,0,0) and also only divide if the passed in value is not 0.

Plane Class

To assist in drawing a single plane, in our case to simulate a surface for other objects to sit on or above, we add a function called setupPlaneMesh(see Listing 4-2).

Listing 4-2. Plane mesh with overridable properties and indexed buffers

```
//plane_mesh.js
function setupPlaneMesh(n, size, translation, color, textured)
{
        size = (typeof size !== 'undefined') ? size : 10.0;
        color = (typeof color !== 'undefined') ? color : [0.5, 0.5, 1.0, 1.0];
        translation = (typeof translation !== 'undefined') ? translation : [0.0, 0.0, 0.0];
        textured = (typeof textured !== 'undefined') ? textured : false;
...
        trianglesNormalBuffers[n] = gl.createBuffer();
...
}
```

In Listing 4-2, n is the index of a global array of VBOs. The size, translation, and color arguments refer to the length and width of the plane, the initial translation amount, and the color. If no arguments are provided, then we use the defaults that we have specified in the ternary operations.

To add a mesh we would make a call like this:

```
setupPlaneMesh(3, 10.0, [0.0, -1.0, 0.0]);
```

The number of parameters to the plane setup function is five, and for more complex meshes, it could be even more. A large number of parameters in a function signature is hard to remember and easy to mix up and cause errors. Instead of the code in Listing 4-2, we will still set default parameters but pass in a JSON object that is more flexible and verbose to encapsulate our data. It is assumed that the reader is familiar with JSON. If you are not, please refer to http://json.org.

We will change the code in Listing 4-2 to this:

```
function setupPlaneMesh(n, options)
{
        options = options || {}; //ensures that we have a JSON object

        size = (typeof options.size !== 'undefined') ? options.size : 10.0;
        color = (typeof options.color !== 'undefined') ? options.color : [0.5, 0.5, 1.0, 1.0];
```

```
        translation = (typeof options.translation !== 'undefined') ? options.translation : [0.0,
        0.0, 0.0];
        textured = (typeof options.textured !== 'undefined') ? options.textured : false;
...
}
```

And we now add a new plane mesh with a call like this:

```
setupPlaneMesh(3, { "translation": [0.0, -1.0, 0.0],
                    "size": 20.0
                }
            );
```

With a set parameter order, if you want to change textured to true, you need to specify any and all parameters in between—size, translation, and color—even if you are using the defaults. This second way of using a JSON object lets us omit parameters that we do not need to override and also not require the parameters to be in any set order.

⬚ **Note**   The code in this chapter is not optimized for performance. Because we only have a few meshes, this will not matter. However, with more complex scenes involving many draw calls, we will need to write optimized code. Please refer to Chapter 9 for best practices and ways to improve performance.

Spheres

To generate a sphere mesh, the function setupSphereMesh is shown in Listing 4-3. The first part lets us set the buffer index, radius, translation, color, divisions, and to use smooth shading or not. Next we generate our mesh using spherical coordinates. When we render a sphere, it is composed of horizontal lines of latitude (if earth is modeled as a sphere, think of lines of latitude as being parallel to the equator) and vertical lines of longitude (think of them running from the North Pole to the South Pole and representing time zones). Where the latitude and longitude lines intersect will be the vertex points. Vertex points will be spaced closer together toward the "poles" and further from each other toward the "equator." The more subdivisions that we have, the closer our approximation to a true sphere the mesh becomes.

⬚ **Note**   The normal value at each point on a unit sphere is the point itself (before scaling or translating). Remember that the normal vector is the direction pointing perpendicularly into or out of a surface, and starting from the origin this direction is the vector itself. The spherical coordinates are of unit length, so this vector is already normalized for us.

Listing 4-3. The file sphere_mesh.js, which generates a sphere mesh

```
function setupSphereMesh(n, options)
{
        options = options || {}; //ensures that we have a JSON object

        color = (typeof options.color !== 'undefined') ? options.color : [1.0, 0.0, 0.0, 1.0];
        translation = (typeof options.translation !== 'undefined') ? options.translation : [0.0,
        0.0, 0.0];
        radius = (typeof options.radius !== 'undefined') ? options.radius : 1.0;
```

```
divisions = (typeof options.divisions !== 'undefined') ? options.divisions : 30;
smooth_shading = (typeof options.smooth_shading !== 'undefined') ? options.smooth_shading
: true;
textured = (typeof options.textured !== 'undefined') ? options.textured : false;

//mesh generation modified from //http://learningwebgl.com/cookbook/index.php/How_to_
draw_a_sphere
    var     latitudeBands = divisions,
            longitudeBands = divisions;

    var     vertexPositionData = [],
            normalData = [],
            colorData = [],
            textureData = [],
            indexData = [];
    for (var latNumber = 0; latNumber <= latitudeBands; latNumber++) {
        var theta = latNumber * Math.PI / latitudeBands;
        var sinTheta = Math.sin(theta);
        var cosTheta = Math.cos(theta);

    for (var longNumber = 0; longNumber <= longitudeBands; longNumber++) {
        var phi = longNumber * 2 * Math.PI / longitudeBands;
        var sinPhi = Math.sin(phi);
        var cosPhi = Math.cos(phi);

        var x = cosPhi * sinTheta;
        var y = cosTheta;
        var z = sinPhi * sinTheta;
        var u = 1- (longNumber / longitudeBands);
        var v = latNumber / latitudeBands;

        textureData.push((x + 1.0) * .5);
        textureData.push((y + 1.0) * .5);

        normalData.push(x);
        normalData.push(y);
        normalData.push(z);
        colorData.push(color[0]);
        colorData.push(color[1]);
        colorData.push(color[2]);
        colorData.push(color[3]);
        vertexPositionData.push(radius * x + translation[0]);
        vertexPositionData.push(radius * y + translation[1]);
        vertexPositionData.push(radius * z + translation[2]);
    }
}

for (var latNumber = 0; latNumber < latitudeBands; latNumber++) {
  for (var longNumber = 0; longNumber < longitudeBands; longNumber++) {
    var first = (latNumber * (longitudeBands + 1)) + longNumber;
    var second = first + longitudeBands + 1;
    indexData.push(first);
    indexData.push(second);
    indexData.push(first + 1);
```

```
        indexData.push(second);
        indexData.push(second + 1);
        indexData.push(first + 1);
      }
    }

    if(!smooth_shading)
    {
        //calculate flat shading normals
    }

    trianglesNormalBuffers[n] = gl.createBuffer();
    gl.bindBuffer(gl.ARRAY_BUFFER, trianglesNormalBuffers[n]);
    gl.bufferData(gl.ARRAY_BUFFER, new Float32Array(normalData), gl.STATIC_DRAW);
    trianglesNormalBuffers[n].itemSize = 3;
    trianglesNormalBuffers[n].numItems = normalData.length / 3;

    trianglesColorBuffers[n] = gl.createBuffer();
    gl.bindBuffer(gl.ARRAY_BUFFER, trianglesColorBuffers[n]);
    gl.bufferData(gl.ARRAY_BUFFER, new Float32Array(colorData), gl.STATIC_DRAW);
    trianglesColorBuffers[n].itemSize = 4;
    trianglesColorBuffers[n].numItems = colorData.length / 4;

    trianglesVerticeBuffers[n] = gl.createBuffer();
    gl.bindBuffer(gl.ARRAY_BUFFER, trianglesVerticeBuffers[n]);
    gl.bufferData(gl.ARRAY_BUFFER,
        new Float32Array(vertexPositionData), gl.STATIC_DRAW);
    trianglesVerticeBuffers[n].itemSize = 3;
    trianglesVerticeBuffers[n].numItems = vertexPositionData.length / 3;

    if(textured)
    {
        trianglesTexCoordBuffers[n] = gl.createBuffer();
        gl.bindBuffer(gl.ARRAY_BUFFER, trianglesTexCoordBuffers[n]);
        gl.bufferData(gl.ARRAY_BUFFER, new Float32Array(textureData),
                    gl.STATIC_DRAW);
        trianglesTexCoordBuffers[n].itemSize = 2;
        trianglesTexCoordBuffers[n].numItems = textureData.length / 2;
    }

    vertexIndexBuffers[n] = gl.createBuffer();
    gl.bindBuffer(gl.ELEMENT_ARRAY_BUFFER, vertexIndexBuffers[n]);
    gl.bufferData(gl.ELEMENT_ARRAY_BUFFER,
        new Uint16Array(indexData), gl.STREAM_DRAW);
    vertexIndexBuffers[n].itemSize = 3;
    vertexIndexBuffers[n].numItems = indexData.length;
}
...
```

We would create a new sphere in our scene like this:

```
setupSphereMesh(0, { "translation": [-1.0, -0.75, 0.0],
                    "color": [1.0, 0.0, 0.0, 1.0],
                    "divisions": 20,
                    "smooth_shading": false
            });
```

Meshes with 5, 10, and 20 subdivisions, as shown within the WebGL Inspector (covered in Chapter 9), are shown in Figure 4-2.

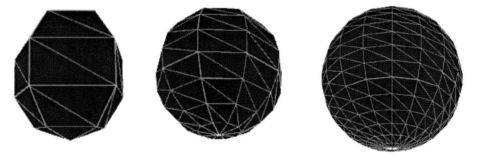

Figure 4-2. *Spheres with 5, 10, and 20 latitude and longitude divisions*

In Listing 4-3, we have omitted the flat shading code. We will come back to this code after we discuss the difference between flat and smooth shading.

Lighting Revisited

Lighting is central to graphics, and we will cover more light implementation details in this chapter starting with shading models, the traditional Phong illumination model, and finally global radiance models.

Shading Models

There are two basic ways to shade a polygon: flatly and smoothly. *Flat shading* means that the entire polygon is one color. We use the same normal vector for all the vertices. As a result, the normals where edges meet may be different for the same vertex depending on what the normal vector value for the entire face is. This variance means that the lighting values on adjacent edges will differ harshly and so you will see where one edge ends and another begins. Contrarily, *smooth shading* means that the color and normal values are interpolated. This can be done in the vertex shader (VS) as in Gouraud shading or in the fragment shader (FS) as in Phong shading. Both of these shading techniques will be covered in detail later on in the chapter.

Normal Vectors Revisited

Let us first examine what the normal vectors of flat shading look like where polygon edges meet and vertices are shared (see Figure 4-3).

As you can see in Figure 4-3, the normals at shared vertices are disjointed. There will be sharp visible jumps between values of adjacent polygons. With flat shading, the specular highlight (recall that specular reflection is light reflected in a specific direction) is omitted if the incoming specular light does not strike a vertex. As such, flat shading usually does not calculate specular reflection at all.

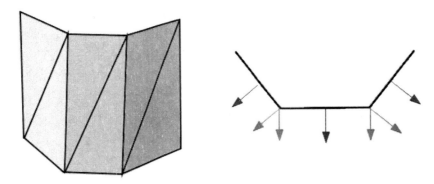

Figure 4-3. *Flat shading: one color, one normal per surface*

With smooth shading, shared vertices are averaged with all the faces it is shared with. The right of Figure 4-4 shows how a new normal vector that is an average of the two shared sides is used. Of course, the left figure also has some vertices that are not shared across multiple triangles and some that are shared by three.

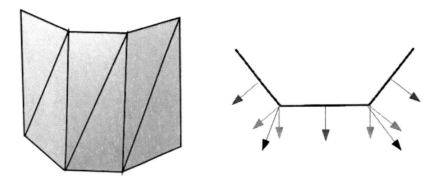

Figure 4-4. *Smooth shading: averaged normals and interpolated color*

There are two main types of smooth shading: Gouraud shading and Phong shading. *Gouraud shading* is performed per vertex, while *Phong shading* is done per pixel and as such captures specular highlights better.

Flat Shading

We will now return to the 04/sphere_mesh.js code and look at the flat shading method that we previously omitted. In WebGL, as the FS interpolates results automatically, it can actually be harder to perform flat shading than smooth shading. For the spheres, we must alter our triangles to have identical normals for each vertex (see Listing 4-4).

Listing 4-4. Calculating flat shading normals

```
if(!smooth_shading)
{
        vertexPositionData = calculateFlattenedVertices(
                        vertexPositionData, indexData);
        colorData = [];
```

```
        for(var i=0; i<indexData.length;++i)
        {
                colorData.push(color[0]);
                colorData.push(color[1]);
                colorData.push(color[2]);
                colorData.push(color[3]);
        }
        normalData = calculatePerFaceNormals(normalData, indexData);
 }
...

function calculateFlattenedVertices(origVertices, indices)
{
        var vertices = [];
        for(var i=0; i<indices.length; ++i)
        {
            a = indices[i]*3;
            vertices.push(origVertices[a]);
            vertices.push(origVertices[a + 1]);
            vertices.push(origVertices[a + 2]);
        }
        return vertices;
}

function calculatePerFaceNormals(origNormals, indices)
{
        var normals = [];
        for(var i=0; i<indices.length; i+=3)
        {
            var a = indices[i]*3;
            var b = indices[i+1]*3;
            var c = indices[i+2]*3;

            n1 = new Vector3(origNormals[a], origNormals[a+1], origNormals[a+2]);
            n2 = new Vector3(origNormals[b], origNormals[b+1], origNormals[b+2]);
            n3 = new Vector3(origNormals[c], origNormals[c+1], origNormals[c+2]);

            nx = (n1.x + n2.x + n3.x)/3;
            ny = (n1.y + n2.y + n3.y)/3;
            nz = (n1.z + n2.z + n3.z)/3;

            v3 = new Vector3(nx,ny,nz);
            normals.push(v3.x);
            normals.push(v3.y);
            normals.push(v3.z);

            normals.push(v3.x);
            normals.push(v3.y);
            normals.push(v3.z);

            normals.push(v3.x);
            normals.push(v3.y);
            normals.push(v3.z);
        }
        return normals;
}
```

In Listing 4-4, we are expanding our data to include color, position, and normal data per each index instead of only each vertex. We are using a constant color, so expanding the color data is trivial. For our vertex positions we pass in the original vertice information that we then use to produce a longer array of all vertex positions (including duplicate values) by looking up the vertice associated with each index. For the normal, we take the average of all three triangle vertex normals and use this new value for each vertex in the triangle. See Figure 4-5.

When we render our spheres, we will use the `drawArrays` method instead of `drawElements` because we are no longer using the index buffer. We still use the `drawElements` method to render the plane:

```
if(i==3){
        gl.drawElements(gl.TRIANGLES, vertexIndexBuffers[i].numItems, gl.UNSIGNED_SHORT, 0);
}else{
        gl.drawArrays(gl.TRIANGLES, 0, trianglesVerticeBuffers[i].numItems);
}
```

Figure 4-5. *Flat shading of spheres with varying subdivisions*

The flat shader example is in the file `04/01_flat.html`.

Lambert Reflection

Lambert reflection gives the intensity of diffuse light at any point of an object. Recall that diffuse light depends on the angle of the incoming light to a surface point, but that the reflection is in all directions. Calculating Lambert reflection involves taking the normal vector N and the direction of the light to the surface L and then computing the cosine of the angle between these vectors. The higher the angle (up to 90 degrees), the lower the cosine will be. As the angle approaches 0, the cosine approaches 1. All other angle values will be between -1 and 1, with 0 occurring when the normal and lighting vectors are perpendicular. Angles in the range of (90, 270) will return negative values because this means that the light is on the opposite side of the surface then the normal vector.

Usually negative values are clamped to 0. To calculate the cosine, we can take the dot product of normalized N and normalized L, which is the Lambert term, `dot(N, L)`. The diffuse component of light is then calculated as the following, where M_D and L_D correspond to the material diffuse component and the light diffuse component:

```
Diffuse = dot(N, L)*M_D*L_D
```

When only diffuse color and an optional global ambient light factor are used, this is sometimes referred to as *Lambert illumination* (see Figure 4-6).

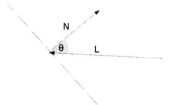

Figure 4-6. *The normal (N) and lighting (L) vectors of a Lambert reflection*

A VS using Lambert illumination is shown in Listing 4-5.

Listing 4-5. Computing Lambert amount

```
<script type="x-shader/x-vertex">
      attribute vec3 aVertexPosition;
      attribute vec3 aVertexColor;
      attribute vec3 aVertexNormal;

      uniform mat3 uNormalMatrix;
      uniform mat4 uMVMatrix;
      uniform mat4 uPMatrix;

      varying highp vec3 vColor;

      void main(void) {
            gl_Position = uPMatrix * uMVMatrix * vec4(aVertexPosition, 1.0);

            vec3 pointLightPosition = vec3(1.0,2.0,-1.0);
            vec3 pointLightDirection = normalize(
                  vec3(pointLightPosition.xyz - aVertexPosition.xyz));
            vec3 ambientColor = vec3(0.1, 0.1, 0.1);

            vec3 L = vec3(uPMatrix * uMVMatrix * vec4(pointLightDirection, 1.0));
            vec3 N = uNormalMatrix * aVertexNormal;
            float lambert = max(dot(normalize(N), normalize(L)), 0.0);
            vColor = aVertexColor * lambert;
      }
</script>
```

Our FS trivially uses the passed in color from the VS:

```
<script id="shader-fs" type="x-shader/x-fragment">
      varying highp vec3 vColor;

      void main(void) {
        gl_FragColor = vec4(vColor, 1.0);
      }
</script>
```

> ■ **Note** In these examples, it would be better to use a uniform value for constants. However, I am trying to keep the application logic the same and vary only the shaders. This lets me more easily show the changes between lighting model improvements, so I am hard-coding constant values within the shader.

The VS in Listing 4-5 and the FS shown previously are also used for the Gouraud shading example that we will show next. The only difference is the normal vector attribute values that are passed into the shaders from the application.

Smooth Shading

Unlike flat shading that uses the same normal value for the entire polygon, in smooth shading every vertex normal and color may be different. The color and normal value used at each pixel is interpolated to produce a smoother, more gradient result. Smooth shading gives the illusion of polygons being curved instead of completely flat.

> ■ **Note** It is possible to use the same geometry multiple times in an application with elementary transformations. However, our sphere geometry calculates the type of normal in the object itself and stores it there. So, if we want to use smooth shading and flat shading at the same time on different instances of the same object, we would have to recalculate the normals in between draw calls.

Gouraud Shading

Gouraud shading, which is named after Henri Gouraud, was the default smooth shading used in early fixed functionality versions of OpenGL. In Gouraud shading, each vertex takes the (normalized) average of surface normals of adjacent polygons that share that vertex as a normal. Lighting calculations are done per vertex and then final values are interpolated. The left of Figure 4-7 is an example of Gouraud shading. The Gouraud shader example is in the file `04/02_gouraud.html`.

Phong shading

Phong shading is named after Bui Tuong Phong, who developed an interpolation method (Phong shading) and reflection model (Phong illumination) in his 1973 Ph.D thesis. It is similar to Gouraud shading because the normals are interpolated in the VS, but the lighting calculations are done inside of the FS. For this reason, Phong shading is more computationally expensive then Gouraud shading, but it also produces better results.

To demonstrate this, imagine a large polygon such as the floor plane found in our chapter examples. It is composed of only four triangles. If a light shines in the middle of a triangle, far away from any corner, the vertex light amounts will be low and so the polygon will be dark with Gouraud shading. However, with Phong shading, the lighting calculation is done per fragment, so the area in which the light is shining will not be missed. The more we subdivide into smaller polygons, the lower the difference between Gouraud and Phong will appear.

The Phong shader with Lambert illumination example is in the file `04/03_phong_lambert.html`(see Listing 4-6).

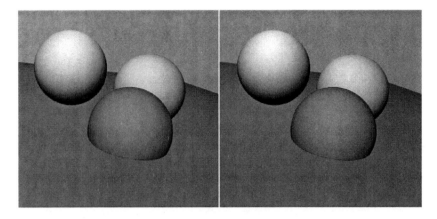

Figure 4-7. Gouraud shading on the left, and Phong on the right. Nearly identical with the Phong shader, providing a little more detail in the plane. Adding a specular component will lead to more variance

Listing 4-6. Shader pair with lighting calculation moved to the FS

```
<script type="x-shader/x-vertex">
      attribute vec3 aVertexPosition;
      attribute vec3 aVertexColor;
      attribute vec3 aVertexNormal;

      varying highp vec3 vColor;
      varying highp vec3 vPosition;
      varying highp vec3 N;

      void main(void) {
            gl_Position = uPMatrix * uMVMatrix * vec4(aVertexPosition, 1.0);

            vColor = aVertexColor;
             vPosition = aVertexPosition;
            N = aVertexNormal;
      }
</script>

<script id="shader-fs" type="x-shader/x-fragment">
      uniform highp mat3 uNormalMatrix;
      uniform highp mat4 uMVMatrix;
      uniform highp mat4 uPMatrix;

      varying highp vec3 vColor;
      varying highp vec3 vPosition;
      varying highp vec3 N;

      void main(void) {
            highp vec3 n = uNormalMatrix * N;

            highp vec3 pointLightPosition = vec3(1.0,2.0,-1.0);
            highp vec3 pointLightDirection = normalize(
                  vec3(pointLightPosition.xyz - vPosition.xyz));
            highp vec3 L = vec3(uPMatrix * uMVMatrix * vec4(pointLightDirection, 1.0));
```

97

```
                highp float lambert = max(dot(normalize(n), normalize(L)), 0.0);
                gl_FragColor = vec4(vColor * lambert, 1.0);
        }
</script>
```

We will now cover adding a specular reflection component in our illumination model.

Phong Illumination Model

We have shown how Lambert illumination can produce decent results. The Phong illumination model (also known as the Phong reflection model) takes into account the specular reflection of objects. In the model, surfaces have diffuse and specular reflection. The diffuse reflection acts more on rough surfaces; the specular reflection occurs more on shiny surfaces. Recall that diffuse reflection is scattered in all directions, while specular reflection is more intense and in a particular direction. Phong noticed that the specular highlights on shiny surfaces are small but intense, while duller surfaces have larger highlights of less-intense value.

With Phong illumination, each light has a RGB specular and diffuse intensity component denoted **i$_s$, i$_d$**. The overall scene has a single ambient component, **i$_a$**.

Each material in the scene has RGB reflection values for specular, diffuse, and ambient light corresponding to the parameters k$_s$, k$_d$, and k$_a$. Each material also has a shininess constant, α, which is larger for smoother, more reflective surfaces. Normally, the constant is set to range from 0 to 128 and is used as an exponent for the specular term.

The calculation of a single point I$_p$, using the Phong reflection model with one light is:

$$I_p = k_a i_a + [k_d * dot(L, N) * i_d + k_s * dot(R, V) * i_s]$$

For more lights, the calculation becomes k$_a$i$_a$ plus the sum of the diffuse and specular calculation for each light (which is the part in square brackets). V is the direction to the viewer, which is sometimes referred to as the eye vector. R is the perfect reflection of the light vector. Given L, the direction of the light to the surface point; and N, the normal vector of the point, R is calculated as:

$$R = 2 * dot(L, N) * N - L$$

In GLSL, the function reflect can compute this value for us. The Gouraud shader with Phong illumination example (see Figure 4-8) is in the file 04/04_gouraud_phong.html.

Figure 4-8. *Gouraud shading (VS), Phong illumination*

The VS for Gouraud-Phong example is shown in Listing 4-7.

Listing 4-7. Gouraud-Phong illumination lighting calculations done in VS

```
<script type="x-shader/x-vertex">
      attribute vec3 aVertexPosition;
      attribute vec3 aVertexColor;
      attribute vec3 aVertexNormal;

      uniform mat3 uNormalMatrix;
      uniform mat4 uMVMatrix;
      uniform mat4 uPMatrix;

      varying vec3 vColor;
      varying float diffuseLambert;
      varying float specular;

      void main(void) {
                gl_Position = uPMatrix * uMVMatrix * vec4(aVertexPosition, 1.0);
                vColor = aVertexColor;

                vec3 pointLightPosition = vec3(1.0,2.0,-1.0);
                  vec3 pointLightDirection = vec3(
                      pointLightPosition.xyz - aVertexPosition.xyz);
                vec3 L = vec3(uPMatrix * uMVMatrix * vec4(pointLightDirection, 1.0));
                vec3 N = normalize(uNormalMatrix * aVertexNormal);
                vec3 V = -vec3(uPMatrix * uMVMatrix * vec4(aVertexPosition,1.0));

                L = normalize(L);
                V = normalize(V);

                vec3 R = reflect(-L, N);
                float shininess = 128.0;

                specular = pow( max(0.0,dot(R,V)), shininess);
                diffuseLambert = dot(L,N);
      }
</script>
```

In Listing 4-7, we calculate the lighting, normal, position, and eye vectors. Then we calculate the reflection vector and Lambert term from the lighting and normal vectors. We then pass these two values to the FS that is shown in Listing 4-8.

Listing 4-8. Gouraud-Phong FS

```
<script id="shader-fs" type="x-shader/x-fragment">
      varying highp vec3 vColor;
      varying highp float diffuseLambert;
      varying highp float specular;

      void main(void) {
          highp float AmbientIntensity = 0.3;
          highp vec3 DiffuseLightIntensity = 0.9;
          highp float SpecularIntensity = 0.5;
```

```
        highp vec3 AmbientColour = vec3(0.1, 0.1, 0.1);
        highp vec3 DiffuseMaterialColour = vColor;
        highp vec3 SpecularColour = vec3(1.0, 1.0, 1.0);

        gl_FragColor = vec4(AmbientColour*AmbientIntensity +
                    diffuseLambert * DiffuseMaterialColour*DiffuseLightIntensity +
                    SpecularColour * specular*SpecularIntensity,1.0);
    }
</script>
```

In Listing 4-8, we take the ambient, diffuse, and specular intensities; light colors; and our specular and Lambert amounts to produce a final color.

For much better specular results, we can move the lighting calculation to the FS. Recall that the VS operates per vertex, so when we pass results to the FS it is a linear interpolation between vertex points that is used for each pixel. However, when we perform the calculation in the FS, the calculation is done at every single pixel. This can produce a more accurate, independent, and detailed range of final values. The result of Phong illumination and shading is shown in Figure 4-9.

Figure 4-9. *Phong shader and illumination*

It is quite remarkable how a little specular highlight can make a scene much more vivid and realistic. The Phong shader with Phong illumination example is in the file 04/05_phong_phong.html.

The VS becomes much simpler. We just pass along the vertex color, position, and normal (see Listing 4-9).

Listing 4-9. Phong VS

```
<script type="x-shader/x-vertex">
     uniform mat4 uMVMatrix;
     uniform mat4 uPMatrix;

     attribute vec3 aVertexPosition;
     attribute vec4 aVertexColor;
     attribute vec3 aVertexNormal;
```

```
        varying highp vec4 vColor;
        varying highp vec3 vPosition;
        varying highp vec3 N;

        void main(void) {
                gl_Position = uPMatrix * uMVMatrix * vec4(aVertexPosition, 1.0);

                vColor = aVertexColor;
                vPosition = aVertexPosition;
                N = aVertexNormal;
        }
</script>
```

Of course, this means that our FS will do the heavy lifting now. In Listing 4-10 we calculate the diffuse and specular reflection light components inside of the FS.

Listing 4-10. Phong FS

```
<script id="shader-fs" type="x-shader/x-fragment">
        uniform highp mat3 uNormalMatrix;
        uniform highp mat4 uMVMatrix;
        uniform highp mat4 uPMatrix;

        varying highp vec4 vColor;
        varying highp vec3 vPosition;
        varying highp vec3 N;

        void main(void) {
                highp vec3 pointLightPosition = vec3(5.0,1.0,5.0);

                highp vec3 pointLightDirection = vec3(
                        pointLightPosition.xyz - vPosition.xyz);

                highp mat4 mvp = uPMatrix * uMVMatrix;

                highp vec3 L = vec3(mvp * vec4(pointLightDirection, 1.0));
                highp vec3 V = -vec3(mvp * vec4(vPosition,1.0));

                highp vec3 l = normalize(L);
                highp vec3 n = normalize(uNormalMatrix * N);
                highp vec3 v = normalize(V);

                highp vec3 R = reflect(l, n);

                highp float diffuseLambert = dot(l,n);
                highp float Roughness = 1.0;
                highp float AmbientIntensity = 0.3;
                highp vec3 DiffuseLightIntensity = vec3(0.9, 0.9, 0.9);
                highp float SpecularIntensity = 0.5;
                highp float shininess = 128.0;

                highp float specular = pow( max(0.0,dot(R,v)), shininess);

                gl_FragColor = vec4(AmbientColour*AmbientIntensity +
                        diffuseLambert * DiffuseMaterialColour*DiffuseLightIntensity +
                        SpecularColour * specular*SpecularIntensity, vColor.a);
```

```
        }
</script>
```

By adjusting the shininess, we can alter the specular highlight as shown in Figure 4-10.

Figure 4-10. Shininess values of 32, 8, and 2 (using the attenuation shader)

A variation of the Phong lighting model uses the half angle H and normal vector N to calculate the specular term. The half angle bisects the angle between the viewer's eye and the lighting vector L.

This variation is known as Blinn-Phong illumination and is the OpenGL 3.1 fixed functionality default. There are times when using the Blinn-Phong lighting model is more computationally expensive than the Phong model because it involves a square root. However, in some cases it only needs to be computed once per light instead of at each pixel and is thus more optimal than the Phong model. Figure 4-11 shows all of the vectors involved in lighting calculations at a given point. The angle between the reflection vector R and normal N will be equal to the angle between the incoming light vector L and N.

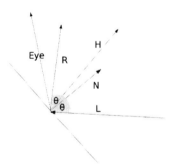

Figure 4-11. All the vectors used in Phong and Blinn-Phong lighting calculations

In Listing 4-10, v is our eye vector. To use Blinn-Phong we calculate the half angle vector as H = (L + v)/length(L + v), that is the normalized sum of L + V. We then compute the specular term as highp float specular = pow(max(0.0,dot(H,N)), shininess);. The Phong and Blinn-Phong specular term will be similar, but produce a slightly different specular highlight.

Attenuation

When we have a point light or spotlight, the light is brightest closest to the light position and decreases as the distance from a point to the light position increases. To emulate this we need to find the length of a point to the light position at every vertex (or pixel for increased accuracy). Then we compute an attenuation factor that is used to model the gradual loss of intensity of the light (see Figure 4-12). Typically, the attenuation factor is `1/(a + b*distance + c*distance²)` where `a`, `b`, and `c` are constant, linear, and quadratic constants, respectively. Experiment with values to see what looks good. I have chosen `0.01`, `0.01`, and `0.02`, respectively, in the example found in the file `04/06_attenuation.html`.

Figure 4-12. *Light attenuation*

The VS is the same as in the last example, shown in Listing 4-9. The FS now adds a per-pixel distance calculation and attenuation factor (see Listing 4-11).

Listing 4-11. Modifications to the FS Which Add an Attenuation Factor

```
highp vec3 pointLightDirection = vec3(pointLightPosition.xyz - vPosition.xyz);
highp float d = length(pointLightDirection);
highp float attenuation = 1.0/(.01 + .01*d+.02*d*d);
…

highp vec3 AmbientColour = vec3(0.1, 0.1, 0.1)*attenuation;
highp vec3 DiffuseMaterialColour = vColor.xyz*attenuation;
highp vec3 SpecularColour = vec3(1.0, 1.0, 1.0)*attenuation;
```

▓ **Note** With additional lights and a high shininess term, it can be easy to have the lighting intensity set too high. The result will look white like an overexposed photo, as shown in Figure 4-13.

Figure 4-13. Setting light values too high

Spotlights

A *spotlight* can be viewed as a cone of light emulating from a point. To model a spotlight, we need to set the angular range of the cone and then determine whether a point lies within it. If it does, we do our lighting calculation; otherwise we do not light the point. Code for a spotlight example can be found in the file 04/07_ spotlight.html.

The VS for the spotlight example does not change from Listing 4-9. The FS adds four variables that correspond to the total angle of the beam, the difference in intensity from the center of the beam to the edges, the direction of the spotlight (in addition to the light position), and a variable to test whether the current light beam is within the spotlight area:

```
//spotlight
highp float spotCosCutoff = -0.1;
highp float spotExponent = 2.0;
highp vec3 spotDirection = vec3(2.0,5.0,1.0);
highp float spotEffect = dot(normalize(spotDirection), l);
```

The new part of the FS involves two tests. The first checks if the Lambert term is greater than 0 (the light is on the proper side of the polygon face), and the second checks if the light to surface point direction falls within the spotlight beam. If either of these tests fails, we paint the pixel black.

```
...
highp float diffuseLambert = dot(l,n);
      //spotlight
      highp float spotCosCutoff = 0.6;
      highp float spotExponent = 2.0;
      highp vec3 spotDirection = vec3(2.5,12.0,1.5);
      highp float spotEffect = dot(normalize(spotDirection), l);
```

```
    if(diffuseLambert > 0.0){
        if(spotEffect > spotCosCutoff){
                        highp float shininess = 32.0;
                        highp float specular = pow( max(0.0,dot(R,v)), shininess);

                        spotEffect = pow(spotEffect, spotExponent);
                        attenuation *= spotEffect;

                        highp float AmbientIntensity = 0.3;
                        highp vec3 DiffuseLightIntensity = vec3(0.9, 0.9, 0.9);

                        highp float SpecularIntensity = 0.5;

                        highp vec3 AmbientColour = vec3(0.1, 0.1, 0.1)*attenuation;

                        highp vec3 DiffuseMaterialColour = vColor.xyz*attenuation;
                        highp vec3 SpecularColour = vec3(1.0, 1.0, 1.0)*attenuation;

                        gl_FragColor = vec4(AmbientColour*AmbientIntensity +
                                    diffuseLambert * DiffuseMaterialColour *
                                    DiffuseLightIntensity +
                                    SpecularColour * specular * SpecularIntensity,
                                    vColor.a);
            }else{
                        gl_FragColor = vec4(0.0,0.0,0.0, 1.0);
            }
    }else{
        gl_FragColor = vec4(0.0,0.0,0.0, 1.0);
    }
...
```

You can further enhance this example by dynamically moving the spotlight like a prison search light or lighthouse beam (see Figure 4-14). Instead of a harsh transition to complete black, you can also use another attenuation factor to ease into darkness.

Figure 4-14. A spotlight

This covers the traditional approach to lighting with an ambient, diffuse, and specular component along with a directional spotlight. Next we will look at additional enhancements that we can make to global light and object interaction.

More Advanced Lighting

The Phong illumination model is fairly good, but it has some shortcomings. Direct illumination models such as Phong (which are traditional in computer graphics) take a small number of light sources and possibly a global ambient term to calculate lighting. What direct illumination fails to account for are the interreflections between objects and self-occlusion.

With global illumination models such as ray tracing, ambient occlusion, hemisphere lighting, and spherical harmonics, a higher degree of realism is achieved by taking these interactions into account and varying the ambient term accordingly. Global illumination models by themselves can look a little dull. A hybrid approach, using direct lights in conjunction with a global illumination model can be optimal. Global illumination can produce vastly more realistic results compared with direct illumination. However, it is slower and much more computationally intensive than direct lighting. For this reason, calculations are often done and then stored for later use.

Global illumination implementation is beyond the scope of this book, but there are several references in Appendix D for those who are interested. The OpenGLSL "Orange" book also discusses several advanced global illumination models.

Lastly, what if a material radiates light? Then we would also need to factor in the emissive light component of the object. We will now show how to model environmental fog and direct shadows with WebGL.

Fog

To produce atmospheric fog (see Figure 4-15), generally one of three equations are used: a linear equation or one of two exponential ones. The linear equation is $Fog = (End_z - z)/(End_z - Start_z)$. `End` and `Start` are between 0 and 1 in the clip space. The first exponential equation is $Fog = e^{-(density*z)}$ and the second exponential equation is $Fog = e^{-(density*z)^2}$.

Figure 4-15. Adding fog

To use the second exponential equation, we add one varying to our VS, which stores the length of our position from the origin. We could also have just stored the z-coordinate:

```
varying float fog_z;
fog_z = length(gl_Position.xyz);
```

In our FS, we set the fog density and color, and then mix the final lighting and material color with the fog color:

```
varying highp float fog_z;
…
//calculate fog
highp float fog_density = 0.25;
highp vec4 fog_color = vec4(0.1, 0.2, 0.1, 0.6);

highp float fogFactor = exp( -fog_density * fog_density * fog_z * fog_z);
fogFactor = clamp(fogFactor, 0.0, 1.0);

highp vec4 materialColor = vec4(AmbientColour*AmbientIntensity +
                    diffuseLambert * DiffuseMaterialColour * DiffuseLightIntensity +
                    SpecularColour * specular * SpecularIntensity, vColor.a);

gl_FragColor = mix( fog_color, materialColor, fogFactor );
```

The fog example can be found in the file 04/08_fog.html. Another example that combines fog and a spotlight is shown in Figure 4-16 and is in the file 04/09_fog_spotlight.html.

Figure 4-16. Fog with a spotlight

Fog is an effect that is fairly easy to implement and can help add character and atmosphere to a scene.

Shadows

The complement of light is darkness, so proper shadows are essential to a realistic scene. With illumination models such as the Phong illumination model, each object has areas of light or darkness. However, objects do not affect one another, which does not look natural. There are several ways to generate shadows and correct this issue. We will discuss two of the most common approaches: ambient occlusion and shadow maps.

Ambient Occlusion

We mentioned that ambient occlusion is a global illumination technique. In direct lighting models, ambient light is modeled as constant throughout a scene. In reality, this is not the case. Ambient light at a point can be blocked by other objects in the scene or another part of the object. As an example, the back of your ears, the creases in your palms, wrinkles, and your belly button all receive less light than other areas such as your forehead, the tip of your nose, and your cheeks.

To determine how accessible light is to a point on an object, we can cast rays from the point and keep track of how many times they reach the boundary of our scene versus how many times they are blocked along the way. The less intersection by other objects, the more visible light gets to the point. The ratio of unblocked rays to total rays is the "occlusion factor" and will vary between 0 for always blocked to 1 for never blocked. By multiplying the occlusion factor with our diffuse light, we darken the resulting image.

The process of sending out light and it being blocked or not is similar to how sonar works. When sound waves hit an object and reflect back, we know that there is an object there. If all our emitted sound waves return, we must be completely enclosed. Going back from this analogy to light rays, if we are completely enclosed than no outside light gets to us.

Ambient occlusion produces soft shadows. By itself it can make an object look dull like the scenery on an overcast day. For this reason it is usually used in combination with a direct lighting model. We will not implement ambient occlusion in this book, but references are provided in Appendix D.

Shadow Maps

A *shadow map* produces harder shadows than ambient occlusion. By *harder shadows* I mean that the luminance of the shadow does not vary much and has well-defined edges, whereas a *softer shadow* has more gradual and subtle edges. To generate the shadow map for a light, we need to view the scene from the light's perspective and then store the nearest depth value of each point, as seen from this view into a buffer for later lookup. When we render the scene, we compare the depth value of the current pixel with that of the stored map and perform the lighting calculation if it is closer than the depth map value. If there are multiple lights, we need to store depth values for each one. In practice, even if a scene has many lights, using the shadow maps of a couple of them is probably sufficient. Because implementing a shadow map involves knowledge of the frame and render buffers, we will explain how to implement a shadow map in Chapter 10. The shadow map of our scene shown from the light's perspective is shown in Figure 4-17.

Figure 4-17. Shadow map of the scene

░ **Note** Desktop versions of the GLSL have a special type for shadows, but the version of GLSL that is currently used for WebGL does not.

Shadows represent the absence of light and so are equally as important as rendering light. However, shadows are often more difficult to render in a visually appealing manner.

Depth Buffer

Our three-dimensional scene is transformed to two dimensions when it is rendered to the <canvas>. As such, many (x,y,z) coordinates may share the same (x,y) value. However there is only one pixel that corresponds to this value when we render to the canvas. So which one do we render?

The answer is determined by the depth buffer (aka the z-buffer), which stores a z-component for each pixel. By default, when WebGL encounters a pixel at (x,y,z), it tests whether the z-value stored at (x,y) in the buffer is farther away and replaces it if the new pixel is nearer. All z-values are clamped to the range [0,1]; 0 is the closest; 1 is the farthest away. So if the viewport z direction is from [40, -40], 40 would be 0.0, 20 would be .25, 0 would be 0.5, -20 would be 0.75, and -40 would be 1.0.

We can set the range of depth values with void depthRange(GLclampf zNear, GLclampf zFar);. zNear needs to be smaller than zFar and both values are clamped to the range [0,1].Imagine we clamp our depth range to the range (0, 5)and that we pass the vertex points (3,-4, 4), (3,-4, 2), (3,-4,5), (3, -4, 1) to our FS. All (x,y) coordinate values in the depth-buffer are initialized to a value of 1.0. The first point (3,-4,4) has a z value of 4, which corresponds to 0.2 in the range [0, 5]. This is lower than 1.0, so it replaces the previous value in the depth buffer. The next z-value for the point, 2, is clamped to a higher value (0.6), so it fails to replace the current pixel. Continuing, the z-value of 5 is clamped to a lower value (0.0), so it replaces the current depth buffer value. Finally, 1 is clamped to (0.8), which does not replace the stored depth value. The final pixel rendered at (3, -4) corresponds to the one at (3, -4, 5).

The depth buffer comparison function is specified with a call to depthFunc(comparision_type), and the default comparision_type is LESS. As we have shown, the LESS comparision test passes if an input z-value is less than the previous pixel stored at the same (x,y)location within the depth buffer. When it passes, the input z-value replaces the stored value.

LESS is the default comparison function. However, we can change how WebGL compares values in the buffer to any one of the values: NEVER, LESS, EQUAL, LEQUAL, GREATER, NOTEQUAL, GEQUAL, or ALWAYS.

We can initialize the value stored in the depth buffer at each pixel with a call to void clearDepth(GLclampf depth).The valid range is 0 to 1, and the default is 1. To enable and disable writing to the depth buffer, you can use the function void depthMask(GLboolean flag);

An alternative to the depth test is blending, as we will cover next.

Blending

Blending lets us determine how to handle pixels that overlap in an alternative manner to the depth test. The depth test discards either the existing pixel or the new pixel, but blending combines the existing fragment color and incoming fragment into a new fragment. Blending can produce transparency, but it is not the same as transparency. To perform blending, you need to disable depth testing and enable blending:

```
gl.enable(gl.BLEND);
gl.disable(gl.DEPTH_TEST);
```

When blending we have a source color (Rs, Gs, Bs, As) and a destination color (Rd, Gd, Bd, Ad). We then can define rules on how to combine the source and destination colors for our new fragment. We do this by using this function:

```
void blendFunc(GLenum sfactor, GLenum dfactor);
```

The first argument is the source factor, and the second is the destination factor. Our resultant color will be Source * sfactor + Destination *dfactor. Our available options for the source factor are ZERO, ONE, DST_COLOR, ONE_MINUS_DST_COLOR, SRC_ALPHA_SATURATE, SRC_ALPHA, ONE_MINUS_SRC_ALPHA, DST_ALPHA and ONE_MINUS_DST_ALPHA and the destination factors are ZERO, ONE, SRC_COLOR, ONE_MINUS_SRC_COLOR, SRC_ALPHA, ONE_MINUS_SRC_ALPHA, DST_ALPHA and ONE_MINUS_DST_ALPHA.

▓ **Note**   Two nice online applications to play around with blend settings are available at http://mrdoob.com/lab/javascript/webgl/blending/blendfunc.html and http://alteredqualia.com/three/examples/webgl_materials_blending_custom.html. The application at the first link is written by the creator of the Three.js framework and the second one is written by the most active contributor to the library. In addition, http://www.khronos.org/registry/gles/specs/2.0/es_full_spec_2.0.25.pdf#nameddest=section-4.1.6 explicitly states the result of each blending factor setting.

Using a blend function value of gl.blendFunc(gl.SRC_ALPHA, gl.ONE) will result in the red component being calculated as follows:

```
Rr = Rs*sfactor + Rd*dfactor
Rr = Rs*As + Rd*1 - Rs*As + Rd
```

The other components (G, B, A) are computed in the same manner. A second example which calculates based on SRC_ALPHA and ONE_MINUS_SRC_ALPHA is:

```
gl.blendFunc(gl.SRC_ALPHA, gl.ONE_MINUS_SRC_ALPHA);
```

```
Rr = Rs*As + Rd*(1-As);
Rr = Rd + As(Rs-Rd);
```

We can also set the blend function to be additive or subtractive by calling void blendEquation(GLenum mode); or void blendEquationSeparate(GLenum modeRGB, GLenum modeAlpha); with FUNC_ADD, FUNC_SUBTRACT or FUNC_REVERSE_SUBTRACT as parameter(s).

FUNC_ADD produces R = Rs*Sr + Rd*Dr, as shown previously for the final red component. FUNC_SUBTRACT produces R = Rs*Sr - Rd*Dr and FUNC_REVERSE_SUBTRACT produces R = Rd*Dr - Rs*Sr.

We can blend with a constant color by using void blendColor(GLclampf red, GLclampf green, GLclampf blue, GLclampf alpha);. To blend RGB and alpha values separately, we can use this function:

```
void blendFuncSeparate(GLenum srcRGB, GLenum dstRGB, GLenum srcAlpha, GLenum dstAlpha);
```

The order of blending is important. Because the depth test and blending are mutually exclusive, we generally need to render completely opaque objects first, followed by semitransparent ones.

An example of blending can be seen in Figure 4-18 and found in the file 04/10_blending.html.

To produce the image in Figure 4-18, only the application changes. The shaders are the same as in the attenuation example, which is shown in code Listings 4-9 to 4-11. In Listing 4-12 the order of rendering is adjusted to render our semitransparent object last. For the plane and first two opaque spheres we enable the depth test and disable blending. Then we alternate these settings, disabling the depth test and enabling blending for our final sphere.

Figure 4-18. *Blending applied to the closest sphere*

Listing 4-12. Using blending

```
var drawOrder = [1,2,3,0];
for(var n=0; n < drawOrder.length; ++n)
{
      var i = drawOrder[n];

      gl.bindBuffer(gl.ARRAY_BUFFER, trianglesVerticeBuffers[i]);
      gl.vertexAttribPointer(vertexPositionAttribute, 3, gl.FLOAT, false, 0, 0);

      gl.bindBuffer(gl.ARRAY_BUFFER, trianglesColorBuffers[i]);
      gl.vertexAttribPointer(vertexColorAttribute, 4, gl.FLOAT, false, 0, 0);

      gl.bindBuffer(gl.ARRAY_BUFFER, trianglesNormalBuffers[i]);
      gl.vertexAttribPointer(vertexNormalAttribute, 3, gl.FLOAT, false, 0, 0);

      if(i==0){
          gl.disable(gl.DEPTH_TEST);
          gl.enable(gl.BLEND);
          gl.blendFunc(gl.SRC_ALPHA, gl.ONE);
          gl.blendEquation(gl.FUNC_ADD);
      }else{
          gl.disable(gl.BLEND);
          gl.enable(gl.DEPTH_TEST);
      }
      gl.bindBuffer(gl.ELEMENT_ARRAY_BUFFER, vertexIndexBuffers[i]);
      gl.drawElements(gl.TRIANGLES, vertexIndexBuffers[i].numItems, gl.UNSIGNED_SHORT, 0);
}
```

There are many combinations of blend factors and varying results obtainable by adjusting them. I encourage the reader to play around with the interactive demos listed in the previous note and/or to calculate the final color of a pixel based on a source and destination color and blend modes.

Reflection and Refraction

To render semitransparent objects such as glass or water, we need to model reflection and refraction. We have shown that when light is reflected off of a surface that the angle between the incoming incident light and surface normal will be equal to the angle between the reflected light ray and the surface normal. For this reason, the larger the light angle to the normal, the duller the specular reflection will be.

Refraction is a change in the direction of light (bending of light) where two varying mediums (of differing optical density) meet. Simple examples of refraction are when air and water or water and glass meet. Consider looking at an object, such as a straw, in a glass of water. The straw will appear to be bent where the water and air meet.

Snell's Law, named after the Dutch astronomer Willebrord Snell who discovered it in the 17th century, describes what happens during refraction as follows:

$$\frac{\sin\theta_1}{\sin\theta_2} = \frac{v_1}{v_2} = \frac{n_2}{n_1}$$

Where θ_1, θ_2 are angles from the normal, v_1, v_2 are velocities, and n_1, n_2 are refractive indices. Refractive indices have no unit of measurement. The faster light travels through a given medium, the lower the medium's refractive index. Because light in a vacuum is the highest speed obtainable, its refractive index is the base of all others to compare against and is given a value of 1. A sampling of increasing refractive indices, are air at standard temperature and pressure, water, glass, and diamond. Figure 4-19 illustrates Snell's Law as we have two distinct mediums meeting. In the diagram, we have the surface normal N, the incoming angle θ_1 and the bent angle θ_2.

■ **Note**　Snell's Law was actually first discovered by the Iranian mathematician Ibn Sahl in the 10th century, though this was not widely known until many centuries later.

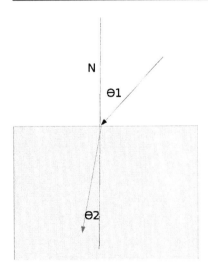

Figure 4-19. *Refraction between two different mediums such as air and water*

Fresnel effect

As we already know, in addition to refraction between mediums, there is also reflection. The Fresnel effect, named after Augustin-Jean Fresnel, states that the amount of specular reflection you see depends on your viewing angle. A viewing angle close to the surface normal (looking down at a surface such as water) will produce low reflection and have high refraction. A greater angle between the viewer and normal (looking across a surface such as water) will result in more reflection and less refraction. In Figure 4-20, part of the incident light ray is reflected as specular reflection off of the surface of the second medium while part of it is refracted into the second medium.

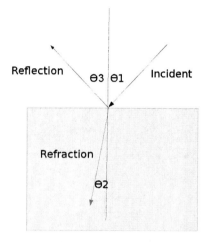

Figure 4-20. *Fresnel effect which shows the relation between incident angle and reflection and refraction components*

Fresnel Shader

A Fresnel shader calculates the reflective and refractive components of light using the GLSL functions `reflect` and `refract`. It uses a texture cube map for the environment. Although covering the complete implementation details of a Fresnel shader is beyond the scope of this book, good examples of Fresnel shaders in action are as follows:

- Bubbles: http://alteredqualia.com/three/examples/materials_shaders_fresnel.html
- Skull: http://www.everyday3d.com/j3d/demo/004_Glass.html

Putting it All Together

We can combine everything that we have learned in this chapter along with texturing to produce a nice final image. Our last example files `04/11_all_techniques.html` contains blending, texturing, atmospheric fog, and Phong illumination, and is shown in Figure 4-21.

Figure 4-21. *Image showing all the techniques discussed in this chapter along with texturing from the last chapter*

Summary

In this chapter we made vast improvements to our lighting model, which made rendering more realistic. Fog, spotlights, and blending added to the quality of our images. We also discussed more-advanced techniques such as global illumination, shadows, and reflection and refraction. The next chapter on physics introduces making the motion of our objects appear more realistic.

CHAPTER 5

■ ■ ■

Physics

In this chapter, we will introduce modeling physical interactions among objects in our scene. Topics that we will cover in this chapter are:

- Position, velocity, acceleration

- Forces such as gravity and friction

- Projectile motion

- Detecting and reacting to collisions

- Elasticity and the conservation of momentum

- Potential and kinetic energy

Background

In addition to lighting, texturing, and other visual cues of realism, how objects physically interact with their surroundings can give credence to the believability of our animations. Interaction that does not follow physical laws can look strange and unrealistic. Of course, this could be the effect that we are after. However, in this chapter, we will concentrate on trying to get our scene to act physically like we would expect objects to interact.

The scope of physical simulation is huge. We could model the ripples and waves of water or the buoyancy of an object, the rotation of tires, the flight of an airplane, and so on. In this chapter we will narrow our scope to basic kinematics: gravity, simple collisions, potential and kinetic energy, and projectiles.

A central requirement when modeling multiple moving objects within a scene is to be able to detect when the objects come into contact with one another. We will build upon methods to detect collisions throughout the chapter.

Forces Acting Upon Us

Every second of every day, we have forces acting upon us. These forces can include gravity, which pulls us down toward the earth; surface normals, which prop us up; friction, which stops us from continually moving; centripetal forces of rotation, wind, objects or people pushing or pulling upon us; and so on. When the sum of these forces balance each other out, we are said to be at rest.

Scalars and Vectors

In physics, we deal with two types of quantities: *scalars* and *vectors*. Scalar quantities have a magnitude but no direction, while vectors have both a magnitude and a direction. For example, speed is a scalar, as is mass and time. We can say that the speed of a car is 50 miles per hour, which is a scalar quantity. If we say that the car is travelling 50 miles an hour east, it is a vector.

Rates of Change

For applications of physics, we are usually interested in vectors. We can measure the vector position or displacement of an object such as 20 m along the x-axis. To calculate the velocity of the object, we take the difference of displacement of the object over a period of time. In other words, velocity is the rate of change of displacement. Acceleration is the rate of change of velocity. Displacement is usually symbolized as d, while velocity is represented as a v, and acceleration is an a. A basic equation to compute the average velocity of an object in the time range from $Time_A$ to $Time_B$, with respective displacements at the endpoints of this range, d_A and d_B, is:

$$v = (d_B - d_A)/(Time_B - Time_A)$$

For example, if d_A = 20m, $Time_A$ = 1s and d_B = 30m, $Time_B$ = 5s then:

$$v = (30m - 20m)/(5s - 1s) = 10m/4s = 2.5m/s$$

Similarly, to calculate the average acceleration over a time interval, we take the velocity at each corresponding time endpoint, v_A and v_B:

$$a = (v_B-v_A)/(Time_B - Time_A)$$

If v_A = 2.5m/s, $Time_A$ = 1s and v_B = 3.0m/s, $Time_B$ = 2s then:

$$a = (3.0m/s - 2.5m/s)/(2s - 1s) = 0.5m/s^2$$

Figure 5-1 shows a sample graph of displacement against time, followed by the velocity plotted against time, and then the acceleration plotted against time. Notice, for example, that we can be moving forward while slowing down and can be moving fast while having zero acceleration.

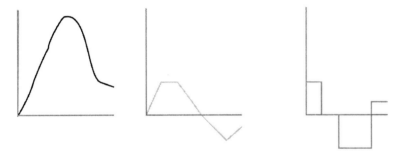

Figure 5-1. *Left: position of an object; center: velocity of the object; right: acceleration of the object*

Our first code example will simulate objects free falling because of the effect of gravity. Here, when we speak of gravity, we are not modeling the universal attraction between all objects. This type of gravity is essential to modeling accurate orbits in astronomy, but in our day-to-day lives while these gravitational forces between objects such as two different people or cars on a road are present, they are negligibly small and not noticed. Instead we will be modeling the type of gravity that we are most familiar with: free fall from an object such as a ball (or human) downward to the surface of the earth.

Code Setup

We will need to be able to keep track of scene elements in a manner that is more conducive to updates and is more flexible by being independent of vertex buffer object (VBO) data. In previous chapters, we used isolated mesh(es) that did not interact. In this chapter, we will have interactions between objects and will need to be able to keep track of physical properties and adjust them. For this, we will create a new sphere object, as shown in Listing 5-1.

Listing 5-1. Object to keep track of physical properties of a sphere

```
SphereObject = function SphereObject (properties) {
  var radius = (properties.radius === undefined) ?  1.0 : properties.radius;
  var position = (properties.position === undefined) ? new Vector3(0.0, 0.0, 0.0) :
        properties.position;
  var velocity = (properties.velocity === undefined) ? new Vector3(0.0, 0.0, 0.0) :
        properties.velocity;
  var acceleration = (properties.acceleration === undefined) ? new Vector3(0.0, 0.0, 0.0) :
        properties.acceleration;

  this.radius = radius;
  this.position = position;
  this.velocity = velocity;
  this.acceleration = acceleration;
  this.vbo_index = properties.vbo_index;
}
```

In the SphereObject of Listing 5-1, we keep track of the radius, position, velocity, and acceleration of a sphere. We also have a vbo_index property that we will use to tie each physical sphere object with the relevant VBO object.

Storing Information

We will store all our SphereObject elements in an array:

```
var sceneElements = [];
```

We declare three spheres and plane mesh as:

```
setupSphereMesh(0,  {
                    "translation": [-1.0, -0.75, 0.0],
                    "color": [1.0, 0.0, 0.0, 1.0],
                }
            );
setupSphereMesh(1,  {
                    "translation": [0.0, 0.0, 1.0],
                    "color": [0.0, 1.0, 0.0, 1.0]
                }
            );
setupSphereMesh(2,  {
                    "translation": [1.0, 0.25, -1.0],
                    "color": [1.0, 1.0, 0.0, 1.0]
                }
            );
setupPlaneMesh(3, {"translation": [0.0, -1.0, 0.0]} );

sceneElements.push(new SphereObject( {"vbo_index": 0} ) );
sceneElements.push(new SphereObject( {"vbo_index": 1} ) );
sceneElements.push(new SphereObject( {"vbo_index": 2} ) );
```

We will be modifying this starting layout as the chapter progresses to a more generic and flexible system. Keeping track of elements is similar to when we create particle systems that are covered in Chapter 6, with the key difference that interactions here are determinalistic, while particle systems are partially unknown or stochastic in nature.

To assist in viewing the scene, we will show how to set up a camera that is adjustable through mouse clicks, drags, and scroll events.

Interactively Adjusting the Camera

First we will zoom out by backing up our viewport along the z-axis:

```
mat4.identity(mvMatrix);
mat4.translate(mvMatrix, [0.0, 0.0, -20.0]);
//other camera transforms
```

We will now demonstrate how to capture the mouse down, up, and move events to adjust the view. Being able to change the view this way will let us look around our scene dynamically.

Using the Mouse to Rotate the View

To implement changing the view with mouse movement, first we need to attach event handlers to our canvas, as shown in Listing 5-2.

Listing 5-2. Capturing mouse events to control the view

```
var     capture = false,
        start = [],
        angleX = 0,
        angleY = 0;

$(document).ready(function(){
        $("#my-canvas").on("mousedown", function(e){
                capture = true;
                start = [e.pageX, e.pageY];
                console.log("start:"+start);
        });

        $("#my-canvas").on("mouseup", function(e){
                capture = false;
                console.log("end capture");
        });

        $("#my-canvas").mousemove(function(e) {
                if(capture)
                {
                    var x = (e.pageX - start[0]);
                    var y = (e.pageY - start[1]);

                    //update start position
                    start[0] = e.pageX;
                    start[1] = e.pageY;

                    angleX += x;
                    angleY += y;
                    //console.log("Angle: ("+angleX+","+angleY+")");
                }
        });
});
```

In Listing 5-2, the mousedown event signals a boolean flag called capture that should capture data on subsequent mousemove events as well as the current mouse position. When the mouseup event occurs, we let the flag know it should stop capturing data. The mousemove event computes the offset from the start position when the mousedown event started. Then we update the start position. This is important; otherwise, we will get very jerky, erratic results. Finally, we increment variables that store the x and y rotation angles.

Then in our application, we update our mvMatrix on each frame, setting the translation amount and then rotation values:

```
mat4.identity(mvMatrix);
mat4.translate(mvMatrix, [0.0, 0.0, -20.0]);
mat4.rotate(mvMatrix, angleX*2*Math.PI/180.0, [0.0, 1.0, 0.0]);
mat4.rotate(mvMatrix, angleY*2*Math.PI/180.0, [1.0, 0.0, 0.0]);
```

▓ **Note**   As an alternative to attaching mouse handlers to the canvas, we can attach them to the entire document. This can be useful in the previous example because moving off of the canvas will currently stop the mouse event capturing and produce unexpected and undesirable results when we move back in to the canvas. The mouse button may still be down, but we will need to first release it and then click and hold it again before events are recaptured.

It is generally best to do scene-wide transformations first, followed by object specific transforms.

Using the Mouse Wheel to Control Zoom

Scrolling the mouse wheel is often used to control zooming in and out of a scene. To do this, we will attach a handler to the mousewheel event:

```
var zoom = 1.0;

...
$(document).ready(function(evt){
    $("#my-canvas").on("mousewheel", function (e){
        var delta = window.event.wheelDelta;
        if(delta>0)
        {
            zoom += 0.1;
        }else{
            zoom -= 0.1;
            //prevent a negative zoom
            if(zoom<0.01)
            {
                zoom = 0.1;
            }
        }
    });
...
mat4.scale(mvMatrix, [zoom, zoom, zoom]);
```

Now, because of browser differences, the above code will not work with Firefox, which uses the DOMMouseScroll event instead of the mousewheel event. To account for this, we can add multiple event handlers:

```
function adjustZoom(delta)
{
    if(delta > 0)
    {
        zoom += 0.1;
    }else{
        zoom -= 0.1;
        if(zoom < 0.01)
        {
            zoom = 0.1;
        }
    }
}
$(document).ready(function(evt){
    $("#my-canvas").on("mousewheel", function (e){
        adjustZoom(window.event.wheelDelta);
    }).on("DOMMouseScroll", function (e){
        //firefox
        adjustZoom(e.originalEvent.detail * -1.0);
    });
...
```

───

■ **Note** The target of the mousewheel and DOMMouseScroll events is the DOM element underneath the current position of the mouse pointer, similar to click events.

───

The detail property has a reverse orientation to the wheelDelta, so we multiply by negative 1 for consistency. The magnitudes of these properties is also different, but we are only concerned with the sign that indicates an up or down scrolling direction. More-robust handling of mouse wheel events can be found in the jQuery mousewheel plugin from https://github.com/brandonaaron/jquery-mousewheel/blob/master/jquery.mousewheel.js.

The shader program for all the examples in this chapter will be the same as the Phong illumination model and shader found in the 04/05_phong_phong.html demo. We are ready to start simulating physical interaction and the first thing we will do is simulate gravity.

Gravity

Gravity, as most nonphysicists are used to, is simply the force that pulls things downward toward the earth. As the saying goes, "What goes up, must come down." We will model dropping three spherical balls toward the ground and make some successive improvements.

Free Falling

Our first attempt to model gravity will simply lower the position of all three spheres each frame. For this example, we will use the code in the 04/05_phong_phong.html file as a starting point, along with the changes outlined previously to keep track of the scene elements. In Listing 5–3, we show how we adjust each sphere by searching for an appropriate vbo_index to determine which objects are spheres and then translating the model view matrix for each.

Listing 5-3. Adjusting select scene elements

```
function searchForObject(arr, index)
{
    for(var i in arr)
    {
        if(arr[i].vbo_index == index)
        {
            return i;
        }
    }
    return -1;
}

function drawScene()
{
    for(var i = 0; i<vertexIndexBuffers.length; ++i)
    {
        mat4.identity(mvMatrix);
        mat4.translate(mvMatrix, [0.0, -1.0, -15.5]);

        var n = searchForObject(sceneElements, i);
        if( n ! = -1)
        {
            mat4.translate(mvMatrix, [  0.0, 5.0 - sceneElements[n].position.y, 0.0 ]);
            sceneElements[n].position.y+= 0.1;
        }
        mat4.toInverseMat3(mvMatrix, normalMatrix);
        mat3.transpose(normalMatrix);
        setMatrixUniforms();

        ...
    }
}
```

In Listing 5-3, we have a helper method, searchForObject, which takes an input array of SphereObjects and finds an appropriate object index based on the input vbo_index value or –1 if no match is found. Extending this approach would allow us to potentially have many different object types in our scene but be able to affect only the VBO objects that match a certain criteria—in this case, being a sphere. If the current VBO index is a match, we translate its model-view matrix and increase the stored y position. The VBO index for the ground mesh will result in a –1 being returned from the search, so it will be stationary.

The result of running this code, which can be found in the 05/01a_gravity.html file, is that the spheres fall indefinitely. They go past the ground, as shown on the left of Figure 5-2. So now let's add our first case of collision detection to prevent this.

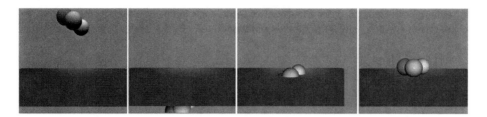

Figure 5-2. *Far left: starting position of spheres; left: free falling with no collision with the ground; right: collision detection not including the radius; far right: proper collision detection*

Falling and Colliding With the Ground

First, we will formalize the initial height of the spheres and ground:

```
var INITIAL_HEIGHT_TRANSLATION_OF_SPHERES = 5.0;
var GROUND_Y = -1.0;

...

setupPlaneMesh(3, { "translation": [0.0, GROUND_Y, 0.0]} );
```

To test whether an object hits the ground, we need to test whether the starting translation amount of our sphere minus the translated y-position is greater than the ground height. If it is not, we stop incrementing the position:

```
...
var n = searchForObject(sceneElements, i);
if( n ! = -1)
{
    if(INITIAL_HEIGHT_TRANSLATION_OF_SPHERES - sceneElements[n].position.y > GROUND_Y)
    {
        sceneElements[n].position.y += 0.1;
    }
    mat4.translate( mvMatrix,
        [0.0, INITIAL_HEIGHT_TRANSLATION_OF_SPHERES - sceneElements[n].position.y, 0.0] );
}
...
```

Running this code stops the spheres, but they get stuck part way through the plane, as shown in the right of Figure 5-2. So let's improve our collision detection to factor in the radius of the sphere:

```
if( ( INITIAL_HEIGHT_TRANSLATION_OF_SPHERES -
    (sceneElements[n].position.y + sceneElements[n].radius) ) > GROUND_Y)
{
    sceneElements[n].position.y += 0.1;
}
```

The result of this adjustment is shown on the far right of Figure 5-2.

Let's make one more code improvement and set the initial translation of the sphere directly in our SphereObject instead of in the setupSphereMesh call:

```
setupSphereMesh(0, { "color": [1.0, 0.0, 0.0, 1.0] } );
setupSphereMesh(1, { "color": [0.0, 1.0, 0.0, 1.0] } );
setupSphereMesh(2, { "color": [1.0, 1.0, 0.0, 1.0] } );
setupPlaneMesh(3, { "translation": [0.0, GROUND_Y, 0.0]} );
```

```
sceneElements.push(new SphereObject( {  "vbo_index": 0,
                                        "position": new Vector3(-1.0, -0.75, 0.0)}) );
sceneElements.push(new SphereObject( {  "vbo_index": 1,
                                        "position": new Vector3(0.0, 0.0, 1.0)}) );
sceneElements.push(new SphereObject( {  "vbo_index": 2,
                                        "position": new Vector3(1.0, 0.25, -1.0)}) );
```

This adjustment lets us keep the local mesh coordinates and color details in the VBO code and the world position in the SphereObject. Because it is outside of the VBO, we can now easily adjust the position without modifying our buffer. We now need to also adjust our x and z positions in the translate call:

```
mat4.translate(mvMatrix,
    [  sceneElements[n].position.x,
       INITIAL_HEIGHT_TRANSLATION_OF_SPHERES  - sceneElements[n].position.y,
       sceneElements[n].position.z
    ]);
```

Our next step is to have the spheres bounce back up.

Falling Down, but Bouncing Back Up

Let's put some spring into these spheres and have them bounce back up upon impact of the plane. So how do we do this? Well if the ground is hit, we need to reverse the direction. One naïve approach to this is to flip the direction of position adjustments upon impact:

```
function isAboveGround(n)
{
    return ( INITIAL_HEIGHT_TRANSLATION_OF_SPHERES -
            (sceneElements[n].position.y+sceneElements[n].radius)>GROUND_Y);
}
...
var n = searchForObject(sceneElements, i);
if( n ! = -1)
{
    if( isAboveGround(n) )
    {
        sceneElements[n].position.y += 0.1;
    }else{
        sceneElements[n].position.y -= 0.1;

    }
...
}
```

The problem with this approach is that the sphere will start traveling upward, but because it is above the ground, it will immediately travel back down on the next iteration. The ground will be reached again, and the sphere will start upward again. It will do this indefinitely and get caught in an alternating loop that makes the object shake slightly but not move much.

A further addition to this approach would be to add a flag signaling that the ground has been hit so that we never pass the test condition to continue falling once the ground has been hit:

```
var flip_direction = [false, false, false];
...
if( isAboveGround(n) &&
    !flip_direction[n]
  )
{
    sceneElements[n].position.y += 0.1;
}else{
    flip_direction[n] = true;
    sceneElements[n].position.y -= 0.1;
}
```

This does eliminate the previous problem, and the ball will bounce back upward upon collision. However, this approach is not a robust or useful solution because once the ball starts traveling upward, it will continue upward forever, never coming back down.

We will now look at how to use velocity and acceleration to properly model a bouncing object.

Falling and Bouncing Up; Repeat

Until now, we have not made use of the velocity or acceleration properties of our SphereObject.

We can rewrite the equation $a = (v_B - v_A)/(Time_B - Time_A)$ as:

$$v_b = v_a + a(Time_B - Time_A)$$

Or equivalently as follows, where f stands for final, i for initial, and t for the time interval:

$$v_f = v_i + at$$

This equation can be used to model our free fall. Until now, the pace of descent has been constant throughout. This is not accurate as objects speed up as they fall—so using this equation will also be an improvement in the realism of the descent. The flexibility of storing information in the SphereObject will present itself when we bounce the balls back upward.

Let's take a closer look at the equation $v_f = v_i + at$. The time, t, can be set to 1 as we can use frame value offset instead of an actual time. Gravity will be the acceleration, a. Usually, gravity has the value of 9.8 m/s² downward, but our scene is not using any specific scale or unit of measurement, so the value that we choose can be anything that looks good—too high a value will make the descent occur too rapidly, and too low will result in it being too slow. Experimentation of values is the key here. With our current scene setup, 0.01 for the acceleration works well. One of the sphere initializations is shown here:

```
sceneElements.push(new SphereObject(
                    {
                        "vbo_index": 0,
                        "position": new Vector3(-1.0, -0.75, 0.0),
                        "acceleration": new Vector3(0.0, 0.01, 0.0)
                    }
                  )
                );
```

Normally, the acceleration is represented as a negative number, but because of the way we are translating each sphere, we are using a positive value. If you want to use a negative value, you can adjust the sign of the translation.

Our initial velocity vector of each sphere is (0, 0, 0), which makes the y-velocity after the next frame:

$$v_{fy} = v_{iy} + a_y t = v_{iy} + 0.01(1) = v_{iy} + 0.01 = 0.01$$

124

So it's v_{fy} = 0.01 after the first frame, 0.02 after the second, 0.03 after the third, and so on linearly. When we apply the velocity to our distance equation of d_{fy} = d_{iy}+v_yt, This will produce displacements relative to the initial displacement of 0.01 after the first frame, 0.03 after the second, 0.06 after the third, and so on increasing and nonlinearly.

In our code, instead of incrementing the position directly, we instead adjust the velocity first and then adjust the position. This allows us to reverse the velocity when contact with the plane is made without getting stuck into a loop:

```
if( isAboveGround(n) )
{
    sceneElements[n].velocity.y += sceneElements[n].acceleration.y;
}else{
    sceneElements[n].velocity.y *= -1.0;
}
sceneElements[n].position.y += sceneElements[n].velocity.y;
```

When you run the program 05/01e_gravity.html, the three balls will continue to bounce up and down indefinitely.

Nonperfect Elasticity

When the balls in the previous example bounce, they do so perfectly elastically. *Perfect elasticity* means that the speed at which they move upward after collision is the same as the speed at which they were falling with at that moment. No momentum is lost to friction or other forms of energy. Except in theory, objects are not perfectly elastic, so we can make the example more realistic by decreasing the elasticity. This will mean that the bouncing will come to a stop at some point. This is very easy to model; we just add the elasticity as a variable and multiply it by the velocity when a collision is made with the ground:

```
var ELASTICITY = -0.8;
...
if( isAboveGround(n) )
{
    sceneElements[n].velocity.y += sceneElements[n].acceleration.y;
    sceneElements[n].position.y += sceneElements[n].velocity.y;
}else{
    //subtract velocity first, which helps prevent getting stuck
    sceneElements[n].position.y -= sceneElements[n].velocity.y;
    sceneElements[n].velocity.y *= ELASTICITY;
}
```

The elasticity value can range from 0.0 for no elasticity (stops dead; think of hitting a brick wall) to 1.0 for perfectly elastic (the greatest rubber ball ever, only theoretically possible). In the previous code, we also made sure to adjust the position before the elasticity factor is multiplied with the velocity. This is to help prevent the ball from coming to a dead stop.

To show why this is necessary, consider an object that is a temporary distance of –0.6 into the ground and has a current velocity of –1.0. It should be able to make its way back above in the next iteration when the direction of velocity switches to 1.0. However, if the object has an elasticity value of 0.4, this dampens the return velocity to a value of 0.4 instead of 1.0. The next position calculated will be –0.2, which means that it is still 0.2 below the surface. This means that the next time through the above ground test, it fails again, and the velocity gets flipped. This is bad news because the object is below the ground and travelling downward again. The velocity is reversed and dampened again to –0.16, which sends it lower into the ground to –0.36, and then flipped to a velocity of 0.064, and so on. The result of this situation is that after a few iterations, an object which could have been travelling fast can stop seemingly dead in its tracks. This looks very odd—to say the least. Adding the velocity to the position before the elasticity is multiplied eliminates this issue. The final version of the bouncing balls is shown in Figure 5-3.

Figure 5-3. *Bouncing balls*

For the next example, we will unleash an arbitrary number of spheres into the world and have initial x, y, and z velocities.

Velocity in Three Dimensions

We will check for hitting the invisible boundaries of our plane and bounce the balls back within our area if they are exceeded. Once we have this set up, we will also test for collisions among the spheres.

Detecting Collisions with Many Walls

We will be adding an arbitrary number of spheres to our scene. First, we will add some code to keep the objects that will have x and z velocity now from going outside of our viewing area. We will test for intersection with our virtual walls of the ground mesh:

```
if(sceneElements[n].position.x>PLANE_SIZE || sceneElements[n].position.x<-PLANE_SIZE)
{
    sceneElements[n].position.x+= (-1.0*sceneElements[n].velocity.x);
    sceneElements[n].velocity.x * = -1.0;
}else{
    sceneElements[n].position.x+= sceneElements[n].velocity.x;
}

if(sceneElements[n].position.z>PLANE_SIZE || sceneElements[n].position.z<-PLANE_SIZE)
{
    sceneElements[n].position.z+= (-1.0*sceneElements[n].velocity.z);
    sceneElements[n].velocity.z * = -1.0;
}else{
    sceneElements[n].position.z+= sceneElements[n].velocity.z;
}
```

So far, we have detected collisions with a moving object and an immovable object. Now we will model moving objects colliding with one another.

Intercollisions

When we want to know whether two objects have collided, it is simpler to test bounding volumes using well-defined shapes. These will be much less computationally expensive. Other volumes exist, such as ellipsoids and cylinders, but boxes and spheres are most commonly used.

Bounding Boxes and Spheres

The bounding volume we choose depends on the shape of the underlying object. Fairly round objects are naturally represented well with a sphere, while many other objects are a much closer fit to a square box. Figure 5-4 shows that a cube does not fit well in a sphere, and vice versa. (We wouldn't want to do either of these things.)

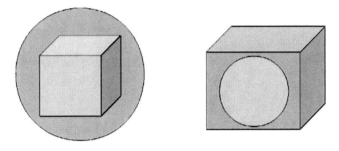

Figure 5-4. *Left: cube in a bounding sphere; right: sphere in a bounding box*

▓ **Note** For a refresher on sphere and cube geometries please refer to http://en.wikipedia.org/wiki/Sphere and http://en.wikipedia.org/wiki/Cube

---

With bounding volumes, we can use simple geometry to handle objects when they are close to one another. For example, we know that two bounding spheres have intersected each other if the distance between their centers is less than the sum of their radii. With bounding volumes, we are guaranteed not to have a collision without knowing about it. If the bounding volume exactly represents the object, the collision is always accurate. However, if the bounding volume is larger than the object being held, there will be some false positives when we think a collision has taken place (but has not). The closer the encapsulated object is to its bounding volume, the fewer false positives of intersection we will encounter.

One way to limit this error is to break an irregularly shaped mesh into smaller bounding boxes or spheres. As the number of smaller bounding volumes (or areas in the 2D case) increases, the amount of error decreases and will approach zero. A 2D irregular shape and bounding rectangles are shown in Figure 5-5, along with several bounding rectangles that more closely approximate the shape but also increase the number of computational checks that we must perform. White space within a bounding rectangle shows areas of collision false positive.

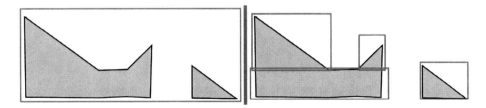

Figure 5-5. *Left: single bounding box; right: four bounding rectangles*

Now we are ready to detect collisions among spheres. First to handle the collisions realistically, we'll need to know a little about momentum and the conservation of it.

Conservation of Momentum

Momentum, p, is the product of an object's mass, m, and velocity, v:

p = mv

When two objects collide, the overall momentum of the system stays the same in theory. In reality, there is friction that also occurs, so no collision is completely elastic.

The equation of the conservation of momentum is the following:

$$P_{1\_initial} + P_{2\_initial} = P_{1\_final} + P_{2\_final}$$

It can be rewritten as this:

$$m_1 v_{1i}^2 + m_2 v_{2i}^2 = m_1 v_{1f}^2 + m_2 v_{2f}^2$$

When you solve for v_{1f} or v2$_f$, you get this:

$$v_{1f} = [(m_1 - m_2)/(m_1 + m_2)]v_{1i} + [2m_2/(m_1 + m_2)]v_{2i}$$

And similarly:

$$v_{2f} = [(m_2 - m_1)/(m_1 + m_2)]v_{2i} + [2m_1/(m_1 + m_2)]v_{1i}$$

When the mass of $m_1 = m_2$, the first equation simplifies to the following:

$$v_{1f} = 0/2m_2 {}^*v_{1i} + 2m_2/2m_2 {}^*v_{2i} = 0{}^*v_{1i} + 1{}^*v_{2i} = v_{2i}$$

And likewise:

$$v_{2f} = v_{1i}$$

So the velocities are simply swapped!

This equation is specific to one dimension, but it also applies to orthogonal (perpendicular) components, so we can apply the equation separately to all three of the x, y, and z dimensions.

Uniform Mass Collisions

As mentioned, when the masses are exactly the same like billiard balls, we can swap the velocities.

For each frame, we will check all the spheres in our scene for collision with other objects in the scene (see Listing 5-4).

Listing 5-4. Checking for collisions among spheres with equal masses

```
checkForCollisions(sceneElements, n);
...

function checkForCollisions(arr, n)
{
    for(var i in arr)
    {
        if(i ! = n)
```

```
    {
        var p1 = arr[n].position;
        var p2 = arr[i].position;
        var v = new Vector3( p1.x - p2.x, p1.y - p2.y, p1.z - p2.z );

        if(v.length()<(2.0 * arr[n].radius) )
        {
            //swap velocities of two vectors
            var tmp = arr[n].velocity;
            arr[n].velocity = arr[i].velocity;
            arr[i].velocity = tmp;

            //move positions so they don't get stuck
            arr[n].position.x += arr[n].velocity.x;
            arr[n].position.y += arr[n].velocity.y;
            arr[n].position.z += arr[n].velocity.z;

            arr[i].position.x += arr[i].velocity.x;
            arr[i].position.y += arr[i].velocity.y;
            arr[i].position.z += arr[i].velocity.z;
        }
    }
  }
}
```

In Listing 5-4, we check for the distance to be less than twice the radius because the radii are the same. If a collision occurs, we swap velocities using a temporary variable. The result of this is shown on the left of Figure 5-6.

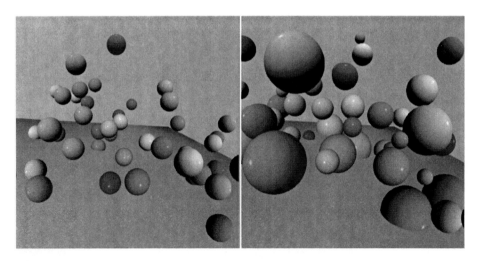

Figure 5-6. *Left: collisions of uniform mass; right: collisions of varying mass*

We will now create spheres with varying radii and masses and compute collisions among them.

Collisions of Different Mass

In our next example, we will now use spheres of varying radii. We will assume that the material of all the spheres is the same and that they are solid. This lets us use the volume to proportionally compare the masses without actually setting or knowing the mass of any sphere. Recall that the volume of a sphere is $V = 4/3*\pi*r^3$.

Suppose we have two spheres: $V_1 = 4/3*\pi*r_1^3$ and $V_2 = 4/3*\pi*r_2^3$. The ratio of these two volumes is $V_1/V_2 = (r_1/r_2)^3$.

If $r_1 = 1$ and $r_2 = 1$, the ratio = $1^3 = 1$. The volumes and (because they are the same material) the masses are also the same. If $r_1 = 2$ and $r_2 = 1$, the ratio = $(2/1)^3 = 8$. So the first sphere has eight times more volume then the second sphere and eight times more mass as well. We can generically use the radii of the two spheres to set our two masses to the following:

$m_1/m_2 = (r_1/r_2)^3/1$

$m_1 = (r_1/r_2)^3$
$m_2 = 1$

■ **Note** For more involved calculations, we can use existing physics libraries such as those discussed in Chapter 8.

We can calculate our final velocity values for each sphere given initial velocities and radius, as shown in Listing 5-5.

Listing 5-5. Checking for collisions among spheres with varying mass

```
function checkForCollisions(arr, n)
{
    for(var i in arr)
    {
        if(i ! = n)
        {
            var p1 = arr[n].position;
            var p2 = arr[i].position;
            var v = new Vector3( p1.x - p2.x, p1.y - p2.y, p1.z - p2.z );

            if(v.length()<(arr[i].radius +  arr[n].radius) )
            {
                //swap velocities of two vectors
                var tmp1 = arr[n].velocity;
                var tmp2 = arr[i].velocity;
                var r1 = arr[n].radius;
                var r2 = arr[i].radius;

                var finalX = findFinalVelocities( tmp1.x, tmp2.x, r1, r2 );
                var finalY = findFinalVelocities( tmp1.y, tmp2.y, r1, r2 );
                var finalZ = findFinalVelocities( tmp1.z, tmp2.z, r1, r2 );

                arr[n].velocity = new Vector3( finalX[0], finalY[0], finalZ[0] );
                arr[i].velocity = new Vector3( finalX[1], finalY[1], finalZ[1] );

                //move positions so they don't get stuck
                arr[n].position.x += arr[n].velocity.x;
```

```
            arr[n].position.y += arr[n].velocity.y;
            arr[n].position.z += arr[n].velocity.z;

            arr[i].position.x += arr[i].velocity.x;
            arr[i].position.y += arr[i].velocity.y;
            arr[i].position.z += arr[i].velocity.z;

        }
      }
    }
}
function findFinalVelocities(v1, v2, r1, r2)
{
    var m1 = (r1*r1*r1)/(r2*r2*r2);
    var m2 = 1.0;
    var f1 = (m1-m2)/(m1+m2)*v1+2*m2/(m1+m2)*v2;
    var f2 = (m2-m1)/(m2+m1)*v2+2*m1/(m2+m1)*v1;
    return [f1, f2];
}
```

In Listing 5-5, we added a helper method findFinalVelocities which takes in two initial velocities and radii and computes and returns the final velocity values. We do this calculation component-wise. Spheres of unequal size are shown interacting on the right of Figure 5-6.

Our next example looks at the path of projectiles.

Projectiles

We are all familiar with the projectile motion of objects, whether it be a cannon ball being fired, an archer's arrow, a baseball being hit or thrown, and so on. Projectiles have a parabolic arc that the object travels along, as shown in Figure 5-7.

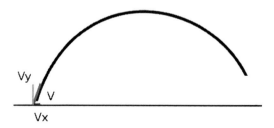

Figure 5-7. *A typical projectile path*

Unless there is a wind or other horizontal force, the horizontal velocity component, v_x, stays constant throughout the flight of the object. The vertical velocity decreases with time due to the force of gravity and is calculated as (v_y+a_yt).

▪ **Note**   Given an initial velocity vector, v, once we calculate the initial orthogonal x and y velocity components, v_x and v_y, we can calculate future velocities separately using these equations:

$v_{fx} = v_{ix} + a_x t$ and $v_{fy} = v_{iy} + a_y t$

There are two basic factors that affect the flight of a projectile (as I am sure anyone who has played "Angry Birds" is familiar with): the angle and magnitude of the initial velocity. An angle of 45 degrees will have an equal initial horizontal and vertical velocity. Between 0 and 90 degrees, any angle higher than 45 degrees will have more vertical velocity while any angle lower will have more horizontal velocity. Given an angle of theta between the velocity vector and the ground, the initial vertical component, v_y is sin(theta), while the initial horizontal component, v_x is cos(theta).

Suppose our initial velocity is 25 m/s, and the angle is 60 degrees. Then $v_y = 21.65$m/s and $v_x = 12.5$m/s. On a flat surface, an object with this initial velocity will hit the ground when the displacement of the y-component distance equation is 0:

d = v_{yi}*t+1/2*a_y*t²

This occurs by solving the following:

0 = t(v_{iy} + 1/2*ay*t)

The first solution occurs trivially at t = 0s. The second solution occurs when:

t = -2v_{iy}/a_y
  = -2(21.65m/s)/(-9.8m/s²)
  = 4.42s

From the hangtime that we just calculated, we can determine the vertical distance that the object will travel as follows:

d = v_{xi}*t+1/2*a_x*t²
  = 12.5m/s*4.42s+0
  = 55.25m

▪ **Note**   To find out the maximum height of a projectile, you can take the initial y velocity, V_{iy}, and solve the equation $V_{fy}^2 = V_{iy}^2 + 2ad$ for when $V_{fy} = 0$. This will correspond to the apex of the projectile path where it starts travelling back downward: $d = -V_{iy}^2/2a = V_{iy}^2/19.6$m/s²

We will now implement a demo that fires a projectile. The main new component of the demo is listening to keystrokes to adjust the angle of a semiopen box mesh that represents the angle of our initial velocity and the speed of our initial velocity. We also listen for a key to fire a sphere from this box. The key shortcuts are shown here:

```
$(document).keyup(function(evt){
    switch(evt.keyCode){
        case 80: //'p'
            paused = !paused;
            break;
        case 83: //'s'
            --angle;
            break;
```

```
            case 68: //'d'
                ++angle;
                break;
            case 37: //'left'
                speed -= 0.1;
                break;
            case 40: //'right'
                speed += 0.1;
                break;
            case 70:
                fire = true;
                console.log("fire!");
                sceneElements[0].position = new Vector3(0.0, 0.0, 0.0);
                sceneElements[0].velocity = new Vector3(
                            speed*Math.cos(angle*.1), speed*Math.sin(angle*.1), 0.0);
                break;
            default:
                break;
        }
});
```

The fire event resets the position of the sphere and then sets the velocity based on the angle. When we perform transformations to our scene, the order in which the translations, rotations, and scalings are performed is important. One new method from the `gl-matrix.js` library that we perform here is to scale our scene smaller so that it is easier to see the path of the projectile:

```
var SCALE = 0.2;
...

mat4.scale(mvMatrix, [SCALE, SCALE, SCALE]);
```

When the f key is pressed and the fire flag is set, we update our sphere position:

```
if(fire){
    sceneElements[0].velocity.y += sceneElements[0].acceleration.y;

    sceneElements[0].position.x += sceneElements[0].velocity.x;
    sceneElements[0].position.y += sceneElements[0].velocity.y;
    sceneElements[0].position.z += sceneElements[0].velocity.z;
}
```

To see the full path of the projectile without clearing the browser along the way, we can tell WebGL to preserve the drawing buffer upon initialization and *not* call `gl.clear` between frames:

```
gl = canvas.getContext("webgl",  {preserveDrawingBuffer: true}) ||
    canvas.getContext("experimental-webgl",  {preserveDrawingBuffer: true});
```

Output showing the full projectile paths is shown on the right of Figure 5-8.

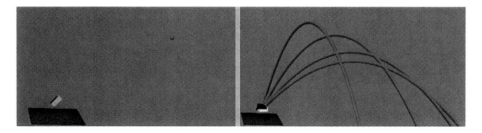

Figure 5-8. *Left: a projectile in flight; right: projectiles without clearing the drawing context*

The full code of this demo is in the 05/05_projectile.html file. I encourage you to play around with projectiles and momentum further. With the knowledge gained here, you could program a simplified version of tennis, for example.

Our final example of the chapter investigates the relation between potential and kinetic energy.

Potential Energy

So far, we have been looking at examples that have kinetic energy, which is the energy of motion. On the other hand, potential energy is stored energy, often because of the height of an object and the force that gravity will exert when the object free falls. A classic example of potential energy is a roller coaster. At the top of the coaster, when the cars are static, the energy in the system is pure potential energy (PE). As each car starts its descent, PE is converted to kinetic energy (KE), and the coaster cars gain velocity. The ratio of KE increases as a car reaches the ground and decreases when the cars travel back upward.

In theory, the total energy of the system is maintained, as shown in Figure 5-9. In the real world, however, energy is lost along the way due to friction.

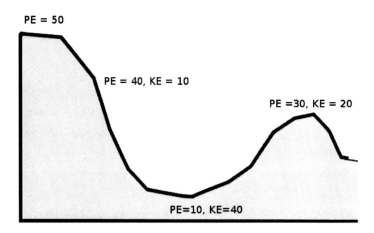

Figure 5-9. *Without friction, the PE and KE of a system are conserved*

For our next example, we will create a small ramp with a jump and have a sphere travel down it. We can adjust the height to determine a value that will produce sufficient velocity to make it across. Figure 5-10 shows a 2D planned outline of the ramp. The actual ramp will be three-dimensional, but a diagram like this is useful to plan the mesh.

Figure 5-10. *Left: side view of ramp; center: side view dissected into triangles; right: side view with edges that will test for collision with the ball*

The first step to modeling this is to define some variables so that we can easily adjust the dimensions:

```
//ramp dimensions
var    HEIGHT_1 = 65.0,
       HEIGHT_2 = 15.0,
       HEIGHT_3 = 20.0,
       HEIGHT_4 = 15.0,
       LENGTH = 60.0,
       LENGTH_2 = 60.0 * 0.5,
       LENGTH_3 = 60.0 * 0.75,
       LANDING_RAMP_START = LENGTH * 2.0,
       LANDING_RAMP_END = LENGTH * 3.0,
       DEPTH = 25.0;
```

The previous heights correspond to the initial maximum height, the height of the flat part of the ramp, and the last peak before the jump/gap and the initial height of the landing ramp. The diagram in Figure 5-10 is not to this scale; it is a guideline that can be resized to any dimensions. The LENGTH determines the distance of the first ramp up to the gap, and the SCALE is used to scale the model into a size that fits better with the rest of our scene.

We will make the ramp all one color, and a way to do this without requiring color data for each vertex is to disable the attribute array for the mesh and specify a single vector instead:

```
gl.disableVertexAttribArray(vertexColorAttribute);
gl.vertexAttrib4f(vertexColorAttribute, 1.0, 0.9, 0.7, 1.0);
```

The full vertex and indice values for the mesh are in the 05/06_ramp.html file, and normals are generated procedurally as in the first four chapters of the book. The ramp mesh and sphere position, along with views of the full path, are shown in Figure 5-11.

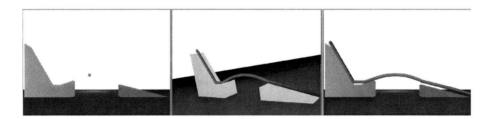

Figure 5-11. *Left: rendered ramp and moving sphere; center: viewing the full path of the sphere; right: an alternate view of the path*

What remains is to calculate the collisions with the four edges shown on the right of Figure 5-10 and also calculate the velocity components relating to the cosine and sine values of each edge angle. In order to achieve this, we will first create a new object to represent a 2D wall that the sphere may encounter as shown in Listing 5-6.

Listing 5-6. An object to store wall properties

```
WallObject = function WallObject (properties) {
    var start_x = (properties.start_x === undefined) ?  0.0 : properties.start_x;
    var start_y = (properties.start_y === undefined) ?  0.0 : properties.start_y;

    var end_x = (properties.end_x === undefined) ?  0.0 : properties.end_x;
    var end_y = (properties.end_y === undefined) ?  0.0 : properties.end_y;

    this.slope = 0.0;
    if( (end_x - start_x)>0.0001 || (end_x - start_x)<-0.001){
        this.slope = (end_y - start_y)/(end_x - start_x);
    }
    this.start_x = start_x;
    this.start_y = start_y;
    this.end_x = end_x;
    this.end_y = end_y;

    var a = [start_x - end_x, start_y - end_y];
    this.angle = 0.0;
    this.angle = Math.atan2( a[1], a[0]);
}
```

We keep track of the two endpoints of each wall line: its slope and angle. We add all four wall representations to an array called ramp_walls. Each insertion into this structure looks like this:

```
var p = {
            "start_x": 0.0,
            "start_y": HEIGHT_1,
            "end_x": LENGTH_2,
            "end_y": HEIGHT_2
        };
ramp_walls.push(new WallObject(p));
```

On each animation frame, check for collisions with each wall, keep track of the total velocity of our sphere, and calculate the x and y velocities and positions as shown in Listing 5-7.

Listing 5-7. Checking for wall collisions and calculating total and component velocity and position

```
function checkForCollisions()
{
    var x = sphere.position.x/SCALE;
    var y = sphere.position.y/SCALE;
    if( sphere.position.y<0.0){ return; } //check for ground contact

    var found = false;
    for(var i in ramp_walls)
    {
        if( x>= ramp_walls[i].start_x && x<= ramp_walls[i].end_x )
        {
            found = true;
            if(ramp_walls[i].slope<-0.001 || ramp_walls[i].slope>0.001)
            {
                if(ramp_walls[i].slope>0.001)
```

```
        {
            sphere.total_velocity -= sphere.acceleration.y;
        }else{
            sphere.total_velocity += sphere.acceleration.y;
        }
        //console.log(sphere.total_velocity);
        sphere.velocity.x = sphere.total_velocity * Math.cos(ramp_walls[i].angle);
        sphere.velocity.y = sphere.total_velocity * Math.sin(ramp_walls[i].angle);

        sphere.position.y += sphere.velocity.y;
    }
        sphere.position.x += sphere.velocity.x;
    }
}
if(!found){
    sphere.velocity.y += sphere.acceleration.y;
    sphere.position.x += sphere.velocity.x;
    sphere.position.y += sphere.velocity.y;
}
}
```

In the preceding code, if we are not in a walled area, found is false and we model freefall. If we are over a walled section, we check the slope and add appropriately to the total_velocity. A slope of zero results in purely horizontal movement with no acceleration (because we are ignoring friction). We calculate the component x and y velocities by taking the sine and cosine of the wall angle multiplied by the total velocity. From Figure 5-11, you can see that the path is close but not entirely precise. Higher velocities would show a more abrupt change between free fall and position on the landing ramp. One way to improve accuracy is to check that the sphere is intersecting a wall before exiting free fall. The sign of the number returned from this function indicates what side of a line that a point is on (zero is on the line):

```
function getSideOfWall(wall, x, y)
{
    var delta = 0.00001;
    var v = (wall.end_x - wall.start_x) * (y - wall.start_y) -
            (wall.end_y - wall.start_y) * (x - wall.start_x);

    if( v<(0.0 - delta) ){
        return -1;
    }elseif( v>(0.0+delta) ){
        return 1;
    }
    return 0;
}
```

It is left to the reader to implement this check. If you are ambitious and want to model a roller coaster, there are even more elements to factor into your calculations, such as centripetal force.

Summary

This chapter introduced some physical properties of objects and modeled gravity, collisions, and projectiles. In the next chapter, we cover the mathematically themed subjects of fractals, height maps, and particle systems. In Chapter 8, we will come back to physics when we introduce some physics libraries that can perform much more complicated calculations.

■ ■ ■

CHAPTER 6

Fractals, Height Maps, and Particle Systems

This chapter presents a hodgepodge of effects that we can achieve with mathematics. Topics that we will cover include:

- painting directly with the GPU
- an introduction to fractals and the Mandelbrot set
- height maps and terrain generation
- rotating the camera with the mouse
- particle systems

Because I have long been enamored with the strong intersection of mathematics and beautiful imagery that it produces, this chapter is particularly fun for me to write about. Even if you do not particularly enjoy mathematics, you can still brush past most of the details/technical explanation and experiment directly with the code. I am sure that the examples and techniques presented here will be of interest to you and can be modified for use inside any WebGL program.

Painting Directly with the GPU

Prior to going over fractal images and the Mandelbrot set, we will show how to paint an image with logic purely contained within the shader program. The only geometry that our WebGL application will use is four triangles from five vertices, which will form a plane. We will then use the fragment shader of the Graphics Processing Unit (GPU) to programmatically set each individual pixel color on the plane. No manipulation of the view will be done. The setup of the square plane is shown in Listing 6-1.

Listing 6-1. Function to create a square in the xy plane composed of two triangles

```
function createSquare(size){
        size = (typeof size !== 'undefined') ? size : 2.0;

        var vertexPositionData = [
                0.0, 0.0, 0.0,
                -size/2.0, -size/2.0, 0.0,
                size/2.0, -size/2.0, 0.0,
                size/2.0, size/2.0, 0.0,
                -size/2.0,size/2.0, 0.0,
        ];
```

```
    var indexData = [0,1,2,0,2,3,0,3,4,0,4,1];

    trianglesVerticeBuffer = gl.createBuffer();
    gl.bindBuffer(gl.ARRAY_BUFFER, trianglesVerticeBuffer);
    gl.bufferData(gl.ARRAY_BUFFER, new Float32Array(vertexPositionData),
                  gl.STATIC_DRAW);
    trianglesVerticeBuffer.itemSize = 3;
    trianglesVerticeBuffer.numItems = vertexPositionData.length / 3;

    vertexIndexBuffer = gl.createBuffer();
    gl.bindBuffer(gl.ELEMENT_ARRAY_BUFFER, vertexIndexBuffer);
    gl.bufferData(gl.ELEMENT_ARRAY_BUFFER, new Uint16Array(indexData), gl.STREAM_DRAW);
    vertexIndexBuffer.itemSize = 3;
    vertexIndexBuffer.numItems = indexData.length;
}
```

The default dimensions of the plane in Listing 6-1 is 2.0 x 2.0.

Our vertex shader takes the x, y input coordinates and passes them on to the fragment shader. The z-value is fixed at 0.0.

```
<script type="x-shader/x-vertex">
      attribute vec3 aVertexPosition;

      varying vec2 position;
      void main(void) {
            position = vec2(aVertexPosition.xy);
            gl_Position = vec4(position, 0.0, 1.0);
      }
</script>
```

Each fragment (pixel) location is interpolated between the five distinct vertice points, and the fragment shader determines the actual color of each pixel. Even though we have only five vertice points, the fragment shader acts on each pixel individually, and we can use any algorithm we want to choose the color.

In our first example, we will draw a circle that has gradient color ranging from pure red at the center to darker toward the edges. The fragment shader to accomplish this is shown here:

```
<script id="shader-fs" type="x-shader/x-fragment">
      varying highp vec2 position;
      void main(void) {
            highp float d = length(position);
            gl_FragColor = vec4(max(0.0, 1.0 - d), 0.0, 0.0, 1.0);
      }
</script>
```

This fragment shader takes the length of each position, which is $\sqrt{x^2 + y^2}$. Then this value is subtracted from the red component of the color. Even though d can be greater than 1, we ensure that the red component is atleast 0.0 by using the max function. This will produce a gradient circle of radius 1 (anything larger than 1 will appear black), as shown on the left of Figure 6-1.

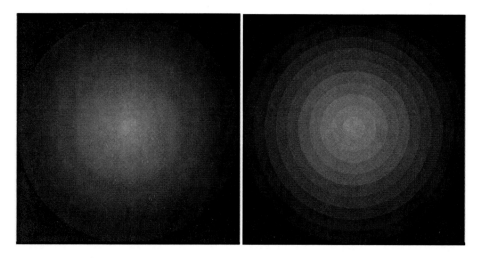

Figure 6-1. *Circle with gradient luminosity (left); concentric rings of varying luminosity (right)*

To draw concentric rings ranging from brightest at the center to darker going out eventually to black, as shown on the right of Figure 6-1, we modify our shader to have discrete steps:

```
<script id="shader-fs" type="x-shader/x-fragment">
    varying highp vec2 position;
    void main(void) {
        highp float d = length(position);
        highp float c = floor( d * 10.0 ) * 0.1;
        gl_FragColor = vec4(max(0.0, 1.0 - c), 0.0, 0.0, 1.0);
    }
</script>
```

Instead of a smooth gradient, we produce ten different color bands with our new fragment shader. To accomplish this, we take our initial distance value d, multiply by 10, and then round to the nearest integer below. For example, a distance of 0.783 will become 7.83, and then the floor function will produce 7. We divide by the same factor of 10 (we multiply by 0.1 in the code) to get a final value of 0.7. In this manner, distances between 0.7 and 0.79999 will all be given a final value of 0.7.

The full source code for this example can be found in the file 06/01_circles.html.

Color Lookups

With the desktop version of the GLSL there is a one-dimensional sampler type, sampler1D, which is often used to store colors for later lookup in a shader. However, this type is not available with the version of GLSL used in OpenGL ES or WebGL. Nonetheless, we can simulate this functionality with a two-dimensional texture.

To create a two-dimensional texture of colors, we need to specify RGBA color values and store them in a texture object, which will then be passed as a uniform to our fragment shader. In Listing 6-2 we specify RGBA integer values in the range 0 to 255.

Listing 6-2. Setting a uniform of color values

```
function setUniforms() {
    var color_data = [
```

```
            255, 0, 0, 255,
            255, 0, 0, 255,
            255, 0, 0, 255,
            255, 0, 0, 255,

            255, 255, 0, 255,
            255, 255, 0, 255,
            255, 255, 0, 255,
            255, 255, 0, 255,

            0, 255, 0, 255,
            0, 255, 0, 255,
            0, 255, 0, 255,
            0, 255, 0, 255,

            0, 0, 255, 255,
            0, 0, 255, 255,
            0, 0, 255, 255,
            0, 0, 255, 255
        ];
        var colors = new Uint8Array(color_data);

        var colorsTexture = gl.createTexture();
        gl.activeTexture(gl.TEXTURE0);
        gl.bindTexture(gl.TEXTURE_2D, colorsTexture);
        gl.texImage2D(     gl.TEXTURE_2D, 0, gl.RGBA, 4, 4, 0,
                           gl.RGBA, gl.UNSIGNED_BYTE, colors);
        gl.texParameteri(gl.TEXTURE_2D, gl.TEXTURE_MAG_FILTER, gl.NEAREST);
          gl.texParameteri(gl.TEXTURE_2D, gl.TEXTURE_MIN_FILTER, gl.NEAREST);
        gl.uniform1i(gl.getUniformLocation(glProgram, "sColors"), colorsTexture);
}
```

In Listing 6-2 we use a typed array of Uint8Array. This will produce four distinct colors - red, yellow, green and blue - represented four times each.

■ **Note**   When we pass in an array of pixel data to the texImage2D function, we must make sure to use a legal WebGL type and JavaScript typed array combo, or else it will generate an INVALID_OPERATION error.

Legal combos are Uint8Array for UNSIGNED_BYTE and Uint16Array for the types: UNSIGNED_SHORT_5_6_5, UNSIGNED_SHORT_4_4_4_4, UNSIGNED_SHORT_5_5_5_1.

Remember that textures need to be powers of 2 in length and width, so we specify our 16 colors to be stored in a texture of dimensions 4 × 4. Lastly, we obtain the uniform location and set its value all within one step:

```
gl.uniform1i(gl.getUniformLocation(glProgram, "sColors"), colorsTexture);
```

By using the WebGL Inspector, which is covered extensively in Chapter 9, you can verify that our texture is indeed 4x4 and visually see what the stored data looks like, as shown in Figure 6-2. For any fixed horizontal s coordinate of our texture, the color will vary as the vertical coordinate t changes. This changing of color looks gradient because of the texture filter settings.

Figure 6-2. Viewing our generated texture of colors

Our vertex shader remains the same as in our last example; however, the fragment shader changes to make use of our sampler:

```
<script id="shader-fs" type="x-shader/x-fragment">
    uniform sampler2D sColors;
    varying highp vec2 position;

    void main(void) {
        highp float t = length(position);
        gl_FragColor = vec4(texture2D(sColors, vec2(0.0, t)).rgb, 1.0);
    }
</script>
```

The result of this shader is seen on the left of Figure 6-3. The s coordinate is fixed as 0.0, and the t coordinate corresponds to the length of the current point.

Figure 6-3. Color lookup (left); playing around with coordinate manipulation (right)

On the right of Figure 6-3 I have played around with the coordinate generation function to produce a more interesting figure:

```
<script id="shader-fs" type="x-shader/x-fragment">
    uniform sampler2D sColors;
    varying highp vec2 position;
```

```
      void main(void) {
            highp float t = length(position);
            highp float x = sin(-position.y)*tan(length(position.xx));
            t = t+x;
            gl_FragColor = mix( vec4(0.0,0.0,0.0,1.0),
                                vec4(texture2D(sColors, vec2(0.0, t)).rgb, 1.0),
                                t);
      }
</script>
```

There is no real rhyme or reason about how I came across the equations to use `sin`, `tan`, and `mix`. I played around with settings until I found something I liked. I encourage you to play around with output and see what other interesting results you generate.

Having produced some images by defining equations in the fragment shader, we will now look at fractals that are capable of producing intricate and complex patterns that can be used to model some natural organisms, terrain, and phenomenon.

Fractals

Informally, *fractals* are images that exhibit self-similarity to the larger structure when zooming in to smaller and smaller regions within. Smaller regions of the object do not have to be identical to the larger structure, only similar. This self-similarity should happen indefinitely, although we are limited by how small a region that we can visualize or calculate, of course. To generate fractal images, repetitive iterations or recursion are often used.

As you shall see, fractals can be pretty cool-looking. However they also have widespread application in and out of graphics; and are used to generate terrain, coastlines, cityscape heights, noise functions, clouds, certain plants and flowers, and patterns found in nature such as seashells. They are also used in image-compression algorithms and other external uses.

Mandelbrot Set

One of the most famous and iconic fractals is the image of the *Mandelbrot set*, a set of points popularized by mathematician Benoit Mandelbrot in the 1970s that relate to this sequence:

$$z_{n+1} = z_n^2 + c$$

In the equation, $z_o = 0$ and c is a complex number of form $(a + ib)$ with real part a and imaginary component b. A starting point c is said to be in the Mandelbrot set if its sequence remains bounded. For example, with c=2=(2+0i), z_1=2, z_2=6, z_3=38..., the sequence clearly goes toward infinity. So c=2 is not in the Mandelbrot set. If we look at c=0, z_1=0, z_2=0, z_3=0... each successive term in the series is always 0 and so the sequence is bounded. Hence, c=0 lies in the set. It can also be shown that when the magnitude (squareroot($a^2 + b^2$)) of a number z_i in the sequence becomes greater than 2, the sequence will become unbounded. Hence, points in the set are limited to the range +/- 2 for both the real and imaginary component.

It is easy to calculate terms in the sequence for numbers with no imaginary component. When there is also an imaginary component, the calculation of the next term is a little more involved. The theory of imaginary numbers is beyond the scope of this book, but further resources are listed in Appendix D for those interested.

What we need to know is that a purely imaginary number multiplied by another imaginary number results in a real number with the opposite sign as you would get if you were multiplying the same two real number magnitudes. For example, 1i*1i=i*i= - 1, 6i * 3i = 18*i^2=-18, and 7i * -2i = 14.

When performing addition, subtraction, and multiplication of complex numbers, real components are grouped together and acted upon separately from the imaginary components. For any $c = a + bi$, and starting term $z_0 = 0 + 0i$, the next two terms in the sequence are:

```
z₁ = z₀² + c = (0 + 0i)² + (a + bi) = a + bi
z₂ = z₁² + c = (a + bi)² + (a + bi) = a² + (b²*i²) + 2*a*bi + (a+bi)
```

And grouping together real and imaginary terms, this can be expressed as:

```
z₂ =[a² - b² + a] + i[2*a*b + b]
```

An alternative way to write this, which is more useful for programming the calculation and keeps the c term separate, is as follows:

```
=[a² - b²] + i[2*a*b] + c
```

Using this form, we can express each successive term in the sequence in terms of the previous z-value's real and imaginary components:

```
zₙ₊₁.real = [zₙ.real² - zₙ.im²] + c.real
zₙ₊₁.imaginary = [2*zₙ.real * zₙ.im] + c.im
```

In our shader, the real value is notated by the x component of the vector, and the imaginary value is the y component.

Listing 6-3. Calculating the next iteration in the Mandelbrot set generation function

```
zₙ₊₁.x = zₙ.x*zₙ.x - zₙ.y*zₙ.y + c.x;
zₙ₊₁.y = 2*zₙ.x*zₙ.y + c.y;
```

Hopefully I haven't lost you. Depending on your level of mathematics this might be nothing new, or it could be Greek to you. Regardless of how the iteration equation in Listing 6-3 is derived, you can now plug it into your fragment shader and use it as shown in Listing 6-4. The vertex shader is unchanged from the previous example, it still simply passes the input point on to the fragment shader.

Listing 6-4. Mandelbrot set fragment shader

```
<script id="shader-fs" type="x-shader/x-fragment">
  varying highp vec2 position;
  const int MAX_ITERATIONS = 250;
  const highp float LIGHTNESS_FACTOR = 1.0;

  void main(void) {
      highp vec2 c = vec2(position.x-0.5, position.y);
      highp vec2 z = c;
      highp vec4 color = vec4(0.0, 0.0, 0.0, 1.0);

      for (int i = 0; i < MAX_ITERATIONS; i++)
      {
          z = vec2(z.x*z.x - z.y*z.y, 2.0*z.x*z.y) + c;

          if (dot(z, z) > 4.0)
          {
              highp float f = LIGHTNESS_FACTOR*float(i) / float(MAX_ITERATIONS);
              color = vec4(vec3(0.1, 0.1, 1.0)*f, 1.0);
              break;
          }
      }
```

```
        gl_FragColor = color;
}
</script>
```

When we plot the values of c with the real values of the x-axis and the imaginary component of the y-axis, the diagram of the numbers that are part of the Mandelbrot set form the (probably) familiar fractal pattern shown in Figure 6-4. In the diagram, the boundary points are what is interesting. Parts of the boundary are visually similar to the overall boundary of the set. As we zoom in closer, smaller regions still have similarity to the overall structure.

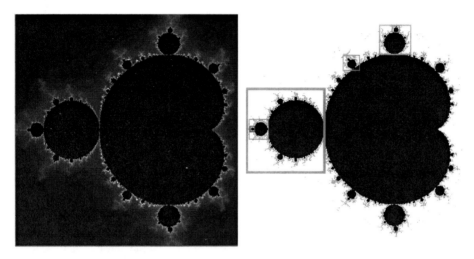

Figure 6-4. Mandelbrot set (left); some regions of self-similarity highlighted (right)

In Listing 6-4, we set constants of the number of iterations to test for each point being in the set and the amount to multiply the color of the boundary points based on the iteration number when a number leaves the set. When setting the c-value, the x coordinate has been moved 0.5 in the negative direction just to center the image better. The first z-value, z_1, equals c,so we set z initially equal to c. We initialize the pixel color to black and start our loop. The next z-value is calculated from the equations that we have derived in Listing 6-3 and then we test the dot product for being over 4. Recall that the dot product is $x^2 + y^2$, which is the magnitude (or length) squared. We know that a magnitude larger than 2 means that the point is outside the set. As $2^2 = 4$, using the squared value is an equivalent but less-expensive calculation because it does not require us to compute a square root. Finally we shade our pixel a value of blue between 0 and 1 based on the current iteration when the pixel becomes unbound in the sequence to the maximum number of iterations. However, it can be hard to see the boundary, so setting the constant LIGHTNESS_FACTOR to a higher value such as 10.0 will help visualize the boundary. Doing so increases the number of white-colored iterations, but this does provide much better contrast.

▪ **Note** If the fragment shader is not loading externally, try placing it inline. I have experienced errors with the for loop when placed in an external file, but have the program working when inline. The actual reason for this is that the comparision sign "<" needs to be escaped in the shader if it is read in as XML. A couple ways to resolve this issue are shown in the debugging section of Chapter 9.The for loop in GLSL is much more restrictive than in JavaScript or C/C++ and requires a constant as the limit condition.

Julia Set

The Julia set is named after French mathematician Gaston Julia, who first wrote about it in a 1918 paper. It is is closely related to the Mandelbrot set and can be generated with the same function:

$$z_{n+1} = z_n^2 + c$$

However, the Julia set restricts the values of c to be those values that lie within the Mandelbrot set and z_o is a coordinate on the complex plane (the xy plane in our shader). The initialization of z and c in our fragment shader becomes this:

```
highp vec2 z = vec2(position.x, position.y);
highp vec2 c = vec2(-0.8, -0.2);
```

c can be any valid point in the Mandelbrot set, and every point will produce a different image! Two such c seed points are (-0.8, 0.2), which produces the left image of Figure 6-5; and (-0.5, 0.62), which produces the right image of Figure 6-5.

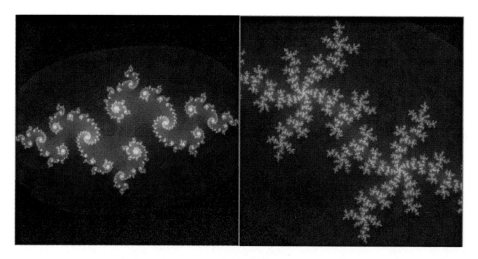

Figure 6-5. Two fractals produced in the Julia set: left - seed value of (-0.8, -0.2); right – seed value of (-0.5, 0.62)

Adding Interactivity

As the fragment shader runs on the GPU, its calculations for the Mandelbrot set will be much faster than calculations implemented on the client side with pure JavaScript. This allows us to add interaction that will have smooth, responsive animation.

The Mandelbrot and Julia sets are pretty cool, and it would be much more enjoyable to explore them if we could adjust the settings with a graphical user interface (GUI) instead of hard-coding values in our fragment shader and rerunning the program to see different results. We will do this now. First we need to think of things that we want to be able to adjust on the fly:

```
//uniform options
var    julia = 0,
       c_seed = [0.0, 0.0],
       zoom = 1.0,
```

```
        offset = [0.0, 0.0],
        color = [0.1, 0.1, 1.0],
        lightness = 1.0;
```

With these variables we are setting up our program to hold options that will allow us to switch between displaying the Mandelbrot and Julia sets, change the c-value when displaying the Julia set, adjust our zoom (magnification) our initial x and y offsets, the highlight color of the fractal, and the brightness.

Adding an HTML Form

Next we will add an HTML form. First we will make some basic styling changes. The form and GUI are not exceptional, but they do the trick. Here I set the canvas and form CSS to float left and the table cells to be vertically aligned:

```
<style>
        body{ background-color: grey; }
        canvas{ background-color: white; float: left; }
        form{ float: left; }
        td{ vertical-align: top; }
</style>
```

Next we set up our form, which uses the HTML5 range type and is shown in Figure 6-6.

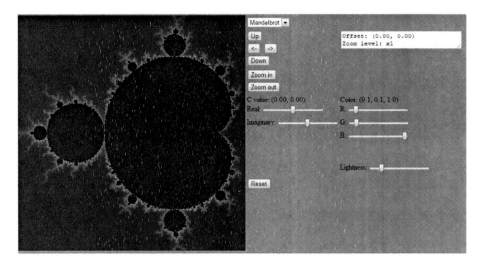

Figure 6-6. *Our WebGL output on the left and form components on the right*

The form consists of several inputs of type submit, several of type range, a select box, a textarea, and some span elements used as labels to show the current values. The code is shown in Listing 6-5.

Listing 6-5. HTML form to adjust Mandelbrot/Julia set settings

```
<form id='fractal-options'>
        <table border="0">
                <tr>
                        <td>
                                <select id="sets">
                                        <option value="mandelbrot">Mandelbrot</option>
                                        <option value="julia">Julia</option>
                                </select>
                        </td>
                        <td>
                        </td>
                </tr>
                <tr>
                        <td>
                                <input type="submit" name="up" value="Up"/><br/>
                                <input type="submit" name="left" value="<-"/>
                                <input type="submit" name="right" value="->"/><br/>
                                <input type="submit" name="down" value="Down"/>
                        </td>
                        <td rowspan="2">
                                <textarea cols="30" rows="2" id="output-text">Offset: (0.00, 0.00)
Zoom level: x1</textarea>
                </tr>
                <tr>
                        <td>
                                <input type="submit" name="zoom-in" value="Zoom in"/><br/>
                                <input type="submit" name="zoom-out" value="Zoom out"/>
                        </td>

                </tr>
                <tr>
                        <td>
                                C value: (<span id="c-value-label">0.00, 0.00</span>)<br/>
                                Real: <input type="range" step="0.01" id="c-real" name="c-real" value="0.0"
min="-2" max="2"/><br/>
                                Imaginary: <input type="range" step="0.01" id="c-imaginary" name="c-
imaginary" value="0.0" min="-2" max="2"/>
                        </td>
                        <td>
                                Color: (<span id="color-label">0.1, 0.1, 1.0</span>)<br/>
                                R: <input type="range" step="0.1" class="color-slider" id="color-r"
name="color-r" value="0.1" min="0.0" max="1.0"/><br/>
                                G: <input type="range" step="0.1" class="color-slider" id="color-g"
name="color-g" value="0.1" min="0.0" max="1.0"/><br/>
                                B: <input type="range" step="0.1" class="color-slider" id="color-b"
name="color-b" value="1.0" min="0.0" max="1.0"/><br/>
                                <br/><br/>
                                Lightness: <input type="range" step="1.0" class="color-slider"
id="lightness" name="lightness" value="10.0" min="1.0" max="50.0"/>

                        </td>
                </tr>
```

```
        <tr>
                <td colspan="2">
                        <input type="submit" name="reset" value="Reset"/>
                </td>
        </tr>
</form>
```

After adding the markup of Listing 6-5, our labels and textarea are currently not adjusted when GUI events occur and our JavaScript global variables that we earlier declared do not get updated.

Adding JavaScript Event Listeners

To add this functionality, we will need to add JavaScript event listeners. They can be written in plain JavaScript, but doing so with jQuery can be more concise and is shown in Listing 6-6.

Listing 6-6. jQuery event listeners for our form

```
<script>
$("#sets").change(function(){
        if($(this).val() == "mandelbrot"){
                julia = 0;
        }else{
                julia = 1;
        }
});
$("#c-real, #c-imaginary").change(function(){
        var range = $(this);
        var value = parseFloat(range.val());
        if(range.attr("id") == "c-real")
        {
                c_seed[0] = value;
        }else if(range.attr("id") == "c-imaginary")
        {
                c_seed[1] = value;
        }

        setCLabel();
});
$(".color-slider").change(function(){
        var range = $(this);
        var value = parseFloat(range.val());

        if(range.attr("id") == "color-r")
        {
                color[0] = value;
        }else if(range.attr("id") == "color-g")
        {
                color[1] = value;
        }else if(range.attr("id") == "color-b")
        {
```

```
                color[2] = value;
        }else if(range.attr("id") == "lightness")
        {
                lightness = value;
        }

        setColorLabel();
});

$("form").on("click", "input:submit", function(evt){
        var name = $(this).attr("name");

        switch(name){
                case 'up':
                        offset[1] += (0.1 * zoom);
                        break;
                case 'down':
                        offset[1] -= (0.1 * zoom);
                        break;
                case 'left':
                        offset[0] -= (0.1 * zoom);
                        break;
                case 'right':
                        offset[0] += (0.1 * zoom);
                        break;
                case 'zoom-in':
                        zoom /= 1.5;
                        break;
                case 'zoom-out':
                        zoom *= 1.5;
                        break;
                case 'reset':
                        resetUniformVariables();
                        $("#c-real").val(0.00);
                        $("#c-imaginary").val(0.00);
                        $("#color-r").val(0.1);
                        $("#color-g").val(0.1);
                        $("#color-b").val(1.0);
                        $("#lightness").val(10.0);
                        $("#sets").val("mandelbrot");
                        setColorLabel();
                        setCLabel();
                        break;
                default:
                        break;
        }

        setTextArea();

        evt.preventDefault();
});
</script>
</body>
```

As you can see, the JavaScript in Listing 6-6 comes immediately before the end `</body>` tag. This lets us be sure that the full Document Object Model (DOM) has loaded and that we can work with it right away. We have three different change listeners and a delegated click listener. We grab DOM elements with the id selector "#" or the class selector " . ".

The first change listener is for the `select` component with id of "sets". The values of the `select` box can be "mandelbrot" or "julia", corresponding to displaying the Mandelbrot or Julia set. We find the current selected value with the `val` function of `$(this)` - a keyword that stores the currently found jQuery object of the `select` element.

The next change listener is for the real and imaginary c-value sliders. We parse the float value of the returned string and update the relevant index of our `c_seed` array by comparing the `id` attribute of the current object. Then we update the C label. We will come back to this and other helper methods in Listing 6-7.

The third change function grabs elements that have a class of "color-slider". We compare the id of the changed object with the ids "color-r", "color-b", and "color-b", and change our color variable value accordingly. Then we update the color label.

Our last event handler matches the form and handles all clicked submit inputs. This is an alternative to defining a separate click handler for each submit input and is preferable as it lets jQuery delegate event handling to the appropriate subitem. In this handler we get the value of the `name` attribute and use a switch statement to adjust our variables accordingly. One case of note within the switch is the "reset" block, which restores our form to the original state.

No matter which submit button is clicked, the `textarea` is updated and `evt.preventDefault` is called. This latter action is very important because without the `preventDefault` call the form will do a full page refresh, and we won't be able to maintain state. Alternatively, we can `return false;` to not submit the form.

Listing 6-7 shows the `resetUniformVariables`, `setColorLabel`, `setCLabel`, and `setTextArea` methods that are called in our event listeners.

Listing 6-7. Helper functions to reset our variables, adjust our labels, and textarea

```
function resetUniformVariables()
{
        c_seed = [0.0, 0.0];
        zoom = 1.0;
        offset = [0.0, 0.0];
        julia = 0;
        color = [0.1, 0.1, 1.0];
        lightness = 10.0;
}

function setColorLabel()
{
        $("#color-label").html( color[0].toFixed(1) + ", " + color[1].toFixed(1) + ", " +
                                color[2].toFixed(1));
}

function setCLabel()
{
        $("#c-value-label").html(c_seed[0].toFixed(2) + ", " + c_seed[1].toFixed(2));
}

function setTextArea()
{
        var zoom_reciprocal = 'MAX_ZOOM';
        if(zoom > 0.00000000001)
        {
```

```
          zoom_reciprocal = 1.0/zoom;
    }
    var settings = "Offset: (" + offset[0].toFixed(2) + "," +offset[1].toFixed(2) + ")\n";
    settings += "Zoom level: x" + zoom_reciprocal;
    $("#output-text").html(settings) ;
}
```

In Listing 6-7 we set the innerHTML of the component with the html function call. The toFixed(2) call formats decimal output to exactly two decimal places.

Passing Information and Animating

At this point, we have listeners for all our form components and update the GUI display to show the current settings. Now we need to pass this information to our shaders and reintroduce an animation loop. We will store the uniform locations as variables within our program so we won't need to repoll the GPU for these locations every time we reanimate the scene:

```
//uniform locations
var     c_seed_uniform = null,
        zoom_uniform = null,
        offset_uniform = null,
        julia_uniform = null,
        color_uniform = null,
        lightness_uniform = null;
```

Limiting GPU get/set calls is a best practice, as will be explained in Chapter 9. The main part of our program now looks like this:

```
getUniformLocations();
(function animLoop(){
    setUniforms();
    setupWebGL();
    drawScene();
    requestAnimationFrame(animLoop, canvas);
})();
```

Where our getUniformLocations helper function is:

```
function getUniformLocations()
{
    c_seed_uniform = gl.getUniformLocation(glProgram, "uCseed");
    zoom_uniform = gl.getUniformLocation(glProgram, "uZoom");
    offset_uniform = gl.getUniformLocation(glProgram, "uOffset");
    julia_uniform = gl.getUniformLocation(glProgram, "uJulia");
    color_uniform = gl.getUniformLocation(glProgram, "uColor");
    lightness_uniform = gl.getUniformLocation(glProgram, "uLightness");
}
```

The first part of our fragment shader now declares our uniforms and their types:

```
<script id="shader-fs" type="x-shader/x-fragment">
    uniform highp vec2 uCseed;
    uniform highp float uZoom;
    uniform highp vec2 uOffset;
    uniform int uJulia;
```

153

```
      uniform highp vec3 uColor;
      uniform highp float uLightness;
```

All that is left is implementing our setUniforms function and updating the rest of our fragment shader. Here is our setUniforms method:

```
function setUniforms() {
      gl.uniform2fv(c_seed_uniform, c_seed);
      gl.uniform1f(zoom_uniform, zoom);
      gl.uniform2fv(offset_uniform, offset);
      gl.uniform1i(julia_uniform, julia);
      gl.uniform3fv(color_uniform, color);
      gl.uniform1f(lightness_uniform, lightness);
}
```

■ **Note**   When defining uniform values, you must always specify the variable size, even if it is 1. For example, in the previous code, 2fv means float vec2, while 1i means int.

Our final fragment shader is shown in Listing 6-8. With the exception of the number of iterations, everything else is configurable by our application passing in uniform values.

Listing 6-8. Configurable fragment shader for Mandelbrot and Julia sets

```
<script id="shader-fs" type="x-shader/x-fragment">
  uniform highp vec2 uCseed;
  uniform highp float uZoom;
  uniform highp vec2 uOffset;
  uniform int uJulia;
  uniform highp vec3 uColor;
  uniform highp float uLightness;

  varying highp vec2 position;
  const int MAX_ITERATIONS = 250;
  void main(void) {
          highp vec2 z = vec2(position.x, position.y) * uZoom + uOffset;
          highp vec2 c = z;
          if(uJulia == 1)
          {
              c = uCseed;
          }

          highp vec4 color = vec4(0.0, 0.0, 0.0, 1.0);

          for (int i = 0; i < MAX_ITERATIONS; i++)
          {
              z = vec2(z.x*z.x - z.y*z.y, 2.0*z.x*z.y) + c;

              if (dot(z, z) > 4.0)
              {
                  highp float f = uLightness*float(i) /
                              float(MAX_ITERATIONS);
                  color = vec4(uColor*f, 1.0);
                  break;
```

```
                }
            }
            gl_FragColor = color;
        }
</script>
```

In Figure 6-7 you can see a small region of the Mandelbrot set zoomed in at more than 16,000 times magnification is still similar to the overall shape (and most likely limited by numeric precision).

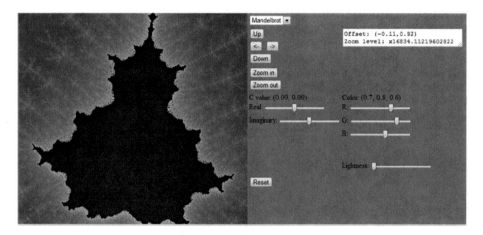

Figure 6-7. *Small region of the Mandelbrot set zoomed in*

In Figure 6-8 you can see two screenshots of the application displaying the Julia set with different C-seed values and magnification levels.

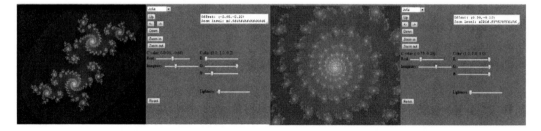

Figure 6-8. *Two screenshots of the Julia set with different c-seed values and magnification levels*

It is left to the reader to extend the program by setting the number of iterations to be adjustable in the GUI and performing other enhancements such as saving and reloading settings or being able to drag the current location around with the mouse or use the mouse wheel for zooming.

Generation of Fractals

There are a number of techniques to generate fractals. Two of these are *iterated function systems* (IFSs) and *Lindenmayer systems* (L-systems). In the former, an image is composed of several copies of itself that decrease each iteration in size and possibly involve affine transforms.

In L-systems, a formal grammar is used with a starting point and replacement rules. For example, the "Sierpinski triangle" has the following rules:

```
Axiom (Start): A
Rules: A->B-A-B, B->A+B+A
```

Where - means turn left 60 degrees, and + means turn right 60 degrees. The first few iterations of this L-system would be:

```
A
(B-A-B)
(A+B+A)-(B-A-B)+(A+B+A)
```

And the resulting images after 1, 2, 3, 4, and 8 iterations are shown in Figure 6-9.

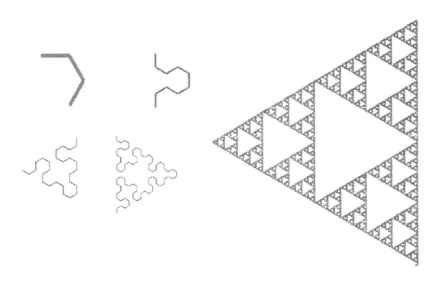

Figure 6-9. *Sierpinski Triangle after the first four iterations on the left and after the eighth iteration on the right*

Similarly, many plants can be graphically represented by L-systems. A fern can be generated with the following L-system rules, where the angle here is 20 degrees and [ ] means to push the operation onto a stack for operator order precedence (see Figure 6-10):

```
Axiom: X
Rules: X -> F[+X]F[-X]+X, F -> FF
```

Figure 6-10. *Plant leaf produced from an L-system fractal*

Rendering a Grid Mesh with One TRIANGLE_STRIP Call

To generate terrain or use a height map (which will be explained later in the chapter), we first need a mesh of points. We will investigate how to render a regular grid mesh of triangles with a single TRIANGLE_STRIP draw call. In Figure 6-11 we have a 2x2 square mesh with triangles subdivided as you might expect, with all divisions along the same diagonal direction (top right to bottom left in this case).

If you attempt to render this with a single triangle strip call, however, your indices would need to be these:

0,3,1,4,2,5,8,7,5,4,…

This presents a problem because vertices 5 and 4 form a triangle with only vertice 7 or 2. So there would need to be repetition of the triangle 5,4,7 and then vertice 6 followed by repeating triangle 7,6,4 again, and so on.

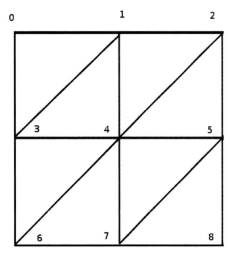

Figure 6-11. *A 2x2 square mesh with the diagonal direction of each triangular bisection consistently being from the lower left corner to upper right corner*

However, if you switch the diagonal cuts on alternating rows, as shown in Figure 6-12, you get a more natural index progression:

0,4,1,5,2,6,3,7,11,6,10,5,9,4,8,12,9,13,10,14,11,15

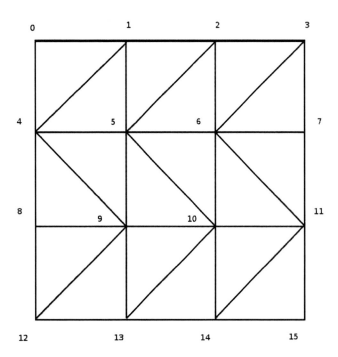

Figure 6-12. *A 3x3 square mesh with triangles having inverted orientation on alternate rows*

We are cheating a little when we switch rows because 3,7,11 is a straight line and not a true triangle, as with 4,8,12. However, you most likely will not see these lines when the grid is rendered, and if you do they will occur at the edges of the mesh.

We want to have meshes with many more subdivisions, but do not want to enter in these vertices or indices manually, so next we need to figure out how to programmatically create this mesh for any number of subdivisions.

First, observe that an nxn grid has $(n+1)^2$ vertice points. In the 3x3 example, notice that we can split the indices into the following groupings:

```
 0, 4, 1, 5, 2, 6, 3, 7,
11, 6,10, 5, 9, 4, 8,
12, 9,13,10,14,11,15
```

If we place the first vertex 0 by itself, we can start to see the pattern emerge:

```
0,
4, 1, 5, 2, 6, 3, 7,
11, 6,10, 5, 9, 4, 8,
12, 9,13,10,14,11,15
```

The triangles formed by these separate groupings are highlighted in Figure 6-13.

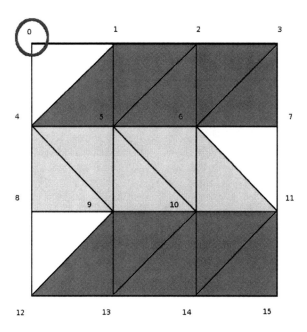

Figure 6-13. *Grouping row vertices*

From Figure 6-13 we can create the following pseudocode:

```
Add 0 to indices
For each row
        If row is odd:
                Alternate bottom and top indices, starting at bottom row (and column indice 0) and
                then top row (starting at column indice 1) and working toward the right
```

```
        Else
                Alternate bottom and top indices, starting at bottom row (and last column indice)
                and then top row (starting at second-last column indice) and working toward the
                left
```

A JavaScript implementation is shown in Listing 6-9, which will produce a flat plane.

Listing 6-9. An arbitrarily divided mesh

```javascript
function createGrid(size, divisions){
        size = (typeof size !== 'undefined') ? size : 1.0;
        divisions = (typeof divisions !== 'undefined') ? divisions : 10;

        var segment_size = size/divisions;
        var vertexPositionData = [];
        for(var i=0;i<=divisions;++i)
        {
                for(var j=0;j<=divisions;++j)
                {
                        vertexPositionData.push(i*segment_size);
                        vertexPositionData.push(0.0);
                        vertexPositionData.push(j*segment_size);
                }
        }

        var indexData = [0];
        for(var row=0;row<divisions;++row)
        {
                if(row%2 == 0)
                {
                        for(var i=0;i<=divisions;++i)
                        {
                                if(i!=0)
                                {
                                        indexData.push( row*(divisions+1) + i);
                                }
                                indexData.push( (row+1)*(divisions+1) + i);
                        }
                }else{
                        for(var i=0;i<=divisions;++i)
                        {
                                if(i!=0)
                                {
                                        indexData.push( (row+1)*(divisions+1) - (i+1) );
                                }
                                indexData.push( (row+2)*(divisions+1) -(i+1) );
                        }
                }
        }
        //assign to buffers
}
```

In Listing 6-9, we set our vertex points evenly spaced along our grid based on the number of divisions. We use the modulus operator, %, to determine whether we are on an even or odd row and push indices into our array appropriately.

Height Maps

A *height map* (aka *heightfield*) is a texture image that stores displacement information, typically for the y-value of an object. Height maps are used in terrain generation but can be used to alter any object or simulate extra detail, as discussed in the bump mapping section.

Taking the grid creation code in Listing 6-9, we can use a texture and our shaders to alter the height of each y point on the xz plane grid. Our vertex and fragment shader pair is shown in Listing 6-10.

Listing 6-10. Vertex and fragment shader to read texture heightfield data

```
<script type="x-shader/x-vertex">
      attribute vec3 aVertexPosition;

      uniform mat4 uPMatrix;
      uniform mat4 uMVMatrix;
      uniform sampler2D uSampler;

      varying highp float height;

      void main(void) {
            height = texture2D( uSampler, vec2(aVertexPosition.xz )).r;
            gl_Position = uPMatrix * uMVMatrix *
                        vec4(aVertexPosition.x, height, aVertexPosition.z, 1.0);
      }
</script>
<script id="shader-fs" type="x-shader/x-fragment">
      varying highp float height;
      void main(void) {

            gl_FragColor = vec4(height, height, height, 1.0);
      }
</script>
```

In the vertex shader of Listing 6-10, we use the x and z coordinate to look up a value in the texture to use as the height value. In the fragment shader, we use the height value to also shade our image, though this is not required. We could have used a lighting model or texturing or have colored the mesh in any other way that we saw fit. The full source of this example is in the file 06/heightmap.html.

■ **Note**   The texture used in this example has gray values using RGBA channels. As such, the luminance can be found by using any of the channels separately. A true grayscale image would have the same result but the texture file used will be physically smaller. If we require a greater range of height values, a RGBA texture can provide this.

In Figure 6-14, we show a texture on the left and the heightfields produced with increasing mesh divisions on the right.

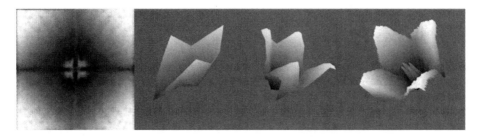

Figure 6-14. *Left: a black-and-white texture; right: using the luminance as a height amount with 3×3, 10×10, and 200×200 grid sizes*

Bump/Normal Mapping

Bump mapping is a technique introduced by Jim Blinn in 1978, which uses a heightmap to simulate extra detail and roughness on a surface without actually changing the geometry of the surface. This is the way bump mapping works:

- Height values of bumps along the surface are stored in a texture
- Surface normals of the height map are calculated
- These normals are combined with the real surface normal and used with a lighting model

Because bump mapping does not actually change the geometry of the object, it is often less computationally expensive then rendering a more complex mesh with actual indentations.

Terrain

There are many ways to model terrain. One way is to use a static heightmap like the one we have just investigated, but using a more appropriate texture. Another method is to dynamically create terrain using fractal generation. We will now show an example of this technique using the midpoint displacement algorithm.

Midpoint Displacement

Midpoint displacement starts with a mesh with four corner points and associated heights. Then the mesh is subdivided between each corner midpoint and then a middle point. In Figure 6-15 you can see that the average of points A and B becomes the value of its midpoint F. Similarly, $G = (A+C)/2$, $H = (B+D)/2$, $I = (C+D)/2$, and point $E = (A+B+C+D)/4$.

Then each new square is subdivided again. In the second subdivision (bottom left of Figure 6-15), only the top-left points are labeled, but these calculations are done to all four squares.

This process of subdividing can continue as long as you want (and can computationally handle). In practice, when computing the midpoint, a random offset is usually added, which is proportional to the size of the midpoint region. So point E could be calculated as $(A + B + C + D)/4 + (Math.Random() -0.5)$, and point J could be $(A + F + G + E)/4 +(Math.Random() -0.5) *0.5$.

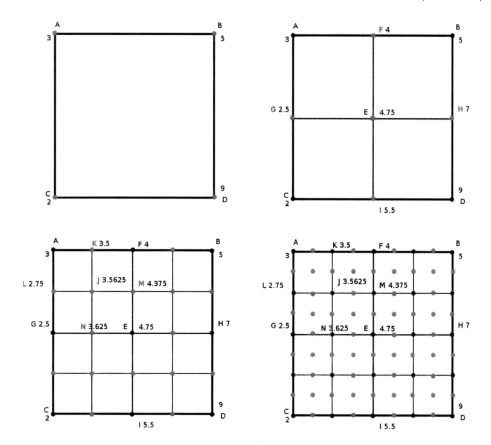

Figure 6-15. *First few iterations of the midpoint displacement algorithm with vertice values shown*

Notice that the dimension of a midpoint displaced grid is always n*n, where n is strictly a power of 2. We can either test that the dimension is in fact a power of 2 and throw an error if it is not, or we can ensure it by modifying the start of our createGrid function to this:

```
function createGrid(size, power){
        size = (typeof size !== 'undefined') ? size : 1.0;
        divisions = (typeof power !== 'undefined') ? (Math.pow(2.0, power) ) : 8;
        divisions = (int)divisions;
```

Every square in the grid will be rendered as two triangles, but we can still use a single TRIANGLE_STRIP call as we have in our height map example. We just need to compute the height of each vertex point. Our first step is to specify heights for the four corners of the mesh:

For each element of an nxn grid, where n = divisions, i is the row index and j is the column index, the array index for the y value of each (x,y,z) point will be calculated as: [(i + j*(n+1))*3 + 1]. Here 3 represents the number of coordinates in the vertex position, (x,y,z). The reason that we add 1 is because we are looking for the middle component, y (x would be an offset of 0, while z would be 2).

```
//seed the corners. Here we will use the values [1.5, 3.5, 2.0, 1.0]
//but these could be randomly generated seed values
vertexPositionData[(0 + 0*(divisions+1))*3+1] = 1.5;  //top-left
vertexPositionData[(divisions + 0*(divisions+1))*3+1] = 3.5; //top-right
```

```
vertexPositionData[(0 + divisions*(divisions+1))*3+1] = 2.0; //bottom-left
vertexPositionData[(divisions + divisions*(divisions+1))*3+1] = 1.0; //bottom-right

midpointDisplacement(
        [0,0],
        [divisions, 0],
        [0, divisions],
        [divisions, divrisions],
        divisions,
        0
);
```

We call the method midpointDisplacement, which takes four corner coordinates as arguments, the number of divisions, and the current iteration of the algorithm. The full method is shown in Listing 6-12.

Listing 6-12. Midpoint displacement recursive function

```
function midpointDisplacement(tl, tr, bl, br, divisions,iteration)
{
        if( (tl[0] + 1) == br[0] || (tl[1] + 1) == br[1] )
        {
                return;
        }

        //array indices
        var midpoint = [(tl[0] + br[0])/2,
                        (tl[1] + br[1])/2
                        ];

        var left_mp = [ tl[0],
                        (tl[1] + bl[1])/2
                        ];
        var right_mp = [ tr[0],
                        (tr[1] + br[1])/2
                        ];
        var top_mp = [ (tl[0] + tr[0])/2,
                        tl[1]
                        ];
        var bottom_mp = [ (bl[0] + br[0])/2,
                          bl[1]
                          ];

        //current height values
        var tl_height = vertexPositionData[(tl[0] + tl[1] * (divisions+1))*3+1];
        var tr_height = vertexPositionData[(tr[0] + tr[1] * (divisions+1))*3+1];
        var bl_height = vertexPositionData[(bl[0] + bl[1] * (divisions+1))*3+1];
        var br_height = vertexPositionData[(br[0] + br[1] * (divisions+1))*3+1];

        //compute five new points
        var top_value = (tl_height + tr_height)/2.0;
        vertexPositionData[(top_mp[0] + top_mp[1] * (divisions+1))*3+1] = top_value;
        var bottom_value = (bl_height + br_height)/2.0;
        vertexPositionData[(bottom_mp[0] + bottom_mp[1] * (divisions+1))*3+1] =
                                                bottom_value;
```

```
var left_value = (tl_height + bl_height)/2.0;
vertexPositionData[(left_mp[0] + left_mp[1] * (divisions+1))*3+1] = left_value;
var right_value = (tr_height + br_height)/2.0;
vertexPositionData[(right_mp[0] + right_mp[1] * (divisions+1))*3+1] = right_value;

//midpoint has random term
vertexPositionData[(midpoint[0] + midpoint[1] * (divisions+1)) * 3 + 1] =
        (tl_height+tr_height+bl_height+br_height)/4.0
        +(-0.5+Math.random())*Math.pow(0.65, iteration-2.0);

//repeat with four quads
midpointDisplacement( tl, top_mp, left_mp, midpoint, divisions, iteration+1 );
midpointDisplacement( top_mp, tr, midpoint, right_mp, divisions, iteration+1 );
midpointDisplacement( left_mp, midpoint, bl, bottom_mp, divisions, iteration+1 );
midpointDisplacement( midpoint, right_mp, bottom_mp, br, divisions, iteration+1 );
}
```

In Listing 6-12, if the top-left and bottom-right corners are only one column and row away from each other, we return immediately. Otherwise, we look up the corner heights and then compute the five new points that we will be adding in this iteration. We then use these new points to recursively call the midpointDisplacement function four more times, once for each quadrant of the original region. In these new calls, we pass in updated corner coordinates and increase the iteration value. The iteration value is used to generate the random portion added to the midpoint height. Sample output from the program is shown in Figure 6-16.

Figure 6-16. *Sample fractal terrain generation*

Once a terrain is dynamically rendered, the height values can be saved to an output texture for later static usage. The full source of this example is in the file 06/fractal_terrain.html.

■ **Note** The midpoint displacement algorithm has visual square–shaped artifacts, and other algorithms such as the diamond-square algorithm produce better results. In Figure 6-16, no lighting or texture data has been applied. Both of these would also dramatically add to the rendered image.

Particle Systems

Particle systems refer to modeling dynamic fluid objects such as smoke, fire, blood splatter, sparks, electricity, dust, glow, sparkle, rain, snow, hail, and clouds. Particle systems were formalized in a landmark paper entitled "Particle Systems: A Technique for Modeling a Class of Fuzzy Objects," by William Reeves in 1983 (while he was working at Lucasfilm).

The phenomena that particle systems model have no fixed shape or rigidity, so they are difficult to model by traditional polygonal methods. Instead they are modeled by clouds of primitive particles that make up the volume of the object.

Each particle in the system is dynamic. It has a lifespan with a birth and a death. It also has attributes that may change throughout its lifespan. Attributes that a particle may have include:

- Position

- Velocity

- Color

- Transparency

- Age

- Size

There can be any other attribute that we want to model and keep track of such as shape, lifetime, previous position and velocity, acceleration, spin, and so on.

Particle system primitives may be points; static lines (rendering the full parametric path of a point particle) for particles such as hair, fur, or grass; triangle primitives; or more advanced primitives such as a falling leaf in a fall forest scene or a fish in a school of fish. Primitives may or may not detect and handle collisions. Particles are usually small and are affected by outside forces like gravity and wind, but not affected by lighting equations or shadows.

A set of rules governs a particle system, but the exact details of each particle are nondeterministic, and the process is stochastic. This means that the overall shape of the object will be unknown until the system is run and will most likely vary when rerun.

The life cycle of a particle in the system is:

1. **Generation/birth**: Initialized within a location of the 'fuzzy object' shape or from within a regular mesh object such as a cube with an added amount of randomness.

2. **Dynamic life**: Attributes vary over time. Often the attribute is defined by a parametric equation using time as the parameter.

3. **Extinction/death**: When the particle's age (which starts at 0 and traditionally is measured in number of frames) reaches a preset lifespan; or the particle hits the ground, another boundary, leaves the frame of view, or some other rule is met, the particle is destroyed.

Particle systems are similar to fractals in that at higher zoom levels, more detail is shown than from far away. An initial seeding of a particle's attribute x is often defined as the average value of that attribute plus a random amount based on a variance:

```
initialₓ = averageₓ + random * varianceₓ
```

Particle systems offer controlled chaos as we set guidelines for particles, but offer an amount of randomness within. We can keep track of a particle's exact state or use parametric equations to calculate new values.

We will now create a particle system with WebGL using point primitives. For this example, we will set the initial position and velocity of each particle at random in the range +/- 1 for each coordinate. We will create a new object type of Particle to hold information, as shown in Listing 6-13.

Listing 6-13. Object to hold particle properties

```
function Particle(position, color){
      if (position === undefined) {
            position = [ ((Math.random()-.5)*.1),
                         ((Math.random()-.5)*.1),
                         ((Math.random()-.5)*.1),
                       ];
      }
      if (color === undefined) { color = [1.0, 0.0, 0.0, 0.5]; }

      this.position = position;
      this.color = color;

      this.velocity = [ ((Math.random()-.5)*.1),
                        ((Math.random()-.5)*.1),
                        ((Math.random()-.5)*.1),
                      ];
      if(
        (Math.abs(this.velocity[0]) < 0.01) &&
        (Math.abs(this.velocity[1]) < 0.01) &&
        (Math.abs(this.velocity[2]) < 0.01)
      )
      {
        //ensure particle is not stagnant
        this.velocity[0] = 0.1;
      }
      this.age = 0;
      this.lifespan = 20;
      this.size = 1.0;
}
```

In Listing 6-13 we set the `position` and `velocity` and initialize the color to red by default. We also set the alpha to 0.5 so that we can blend our particles. We initialize the age to 0 and set the lifespan to 20. Next we define a function to control how our particles are updated in Listing 6-14.

Listing 6-14. Our particle update function

```
Particle.prototype.update = function(){
      this.position[0] += (0.1 * this.velocity[0]);
      this.position[1] += (0.1 * this.velocity[1]);
      this.position[2] += (0.1 * this.velocity[2]);
      var x = Math.abs(this.position[0]);
      var y = Math.abs(this.position[1]);
      var z = Math.abs(this.position[2]);

      var distance = x*x + y*y + z*z;
      if(distance > 4)
      {
            this.position = [ (Math.random()*2.0)-1.0,
                              (Math.random()*2.0)-1.0,
                              (Math.random()*2.0)-1.0
                            ];
```

```
this.velocity = [ (Math.random()*2.0)-1.0,
                  (Math.random()*2.0)-1.0,
                  (Math.random()*2.0)-1.0
];
if(this.age < 10)
{
        this.color = [1.0, 1.0, 1.0, 0.75];
}else if(this.age < this.lifespan)
{
        this.color = [0.0, 0.0, 1.0, 0.75];
}else
{
        this.color = [1.0, 1.0, 1.0, 0.0];
}
this.age++;
}
}
```

There is more than one way to model a system. Here I check the squared distance of each point to the origin. If it is over some set amount, we increment the age of the particle and rerandomize the position and velocity. On the first increment of the age up until the age of 10, the color is set to white. Between 10 and the lifespan of the particle, it is then blue. When the particle reaches the lifespan, the alpha channel is set to 0 so that the particle does not show (but is still stored in memory). The range of the velocity once the age increments is much higher than for the red particles. As such, red particles often exist longer then older white and blue counterparts at the end of the animation. The full code can be found in the file 06/particle_systems.html, and screenshots during the life of the program are shown in Figure 6-17.

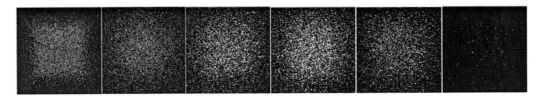

Figure 6-17. A basic particle system with slow-moving red particles that give way to faster white and blue particles and then eventually disperse

Enhancements

There are several enhancements that we can make to our previous example:

- Limiting how many particles are spawned at once

- Using time for parametric movement

- Having a more controlled model instead of complete randomness

- Having particles die and fade away

When using particle systems in WebGL, remember that the GPU is much faster than JavaScript for calculations and offset as much of the calculation to it as possible. In the previous example, if you increase the number of particles to an amount that your computer cannot easily handle; for me 1,000,000 grinds it to a halt, then we can see that using the GPU for calculation would be an improvement. The downside of using the GPU is that it does not maintain as much state, so our effects need to be simpler or pass in extra data that is stored in a vertex buffer object (VBO) or texture.

For our next example, we will pass the frame count of each particle to use as time into the GPU. We will use parametric equations in our shader to define the path of each particle according to the basic physics equation of *position = initial position + velocity*time + 0.5*acceleration*time², (Df = Di + v*t + 0.5*a*t^2)*, which was discussed in the previous chapter. This allows us to calculate the point of each particle purely from the time value passed to the shader instead of using JavaScript and the Particle object that we previously used.

We will define a total of seven properties that are passed to the shader each frame:

```
x,y,z, age (in frames), velocity X, velocity Y, size
```

In each frame, our JavaScript removes old particles, updates the age of particles, and spawns new ones, as shown in Listing 6-15. We will be simulating a stream of water initially travelling upwards.

Listing 6-15. JavaScript to spawn, update, and remove particles

```
function adjustParticles(){
        var particles_old = particles.slice(); //copy
        particles = [];
        for( var i=0; i<particles_old.length; i+=PARTICLE_COMPONENTS )
        {
                //remove old particles
                //if past lifespan or below the start position, do not readd particle
                if(     (particles_old[i+3] < LIFESPAN) &&
                        (particles_old[i+1] > (START_Y - 0.001) )
                        )
                {       var old = particles_old.slice(i, i+PARTICLE_COMPONENTS );
                        old[3] += 1.0; //age
                        particles = particles.concat(old);
                }
        }

        currentNumberParticles = particles.length/PARTICLE_COMPONENTS;

        //spawn new particles
        if( currentNumberParticles + MAX_SPAWN_PER_FRAME < MAX_NUMBER_OF_PARTICLES )
        {
                for( var n=0; n<MAX_SPAWN_PER_FRAME; ++n )
                {
                particles.push(.5*Math.random()-.25);        //X
                particles.push(START_Y);                     //Y
                particles.push(Math.random() - .5);          //Z
                particles.push(0.0);    //age

                particles.push(5.0*Math.random() - 10.0);    //velX
                particles.push(14.0 + 12.0*Math.random());   //velY
                particles.push(0.5 + Math.random() *4.0);    //size
                ++currentNumberParticles;
                }
        }
}
```

The x,y,z, and age component are stored in one attribute, aVertexPosition, with the age accessible via the w component. The x,y velocity and size are stored in another attribute called aVertexVelocity, with the size the z component. The vertex and fragment shader are shown in Listing 6-16.

Listing 6-16. Parametric vertex and fragment shader for particle system

```
<script type="x-shader/x-vertex">
        attribute vec4 aVertexPosition;
        attribute vec4 aVertexVelocity;

        uniform mat4 uPMatrix;
        uniform mat4 uMVMatrix;

        varying highp float parametricTime;
        void main(void) {
              parametricTime = (aVertexPosition.w/100.0);

              vec3 currentPosition = vec3(aVertexPosition.x + (aVertexVelocity.x *
              parametricTime),

                  aVertexPosition.y + (aVertexVelocity.y * parametricTime),
                  aVertexPosition.z + (aVertexVelocity.x * parametricTime)
              );

              currentPosition.y -= 4.9*parametricTime*parametricTime;

              gl_Position = uPMatrix * uMVMatrix * vec4(currentPosition.xyz, 1.0);
              gl_PointSize = aVertexVelocity.z;
        }
</script>

<script id="shader-fs" type="x-shader/x-fragment">
      varying highp float parametricTime;
      void main(void) {
            gl_FragColor = vec4(parametricTime*.8, parametricTime*.8, 1.0,
                          0.9-(parametricTime*.4));
      }
</script>
```

The shader code has the particles change from blue to white with age and is used to model a stream of water, as shown in Figure 6-18. The full source of this example is in the file 06/particle_systems_gpu.html.

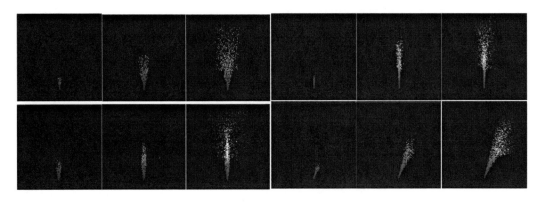

Figure 6-18. *Water stream with varying parameters modeled as a particle system*

Summary

This chapter showed that we can use algorithms directly in the GPU to render complex images. We demonstrated how cool and useful fractals can be and we generated terrain. We investigated particle systems, discussed how to use height maps, and explained how bump mapping can create the illusion of more noise on a surface.

The next chapter will look at the popular WebGL framework Three.js. We will show how to get started developing with it and demonstrate how its API abstraction can simplify and expediate development.

CHAPTER 7

■ ■ ■

Three.js Framework

There are many WebGL frameworks that are available to abstract away the lower-level application programming interface (API) calls that we have covered in the first six chapters of the book. This abstraction helps to make WebGL development easier and more productive. We will discuss several WebGL frameworks in the next chapter. In this chapter we will concentrate on one of the most widely used frameworks – Three.js. We will cover the following:

- A background of the library

- How to start development with Three.js

- Falling back to a 2D canvas context for rendering if WebGL is not supported

- Three.js API calls to easily create cameras, objects, and use lighting models

- Show the equivalent Three.js code to some examples found in previous chapters, which used direct low-level WebGL API calls

- Introduce tQuery, a library that blends Three.js with jQuery selectors

Background

Three.js was created by Ricardo Cabello, aka Mr.Doob, and has been on gitHub since 2010. Since that time, it has received added help from many contributors and its user base has grown to a large size.

Three.js provides several different draw modes and can fall back to the 2D rendering context if WebGL is not supported. Three.js is a well-designed library and fairly intuitive to use. Default settings reduce the amount of initial work or "boilerplate" needed. Settings can be overridden as parameters passed in upon object construction or by calling the appropriate object methods afterwards.

■ **Note** There can be a mistaken notion among people starting out with WebGL that Three.js and WebGL development are one and the same. Just as the JavaScript framework, jQuery, is not the same as JavaScript, Three. js (or any other framework) is not the same as pure WebGL development.

If you are adept with an underlying language, you can usually understand framework code for it. The reverse is not true. Knowing a framework in no way guarantees that you know a language, so learning the low-level language is highly beneficial.

Features

Here are some of the many features of the Three.js framework:

- Gracefully falls back to 2D context when WebGL is not supported

- Built-in vector and matrix operators

- API wrapper implementation of cameras, lights, materials, shaders, objects, and common geometries

- Import and export utilities

- Good documentation and examples

Setup

We will now go over how to obtain the Three.js library code, its directory structure, and core objects.

Obtaining the Library

The Three.js project is hosted on github at `https://github.com/mrdoob/three.js`. The latest release can be downloaded from `https://github.com/mrdoob/three.js/downloads`. Or if you are familiar with git, you can clone the repository:

`git clone https://github.com/mrdoob/three.js.git`.

The library is under active development, and changes to the API are not uncommon. The latest complete API documentation can be found at the URL `mrdoob.github.com/three.js/docs/latest/`, which will redirect to the current version. There is a wiki page at `https://github.com/mrdoob/three.js/wiki/`, and there is no shortage of demos that use Three.js or articles about Three.js development on the Web. Some of the better articles are listed in Appendix D.

Directory Structure

Once you download or clone the repository, you can place the files within your active development folder. The directory structure shows the following folder layout:

```
/build      compressed versions of the source files
/docs       API documentation
/examples   examples
/gui        a drag-and-drop GUI builder that exports Three.js source
/src        source code, including the central Three.js file
/utils      utility scripts such as exporters
```

Within the `src` directory, components are split up nicely into the following subfolders:

```
/src
    /cameras        camera objects
    /core           core functionality such as color, vertex, face, vector, matrix, math
                    definitions, and so on
    /extra          utilities, helper methods, built-in effects, functionality, and plugins
    /lights         light objects
    /materials      mesh and particle material objects such as Lambert and Phong
    /objects        physical objects
```

```
/renderers      render mode objects
/scenes         scene graph object and fog functions
/textures       texture object
Three.js        central file
```

Basic Elements

There are several core object types in Three.js (see Table 7-1).

Table 7-1. *Core Objects in Three.js*

Base Object	Description
THREE.Renderer	The object that actually renders the scene. Implementations can be CanvasRenderer, DOMRenderer, SVGRenderer, or WebGLRenderer.
THREE.Scene	Scene graph that stores the objects and lights contained within a scene.
THREE.Camera	Virtual camera; can be PerspectiveCamera or OrthographicCamera.
THREE.Object3D	Many object types, including Mesh, Line, Particle, Bone and Sprite.
THREE.Light	Light model. Types can be AmbientLight, DirectionalLight, PointLight, or SpotLight

Two other notes about the object hierarchy: THREE.Mesh objects have an associated THREE.Geometry and THREE.Material objects, and in turn each THREE.Geometry contains THREE.Vertex and THREE.Face objects.

Basic Usage

Now that we have obtained the Three.js library, we are ready to start using it. We need to include the script, either from local sources, as follows:

```
<script src="./three.js/build/Three.js"></script>
```

Or remotely—from github, for example:

```
<script src="https://raw.github.com/mrdoob/three.js/master/build/Three.js"></script>
```

Hello World!

Using Three.js is very easy compared with the low-level coding that we have done so far. Having learned the base WebGL API calls already, though, we can fully appreciate the speedup of a framework while knowing (or at least presuming to know without actually checking the library code) what is going on underneath the surface Three.js API calls.

In our first example, shown in Figure 7-1, we will render an unlit rectangular cuboid in Three.js.

Figure 7-1. A rectangular cuboid rendered with Three.js. No light makes the cuboid appear flat

The full code of the example is fairly short compared with pure WebGL (see Listing 7-1). We will go into each section of the code in detail after the listing.

Listing 7-1. Rendering an unlit rectangular cuboid

```
<!doctype html>
<html>
      <head>
            <title>Three.js Cube Test</title>
            <style>
                  body{ background-color: grey; }
                  canvas{ background-color: white; }
            </style>
            <script src="./Three.js/build/Three.js"></script>
            <script>
                  var     CANVAS_WIDTH = 400,
                          CANVAS_HEIGHT= 300;

                  var     renderer = null,      //WebGL or 2D
                          scene = null,         //scene object
                          camera = null;        //camera object

                  function initWebGL()
                  {
                          setupRenderer();
                          setupScene();
                          setupCamera();

                          renderer.render(scene, camera);
                  }

                  function setupRenderer()
                  {
                          renderer = new THREE.WebGLRenderer();
                          renderer.setSize( CANVAS_WIDTH, CANVAS_HEIGHT );
```

```
                              //where to add the canvas element
                              document.body.appendChild( renderer.domElement );
                      }

                      function setupScene()
                      {
                              scene = new THREE.Scene();
                              addMesh();
                      }

                      function setupCamera()
                      {
                              camera = new THREE.PerspectiveCamera(
                                 35,                              // Field of view
                                 CANVAS_WIDTH / CANVAS_HEIGHT,    // Aspect ratio
                                 .1,                             // Near clip plane
                                 10000                           // Far clip plane
                              );
                              camera.position.set( -15, 10, 10 );
                              camera.lookAt( scene.position );
                              scene.add( camera );
                      }

                      function addMesh()
                      {
                              var cube = new THREE.Mesh(
                                      new THREE.CubeGeometry( 5, 7, 5 ),
                                      new THREE.MeshBasicMaterial( { color: 0x0000FF } )
                              );
                              scene.add(cube);
                      }
              </script>
       </head>
       <body onload="initWebGL()"></body>

</html>
```

The code in Listing 7-1 is very straightforward. When scanning the listing, notice that we have not written vertex or fragment shaders or included a < canvas > tag. The shaders have been written for us by the library when the code is rendered and are based on our scene and camera setup. We will show later in the chapter how to specify shaders if needed.

Going through Listing 7-1, the first thing we do is add variables that will be used to set the size of our canvas and hold Three.js WebGLRenderer, Scene, and PerspectiveCamera objects:

```
var    CANVAS_WIDTH = 400,
       CANVAS_HEIGHT = 300;

var    renderer = null,     //WebGL or 2D
       scene = null,        //scene object
       camera = null;       //camera object
```

Then, as with low-level WebGL, we have an onload event. In Listing 7-1, the onload event calls the initWebGL function:

```
function initWebGL()
{
        setupRenderer();
        setupScene();
        setupCamera();

        renderer.render(scene, camera);
}
```

The names of the function give hints that we are going to set up a WebGLRenderer object, a Scene object, and a Camera object; and then run the renderer with our scene and camera objects. Each of the setup function calls are small and straightforward, starting with setupRenderer:

```
function setupRenderer()
{
        renderer = new THREE.WebGLRenderer();
        renderer.setSize( CANVAS_WIDTH, CANVAS_HEIGHT );

        //where to add the canvas element
        document.body.appendChild( renderer.domElement );
}
```

We choose the WebGLRenderer object as our renderer type and create a new instance of it. Then we set the renderer size to our canvas dimensions and attach the domElement of the renderer (a < canvas > element) to our document < body > tag.

Next we call setupScene:

```
function setupScene()
{
        scene = new THREE.Scene();
        addMesh();
}
```

We create a new Scene object that will store objects such as meshes and lighting. The addMesh function is this:

```
function addMesh()
{
        var cube = new THREE.Mesh(
                new THREE.CubeGeometry( 5, 7, 5 ),
                new THREE.MeshBasicMaterial( { color: 0x0000FF } )
        );
        scene.add(cube);
}
```

In this example, we create a cuboid mesh of dimensions 5x7x5. We create a MeshBasicMaterial object with color property set to blue and do not add any lighting. Cuboid faces are not distinct in the rendering of Figure 7-1 because each face is the same color, and no lighting means that no normal vectors are used. Finally, in the addMesh function, we add this mesh to our scene object.

The setupCamera method creates and sets up a PerspectiveCamera object:

```
function setupCamera()
{
        camera = new THREE.PerspectiveCamera(
                45,                            // Field of view
                CANVAS_WIDTH / CANVAS_HEIGHT,  // Aspect ratio
```

```
            .1,                        // Near clip plane
            10000                      // Far clip plane
        );
        camera.position.set( 10, 10, 10 );
        camera.lookAt( scene.position );
        scene.add( camera );
}
```

We position our camera and tell it which direction to look. Then we add the camera object to the scene.

■ **Note** There is an equivalent orthogonal camera API call: THREE.OrthogonalCamera(float left, float right, float top, float bottom, float near, float far). Recall that an orthogonal camera is useful if we want objects with same-sized dimensions to appear the same size regardless of their distances within a scene.

Lastly we have the call:

```
renderer.render(scene, camera);
```

This call will render the scene using the scene graph object, which contains all the physical objects in the scene along and with the virtual camera object. The renderer object takes care of context handling and drawing to the underlying canvas element.

Let's examine all the details in Listing 7-1 that have been abstracted:

- No vertex points were specified; just the dimensions of the cuboid.

- The modelview or perspective matrices were not explicitly set. The PerspectiveCamera position and lookAt functions, along with the scene.position vector, were used to calculate them and pass along to the shaders for us.

- The shader pair in this example is completely computed for us.

- The < canvas > element is automatically added to our document.

- No vertex buffer objects or draw call is made by us. Which is used: drawArrays or drawElements? We cannot tell without looking at the source code of the library.

These are some nice abstractions for a basic scene to help an absolute beginner get started with three-dimensional animation. For more complex scenes, the amount of abstraction is even greater and can further increase productivity. Having a knowledge of the underlying workings of WebGL as we now do is also great because it allows us to understand the library code to help us troubleshoot when things do not work as expected.

Adding Some Details

We will now look at adjusting color, lighting, and mesh objects with Three.js.

Color

In Three.js, colors are initialized with hex values, which look similar to CSS but are numeric values prefixed with 0x instead of a hash (#) tag. So pure red would be 0xFF0000, and we would create a new red Color object with:

```
var myColor = new THREE.Color( 0xff0000 );
```

After initialization, color components are converted to RGB values between 0 and 1, and are available as the object properties r, g, and b. If you want to set the color component-wise yourself, you can use the function setRGB. To change the color to blue looks like this:

```
myColor.setRGB(0.0, 1.0, 0.0);
```

The Clear Color

To set the clear color in Three.js, we use the renderer method setClearColor or setClearColorHex:

```
var alpha = 1.0;
renderer.setClearColor(myColor, alpha);
```

Or equivalently:

```
renderer.setClearColorHex(0x00ff00, 1.0);
```

■ **Note**   We can also specify the clear color in the WebGLRenderer constructor, along with other options. The default properties are shown here:

```
new THREE.WebGLRenderer({
    antialias: false,
    canvas: document.createElement( 'canvas' ),
    clearColor: 0x000000,
    clearAlpha: 0,
    maxLights: 4,
    stencil: true,
    preserveDrawingBuffer: false
});
```

When setting the clearColor in this manner, make sure to also set the clearAlpha to a nonzero value, such as this:

```
renderer = new THREE.WebGLRenderer( { clearColor: 0x007700, clearAlpha: 1 } );
```

Lighting

We will now add a light to our scene by adjusting setupScene and addMesh and adding a new method called addLight, which is shown in Listing 7-2. Changes are shown in bold.

Listing 7-2. Adding a light to the scene

```
function setupScene()
{
        scene = new THREE.Scene();
        addMesh();
        addLight();
}
```

```
function addMesh()
{
        var cube = new THREE.Mesh(
                        new THREE.CubeGeometry( 5, 7, 5 ),
                        new THREE.MeshLambertMaterial( { color: 0x0000FF } )
                );
        scene.add(cube);
}

function addLight()
{
        var light = new THREE.PointLight( 0xFFFFFF );
        light.position.set( 20, 20, 20 );
        scene.add(light);
}
```

The result of our code modifications can be seen in Figure 7-2 and are in the 07/basic_lighting.html file. In the addLight method of Listing 7-2 it takes only three lines of code to add a point light, specify the color and location of the light, and add it to our scene. It only takes changing the type of our Mesh material from MeshBasicMaterial to MeshLambertMaterial to use the Lambert shading model that was discussed in Chapter 4. We still have not needed to adjust the shader code.

Figure 7-2. *Cuboid with clear color set to gray and a light that makes the 3D shape visible*

So far, we have used only the built-in CubeGeometry object. We will now cover the Geometry and Mesh objects in more detail.

Meshes

The basic THREE.Mesh object extends THREE.Object3D and stores a Geometry object and a Material object (among other things):

var myMesh = new THREE.Mesh(*geometry, material*);

As shown in Listing 7-1 and Listing 7-2, the material can be a Lambert model and created like this:

var material = new THREE.MeshLambertMaterial({ color: 0x0000FF });

Preset geometry objects can be found in the /src/extras/geometries folder similar to the one we have used so far: CubeGeometry. If you look at the TorusGeometry.js source, the function signature is:

```
THREE.TorusGeometry = function ( radius, tube, segmentsR, segmentsT, arc ){ … }
```

To render a torus, we simply change the Geometry object in the addMesh code of Listing 7-2 to this:

```
function addMesh()
{
        var mesh = new THREE.Mesh(
                        new THREE.TorusGeometry( 4, 1.5, 20, 20 ),
                        new THREE.MeshLambertMaterial( { color: 0x0000FF } )
                );
        scene.add(mesh);
}
```

Figure 7-3 shows a torus geometry obtained by switching the Geometry object of a mesh.

Figure 7-3. *A torus geometry rendered in Three.js*

Having existing geometries available is really nice. You do not need to understand or implement the math involved; someone has already done this for you! Each of these geometries extends the THREE.Geometry object found in /src/core/Geometry.js. In the base Geometry object are many properties such as vertices, colors, and faces along with built-in functionality such as computing normal vectors and bounding boxes, which are useful for collision detection.

Smooth shading is the default shading model, but we can also perform flat shading and show wireframe models very easily, as shown in Figure 7-4. To perform flat shading we adjust the material properties like so:

```
new THREE.MeshLambertMaterial( {
        color: 0x0000FF,
        shading: THREE.FlatShading
} )
```

Similarly to show the wireframe, we adjust the material properties to:

```
new THREE.MeshLambertMaterial( {
        color: 0x0000FF,
        wireframe: true
} )
```

On the left of Figure 7-4 is a flat shaded torus geometry; the wireframe of a torus is displayed on the right.

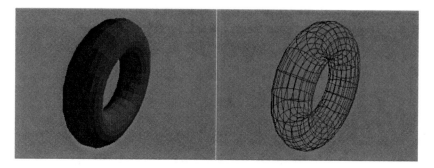

Figure 7-4. Left: flat shading; right: wireframe

Three.js caches values for performance improvements. If you change a Geometry object's properties, you need to inform Three.js to use the new values as we will now discuss.

Updating Objects

In Three.js, some values are updated automatically when adjusted, such as matrix transforms and cameras. However, for performance some values are not automatically updated. Instead you need to set a flag telling Three.js that the object needs updating.

For a Geometry object, update flag properties are verticesNeedUpdate, elementsNeedUpdate, morphTargetsNeedUpdate, uvsNeedUpdate, normalsNeedUpdate, colorsNeedUpdate, and tangentsNeedUpdate. For instance, you would tell Three.js that the normal vectors have been changed on an object named geometry by setting the normalsNeedUpdate flag with this:

geometry.normalsNeedUpdate ;

Meshes also need their dynamic flag set:

geometry.dynamic = true;

Other objects such as textures may require flags as well. To update a texture you would set this:

texture.needsUpdate = true;

Complete details of how to update Three.js objects are available at https://github.com/mrdoob/Three.js/wiki/Updates.

Falling Back to the 2D Canvas Context

One of the really nice things about Three.js is the ability to fall back to the 2D canvas context if WebGL is not supported. We can do this with the new code shown in bold text in Listing 7-3.

Listing 7-3. Testing for WebGL support and falling back to the 2D canvas context if needed

```
function setupRenderer()
{
        var test_canvas = document.createElement('canvas');
        var gl = null;
        try{
```

```
                   gl = (  test_canvas.getContext("webgl") ||
                           test_canvas.getContext("experimental-webgl")
                     );
     }catch(e){
     }

     if(gl)
     {
             renderer = new THREE.WebGLRenderer();
             console.log('webgl!');
     }else{
             renderer = new THREE.CanvasRenderer();
             console.log('canvas');
     }
     test_canvas = undefined;

     renderer.setSize( CANVAS_WIDTH, CANVAS_HEIGHT );
     renderer.setClearColorHex(0x777777, 1.0);

     //where to add the canvas element
     document.body.appendChild( renderer.domElement );
}
```

This output of the code in Listing 7-3 run in two browsers, one with and one without WebGL support, is shown in Figure 7-5. The images are not identical, but compared to not rendering anything, this ability to fall back with no code alterations other than that of Listing 7-3 is fantastic! It provides graceful degradation for users who do not have a browser with WebGL capabilities.

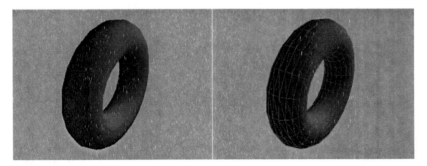

Figure 7-5. *Left: browser supporting WebGL; right: falling back to canvas context*

Shaders

To use shaders in Three.js, set the object material to be of type ShaderMaterial, where vs_source and fs_source are loaded sources from either embedded code or external files:

```
var material=new THREE.ShaderMaterial({
        vertexShader: vs_source,
        fragmentShader: fs_source
});
```

In addition, the constructor takes other optional parameters such as attributes and uniforms, which we will examine later on in the chapter.

Revisiting Earlier Book Code

We will now reproduce some of the earlier examples of the book using Three.js so that an adequate comparison can be made in terms of using a framework versus lower-level API usage. Along the way, we will uncover new Three.js API functions and configuration parameters, so porting our existing code is a great way to get our feet wet in a new API.

2D Rendering

Remember the "bowtie" two-triangle example of Chapter 1 (Figure 1-4)? Let's reproduce it with Three.js. At this point, we have used only built-in meshes, but we do not know how to create a custom mesh, even a simple one, with Three.js.

Custom Mesh

To build a custom mesh, we first create a new Geometry object. Then we create Vector3 objects for each vertice and add them to the Geometry object's vertices property array. We then add vertice triplets to the faces array property of the Geometry object. Finally, we add our Geometry object to a new Mesh object. This is shown in Listing 7-4.

Listing 7-4. Creating a custom mesh with Three.js

```
function addMesh()
{
        var triangleVertices = [
                //left triangle
                -0.5, 0.5, 0.0,
                 0.0, 0.0, 0.0,
                -0.5, -0.5, 0.0,

                //right triangle
                0.5, 0.5, 0.0,
                0.0, 0.0, 0.0,
                0.5, -0.5, 0.0
        ];

        var geometry = new THREE.Geometry();
        for(var i=0; i<triangleVertices.length; i += 3)
        {
                var vertex = new THREE.Vector3(
                                triangleVertices[i],
                                triangleVertices[i + 1],
                                triangleVertices[i + 2]
                                );
                geometry.vertices.push(vertex);
        }
```

```
geometry.faces.push( new THREE.Face3(0, 1, 2) );
geometry.faces.push( new THREE.Face3(3, 4, 5) );

var mesh = new THREE.Mesh(
        geometry,
        new THREE.MeshBasicMaterial( { color: 0xFFFFFF } )
);

scene.add(mesh);
}
```

Now when we run the code, we produce the image on the left of Figure 7-6. Only one triangle is rendered. This is because the winding order is opposite in our triangles. To fix this, we have two options. First, we can render both sides of the mesh:

```
mesh.doubleSided = true;
```

However, this is a performance hit and we do not want to get into the habit of doing this. The other option is to fix the winding order of the second face:

```
geometry.faces.push( new THREE.Face3(3, 5, 4) );
```

After this adjustment, we get the image on the right of Figure 7-6. The full code is in the file 07/bowtie.html. Notice that even though we have specified the vertex data, we are not responsible to bind it to a VBO.

Figure 7-6. *Left: triangle faces with opposite winding order, only one is visible; right: triangle faces with the same winding order*

Separate Vertex Colors

To have separate colors per vertex, we need to assign them to the geometry.faces[n].vertexColors attributes and NOT the geometry.colors attribute. The geometry.colors attribute is used for other objects such as particles, but not for meshes. Instead of setting the color property of our mesh material, we now set the vertexColors property:

```
new THREE.MeshBasicMaterial(
{
        vertexColors: THREE.VertexColors
```

▓ **Note**   If we do not need per vertex coloring, we can also set the color of each face with geometry.faces[n]. color and using vertexColors: THREE.FaceColors in our Material setup.

186

Changing the addMesh code to that in Listing 7-5 will produce the same colored output as in Figure 1-8. A working example can be found in the 07/bowtie_color.html file.

Listing 7-5. Per vertex color values

```
function addMesh()
{
        var triangleVertices = [
                //left triangle
                -0.5, 0.5, 0.0,
                 0.0, 0.0, 0.0,
                -0.5, -0.5, 0.0,

                //right triangle
                0.5, 0.5, 0.0,
                0.0, 0.0, 0.0,
                0.5, -0.5, 0.0
        ];
        var triangleVerticeColors = [
                //left triangle
                1.0, 0.0, 0.0,
                1.0, 1.0, 1.0,
                1.0, 0.0, 0.0,

                //right triangle
                0.0, 0.0, 1.0,
                0.0, 0.0, 1.0,          //these two colors are switched
                1.0, 1.0, 1.0,          //from the chapter 1 example as the
                                        //vertice order is changed here
        ];
        var geometry = new THREE.Geometry();
        var colors = [];

        for(var i=0; i<triangleVertices.length; i += 3)
        {
                var vertex = new THREE.Vector3();
                vertex.set(
                                triangleVertices[i],
                                triangleVertices[i + 1],
                                triangleVertices[i + 2]
                        );
                geometry.vertices.push(vertex);

                var color = new THREE.Color();
                color.setRGB(
                        triangleVerticeColors[i],
                        triangleVerticeColors[i + 1],
                        triangleVerticeColors[i + 2]              );
                colors.push(color);
        }
```

```
        geometry.faces.push( new THREE.Face3(0, 1, 2) );
        geometry.faces.push( new THREE.Face3(3, 5, 4) );

        var f = 0;
        for(var i=0; i < colors.length; i+=3)
        {
                geometry.faces[f].vertexColors.push(colors[i]);
                geometry.faces[f].vertexColors.push(colors[i+1]);
                geometry.faces[f].vertexColors.push(colors[i+2]);
                ++f;
        }

        var mesh = new THREE.Mesh(
                geometry,
                new THREE.MeshBasicMaterial(
                        {
                          vertexColors: THREE.VertexColors
                        }
                    )
        );
        scene.add(mesh);
}
```

The next component of Chapter 1's bowtie example was adding movement, which we will now cover with Three.js.

Movement

We will now move our two triangles, as we did in the first chapter. We do this a little differently from how we did in Listing 1-9. First, we will make the geometry, mesh, and triangleVertices that were local variables in Listing 7-5 globally available:

```
var     mesh = null,
        geometry = null,
        triangleVertices = [],
        angle = 0;
```

We also have added a variable to keep track of an angle. To animate the scene, we can use the same animation loop using the renderAnimationFrame polyfill that we discussed in Chapter 1 and have been using since. However, Three.js includes the polyfill, so we do not need to include an extra file just for it:

```
function initWebGL()
{
        setupRenderer();
        setupScene();
        setupCamera();

        (function animLoop(){
                updateGeometry();
                renderer.render(scene, camera);
                requestAnimationFrame( animLoop );
        })();
}
```

In our addMesh method of Listing 7-5, we need to add this line:

```
geometry.dynamic = true;
```

This informs Three.js that properties of the geometry will change. Lastly, we define the `updateGeometry` function, which controls how the vertices change:

```
function updateGeometry()
{
        var x_translation = Math.sin(angle)/2.0;

        for (var i = 0; i < geometry.vertices.length; i++) {
                geometry.vertices[i].x = triangleVertices[i*3] + x_translation;
        }

        angle += 0.01;
        geometry.verticesNeedUpdate = true;
}
```

The preceding code loops through each vertex and adjusts the x component to its original value from the `triangleVertices` array plus a translation amount. We will look at a simpler way to move an entire mesh in the next example. To see movement, it is essential that we tell Three.js that the vertices need to be updated with this line:

```
geometry.verticesNeedUpdate = true;
```

The Triangular Prism

Our next code revisits producing the triangular prism shown in Figure 1-16 and found in the file 01/triangular_prism_depth_test.html. Our array data is the same as in Listing 1-11, and we will not relist it here. The rest of the addMesh method for a triangular prism is shown in Listing 7-6.

Listing 7-6. Add mesh function for triangular prism

```
function addMesh()
{

        var triangleVertices,         //same as in Listing 1-11
          triangleVerticeColors,      //same as in Listing 1-11
          triangleVertexIndices;      //same as in Listing 1-11
        ...

        var colors = [];

        for(var i=0; i<triangleVertexIndices.length; i += 3)
        {
                var vertex = new THREE.Vector3();
                var color = new THREE.Color();
                vertex.set(
                        triangleVertices[i],
                        triangleVertices[i + 1],
                        triangleVertices[i + 2]
                );
                geometry.vertices.push(vertex);

                color.setRGB(
                        triangleVerticeColors[i],
```

```
                        triangleVerticeColors[i + 1],
                        triangleVerticeColors[i + 2]
                );
                colors.push(color);
        }
        for(var i=0; i<triangleVertexIndices.length; i += 3)
        {
                geometry.faces.push( new THREE.Face3(
                        triangleVertexIndices[i],
                        triangleVertexIndices[i + 1],
                        triangleVertexIndices[i + 2]
                ) );
        }

        var f = 0;
        for(var i=0; i<triangleVertexIndices.length; i +=3 )
        {
                geometry.faces[f].vertexColors.push(colors[triangleVertexIndices[i]]);
                geometry.faces[f].vertexColors.push(colors[triangleVertexIndices[i + 1]]);
                geometry.faces[f].vertexColors.push(colors[triangleVertexIndices[i + 2]]);
                ++f;
        }

        geometry.dynamic = true;

        mesh = new THREE.Mesh(
                geometry,
                new THREE.MeshBasicMaterial(
                        {
                          vertexColors: THREE.VertexColors
                        }
                )
        );
        mesh.doubleSided = true;

        scene.add(mesh);
}
```

The code in Listing 7-6 generates our vertices, faces, and vertexColors properties of our geometry. We also set the mesh to doubleSided for this example instead of making the winding consistent. To rotate and translate the mesh, we will act directly on the Mesh object instead of each vertice property, as we did in the previous example:

```
function initWebGL()
{
        setupRenderer();
        setupScene();
        setupCamera();

        var original_mesh_x = mesh.position.x;

        (function animLoop(){
                //rotate mesh round y-axis
                mesh.position.x = original_mesh_x + 2.0*Math.cos(angle);
                mesh.rotation.y = angle;
                angle += 0.05;
```

```
        renderer.render(scene, camera);
        requestAnimationFrame( animLoop );
    })();
}
```

The key to this technique is storing the original x position. A working implementation can be found in the 07/triangular_prism.html file.

Texturing

Our next example will texture the triangular prism as we did in Chapter 3, in the 03/multitexture.html file. Some of the built-in geometries will automatically calculate default texture coordinates. This is not the case for our custom mesh, but we will now go over how to assign custom coordinates.

First, we load our textures:

```
var     texture = [],
        textureImage = [],
        STONE_TEXTURE = 0,
        WEBGL_LOGO_TEXTURE = 1;
...
setupTexture();
...
function setupTexture()
{
        texture[STONE_TEXTURE] = THREE.ImageUtils.loadTexture(
                            "textures/stone-128px.jpg");
        texture[WEBGL_LOGO_TEXTURE] = THREE.ImageUtils.loadTexture(
                            "textures/webgl_logo-512px.png");

        for(var i=0; i<texture.length;++i)
        {
                texture[i].wrapT = texture[i].wrapS = THREE.RepeatWrapping;
                texture[i].needsUpdate = true;
        }
}
```

▥ **Note** We need to ensure that THREE.ImageUtils.loadTexture() finishes before our scene is rendered. We show a couple approaches to guarantee this later in the chapter.

And now we will set our per vertex texture coordinates, which are stored as an array in the geometry's faceVertexUvs property:

```
function addMesh()
{
        ...
        var uvs = [];
        for(var i=0; i<triangleVertexIndices.length; i += 3)
        {
                var vertex = new THREE.Vector3();
                var color = new THREE.Color();
                vertex.set(
```

```
                              triangleVertices[i],
                              triangleVertices[i + 1],
                              triangleVertices[i + 2]
                    );
            geometry.vertices.push(vertex);

            var tex = [];
            for(var j=0; j<3;++j)
            {
                    var a = triangleVertexIndices[i+j];
                    var s = null,
                        t = null;

                    if(i >= 24)
                    {
                            s = triangleVertices[a*3 + 1];
                            t = triangleVertices[a*3 + 2];
                    }else{
                            s = triangleVertices[a*3];
                            t = triangleVertices[a*3 + 1];
                    }
                    s = (s+2.0) * .25;
                    t = (t+2.0) * .25;
                    tex.push(new THREE.UV(s, t));
            }
            uvs.push(tex);

            color.setRGB(
                    triangleVerticeColors[i],
                    triangleVerticeColors[i + 1],
                    triangleVerticeColors[i + 2]
            );
            colors.push(color);
    }

    ...

    geometry.faceVertexUvs = [];
    for(var z=0;z<uvs.length;z++){
            geometry.faceVertexUvs.push(uvs);
    }

    ...

    mesh = new THREE.Mesh(
            geometry,
            new THREE.MeshBasicMaterial(
                            {
                               map: texture[STONE_TEXTURE]
                            }
                    )
    );

    mesh.doubleSided = true;
    scene.add(mesh);
}
```

The preceding code applies the stone texture, and the example can be run from the `07/triangular_prism_textured.html` file.

How do we use two textures, one as a decal as we did in Chapter 3? To accomplish this, we will have to do our only shader coding with Three.js in this chapter, using the `ShaderMaterial` object.

ShaderMaterial

As mentioned earlier, the `ShaderMaterial` requires vertex and fragment shader sources. We also can provide `uniform` and `attribute` values. Three.js automatically sets many mesh properties such as vertex position and texture coordinates assigned as program attributes from our object properties. In addition, the model view and perspective uniforms are also assigned. This is nice, but may appear a little magical as well.

To decal a texture on top of another texture, as we did in the `03/multitexture.html` file, we first assign variables for our uniforms and shader material:

```
var     uniforms = null,
        shaderMaterial = null;
```

Next we adjust our addMesh method:

```
function addMesh()
{
        ...
        setupShaderMaterial();
        mesh = new THREE.Mesh(
                geometry,
                shaderMaterial
        );

        mesh.doubleSided = true;
        scene.add(mesh);
}
```

The `setupShaderMaterial` method is shown in Listing 7-7. In the method we set our textures as uniform variables. The type parameter represents the variable type: texture, int, float, and so on. Then we load our sources with Ajax (again, this could be embedded sources instead) and then create and store a new `ShaderMaterial` object.

Listing 7-7. Using a ShaderMaterial

```
function setupShaderMaterial()
{
        uniforms = {
                uSampler: { type: "t", value: 0, texture: texture[STONE_TEXTURE] },
                uSampler2: { type: "t", value: 1, texture: texture[WEBGL_LOGO_TEXTURE] }
        };

        var     vs_source = null,
                fs_source = null;

        //get shader sources with jQuery Ajax

        $.ajax({
            async: false,
            url: './multitexture.vs',
            success: function (data) {
```

```
            vs_source = data.firstChild.textContent;
        },
        dataType: 'xml'
    });

    $.ajax({
        async: false,
        url: './multitexture.fs',
        success: function (data) {
            fs_source = data.firstChild.textContent;
        },
        dataType: 'xml'
    });

    shaderMaterial = new THREE.ShaderMaterial( {
            uniforms: uniforms,
            vertexShader: vs_source,
            fragmentShader: fs_source
    } );

}
```

We define our shaders, which are different from the ones written in Chapter 3. The shader program pair is shorter now and uses some "magically set" attributes and uniforms in Listing 7-8.

Listing 7-8. A Three.js shader program for two textures

```
<script type="x-shader/x-vertex">
        varying highp vec2 vTextureCoord;

        void main(void) {
                gl_Position = projectionMatrix * modelViewMatrix * vec4(position, 1.0);
                vTextureCoord = uv;
        }
</script>

<script id="shader-fs" type="x-shader/x-fragment">
        varying highp vec2 vTextureCoord;
        uniform sampler2D uSampler;
        uniform sampler2D uSampler2;

        void main(void) {
                highp vec4 stoneColor = texture2D(uSampler, vec2(vTextureCoord.st));
                highp vec4 webglLogoColor = texture2D(uSampler2, vec2(vTextureCoord.st));
                gl_FragColor = mix(stoneColor, webglLogoColor, webglLogoColor.a);
        }
</script>
```

In Listing 7-8, the `projectionMatrix` and `modelViewMatrix` variables are uniforms passed in from Three.js for our projection and model view transforms. The vertex positions values are passed in as the `position` variable attribute.

▓ **Note** It is important to realize that Listing 7-8 is not a valid shader program on its own. These sources are not passed directly to the `shaderSource`, and `compileShader` WebGL methods. Instead, behind the scenes, Three. js checks for set values and inserts attributes and uniforms into the shader source before finalizing the source and compiling it. You can observe this by viewing the source of your browser and demonstrated in Figures 7-7 and 7-8. Then Three.js attaches and links the shader program and selects to use it as we manually do in other book chapters.

Part of the vertex shader produced is shown in Figure 7-7.

```glsl
uniform mat4 viewMatrix;
uniform mat3 normalMatrix;
uniform vec3 cameraPosition;
attribute vec3 position;
attribute vec3 normal;
attribute vec2 uv;
attribute vec2 uv2;
#ifdef USE_COLOR
attribute vec3 color;
#endif
#ifdef USE_MORPHTARGETS
attribute vec3 morphTarget0;
attribute vec3 morphTarget1;
attribute vec3 morphTarget2;
attribute vec3 morphTarget3;
#ifdef USE_MORPHNORMALS
attribute vec3 morphNormal0;
attribute vec3 morphNormal1;
attribute vec3 morphNormal2;
attribute vec3 morphNormal3;
#else
attribute vec3 morphTarget4;
attribute vec3 morphTarget5;
attribute vec3 morphTarget6;
attribute vec3 morphTarget7;
#endif
#endif
#ifdef USE_SKINNING
attribute vec4 skinVertexA;
attribute vec4 skinVertexB;
attribute vec4 skinIndex;
attribute vec4 skinWeight;
#endif

varying highp vec2 vTextureCoord;

void main(void) {
    gl_Position = projectionMatrix * modelViewMatrix * vec4(position, 1.0);
    vTextureCoord = uv;
}
```

Figure 7-7. Part of the final vertex shader produced by Three.js from the initial vertex shader in Listing 7-8

The full fragment shader generated code is shown in Figure 7-8. Compare the source code in these two figures with what we specify in Listing 7-8.

```
precision highp float;
#define MAX_DIR_LIGHTS 0
#define MAX_POINT_LIGHTS 0
#define MAX_SPOT_LIGHTS 0
#define MAX_SHADOWS 0

#define DOUBLE_SIDED

#define SHADOWMAP_SOFT


uniform mat4 viewMatrix;
uniform vec3 cameraPosition;

    varying highp vec2 vTextureCoord;
    uniform sampler2D uSampler;
    uniform sampler2D uSampler2;

    void main(void) {
        highp vec4 stoneColor = texture2D(uSampler, vec2(vTextureCoord.st));
        highp vec4 webglLogoColor = texture2D(uSampler2, vec2(vTextureCoord.st));
        gl_FragColor = mix(stoneColor, webglLogoColor, webglLogoColor.a);
    }
```

Figure 7-8. *Final fragment shader produced by Three.js from initial fragment shader in Listing 7-8*

Finally, we make setupTexture the document onload event now. In the setupTexture function, I have nested callbacks in the loadTexture function calls to ensure that the textures are loaded before initializing WebGL:

```
function setupTexture()
{
        texture[STONE_TEXTURE] = THREE.ImageUtils.loadTexture(
                "textures/stone-128px.jpg",
                {}, function() {
                texture[WEBGL_LOGO_TEXTURE] = THREE.ImageUtils.loadTexture(
                        "textures/webgl_logo-512px.png",
                        {}, function() {
                                for(var i=0; i<texture.length;++i)
                                {
                                        texture[i].wrapT = texture[i].wrapS =
                                                THREE.RepeatWrapping;
                                        texture[i].needsUpdate = true;
                                }
                                initWebGL();
                        }
                );
                }
        );
}
```

Obviously, if we had more than a couple of textures, this approach would be very hard to read, and an alternate code structure would be preferable. We will show an alternate code structure later in the chapter. The full code of this example can be found in the 07/triangular_prism_textured_decal.html file.

Lighting and Texturing

Our next example will be to re-create the three spheres and plane demonstrated in Chapter 4. We will use Phong lighting, blending, fog, and texturing. In this example, we do not use multiple textures per object and can accomplish everything without explicitly setting our shaders in Three.js. The final result is shown in Figure 7-9.

Figure 7-9. *Achieving a similar result to the examples in Chapter 4; this time with Three.js*

Here are the new variables that we will use in this example:

```
var     texture = [],
        STONE_TEXTURE = 0,
        GLASS_TEXTURE = 1,
        WATER_TEXTURE = 2,
        number_textures = 3,
        loaded_textures = 0,
        meshes = [],
        NUM_SPHERES = 3,
        PLANE_INDEX = 3;
```

To load our textures instead of nested callbacks, we now use the code in Listing 7-9. The advantage of it is that it is easier to read and adjust if we add more textures. Each time the callback is called, a global counter of loaded textures is incremented. When the expected number of textures loaded is reached, we call the initWebGL method.

Listing 7-9. Callback to adjust our loaded textures

```
function adjustLoadedTexture( tex )
{
        loaded_textures++;

        tex.wrapS = THREE.RepeatWrapping;
        tex.wrapT = THREE.RepeatWrapping;
        tex.needsUpdate = true;

        if( loaded_textures == number_textures )
```

```
        {
                initWebGL();
        }
}

function setupTexture()

{
        var texture_files = [
                "textures/stone-256px.jpg",
                "textures/glass-256px.jpg",
                "textures/water-256px.jpg"
        ];

        loaded_textures = 0;
        for(var i=0; i<texture_files.length;++i)
        {
                texture[i] = THREE.ImageUtils.loadTexture(
                        texture_files[i], {}, adjustLoadedTexture
                );
        }
}
```

▮ **Note**   The callback automatically passes the object returned from the `loadTexture` call as a parameter in the callback function, `adjustLoadedTexture`. Both of the following alternate function calls will not work:

```
texture[i] = THREE.ImageUtils.loadTexture(
        texture_files[i], {}, adjustLoadedTexture()
);
texture[i] = THREE.ImageUtils.loadTexture(
        texture_files[i], {}, adjustLoadedTexture( texture[i] )
);
```

To add fog to our scene, we do not need to implement this within a shader. We just assign a value to the `scene.fog` parameter by calling the method `THREE.FogExp2`:

```
  scene.fog=new THREE.FogExp2( 0x775555, 0.11 );
```

The second parameter is the density of the fog. FogExp2 is the exponent version of the fog equations that we discussed in Chapter 4. To perform the linear version, we would use `THREE.Fog(color, near, far)`.

Other interesting adjustments that we have made for this example are to change the material used:

```
var material = new THREE.MeshPhongMaterial(
                {       ambient: 0xffffff,
                        color: colors[i],
                        specular: 0x555555,
                        shininess: 30,
                        map: tex
                }
        );
```

In this declaration, tex is a texture object. We specify blending on one of the spheres with this:

```
if(i == 2)
{
        material.blending = THREE.AdditiveBlending;
        material.blendSrc = THREE.SrcAlphaFactor;
        material.blendDst = THREE.OneFactor;
        material.transparent = true;
        material.depthTest = false;
}
```

Lastly, we have added a few more lights:

```
function addLight()
{
        var ambientLight = new THREE.AmbientLight( 0x111111 );
        scene.add(ambientLight);

        var pointLight = new THREE.PointLight( 0xFFFFFF );
        pointLight.position.set( 0, 10, 0 );
        scene.add(pointLight);

        var directionalLight = new THREE.DirectionalLight( 0xFFFFFF );
        directionalLight.position.set( 1, 2, 1 ).normalize();
        scene.add( directionalLight );
}
```

The point and directional light can have attenuation and intensity variations as with the lighting models that we implemented in Chapter 4.

Particle System

For our last example of the chapter, we will produce a particle system with Three.js similar to the one we created in Chapter 6. The result of the code is shown in Figure 7-10.

Figure 7-10. *Particle system produced with Three.js*

Creating our particle system is similar to the way we implemented it in Chapter 6, except now we place our particles inside of a Geometry as shown in Listing 7-10. Remember that particles are usually represented as single points, and we can also use a texture image mapped onto each point.

Listing 7-10. Initializing particles

```
function setupParticles()
{
        particleGeometry = new THREE.Geometry(),
        particleMaterial =
                new THREE.ParticleBasicMaterial({
                color: 0xFFFFFF,
                size: (Math.random() + 1.0) * .25
        });

        //fill empty data to capacity
        for( var i=0; i<MAX_NUMBER_OF_PARTICLES; ++i )
        {
                particleGeometry.vertices.push( initializeParticle() );
        }
}

function initializeParticle()
{
        var particle = new THREE.Vector3(
                                .5 * Math.random() - .25,
                                START_Y,
                                3.0);

        //add extra data
        particle.age = 0;
        particle.original = new THREE.Vector3(particle.x, particle.y, particle.z);
        particle.velocity = new THREE.Vector3(
                        5.0 * Math.random() - 10.0,
                        12.0 * Math.random() + 14.0,
                        0.5 + Math.random() * 4.0); //velocity [x,y,z]
        }
        return particle;
}
```

Next we set up a particle system that is basically a wrapper for a mesh and material:

```
//particle system
particleSystem = new THREE.ParticleSystem(
                        particleGeometry,
                        particleMaterial
                );
scene.add(particleSystem);
```

■ **Note**   The object THREE.Particle also exists, but is used for CanvasRenderer, whereas THREE.ParticleSystem is used for the WebGLRenderer.

Finally, we adjust the particles during each iteration of the render loop, as shown in Listing 7-11.

Listing 7-11. Updating particles in the render loop

```
function adjustParticles(){
        var particles_old = particleGeometry.vertices.slice(); //copy
        particleGeometry.vertices = [];
        for( var i=0; i<particles_old.length; ++i )
        {
                //remove old particles
                //if past lifespan or below the start position, do not readd particle
                if(     ( particles_old[i].age < LIFESPAN ) &&
                        ( particles_old[i].y > (START_Y - 0.001) )
                  )
                {
                        particles_old[i].age += 1.0; //age
                        var pTime = particles_old[i].age/100.0;
                        particles_old[i].x = particles_old[i].original.x
                                        + particles_old[i].velocity.x * pTime;
                        particles_old[i].y = particles_old[i].original.y
                                        + particles_old[i].velocity.y * pTime
                                        - 4.9 * pTime * pTime;
                        particleGeometry.vertices =
                        particleGeometry.vertices.concat(particles_old[i]);
                }
        }

        currentNumberParticles = particleGeometry.vertices.length;

        //spawn new particles
        if( currentNumberParticles + MAX_SPAWN_PER_FRAME < MAX_NUMBER_OF_PARTICLES )
        {
                for( var n=0; n<MAX_SPAWN_PER_FRAME; ++n )
                {
                        var particle = initializeParticle();

                        particleGeometry.vertices.push(particle);
                        ++currentNumberParticles;
                }
        }
        particleGeometry.verticesNeedUpdate = true;
}
```

The working example can be found in the file 07/particle_system.html.

Advanced Usage

There are many advanced built-in functions and algorithms in the Three.js library and currently more than 150 included examples that demonstrate usage. We cannot cover them in this book, but I encourage you to explore the API, examples, and source code of the library.

Import/Export

Files to import mesh files are available in the /src/loaders and /src/extra/loaders directories while files to export are in the /utils/exporters directory. We will show how to import a mesh which is converted to a JSON format specifically for Three.js in the next chapter.

tQuery

A promising looking project in development is called tQuery, which stands for: **Three.js** + **jQuery**. This library is written by Jerome Eteinne, who also writes the blog http://learningthreejs.com. tQuery is a thin wrapper on top of the Three.js library, which mimics jQuery chainability and can produce scenes with even less boilerplate code to get up and running than using Three.js alone. The project is available on gitHub at https://github.com/jeromeetienne/tquery.

The following code with tQuery produces the cylinder in Figure 7-11:

```
<!doctype html>
<html>
        <head>
                <title>tQuery Cylinder Example</title>
                <script
src="https://raw.github.com/jeromeetienne/tquery/master/build/tquery-all.js">
                </script>
        </head>
        <body>
                <script>
                        var world = tQuery.createWorld().boilerplate().start();
                        var object = tQuery.createCylinder().addTo(world);
                </script>
        </body>

</html>
```

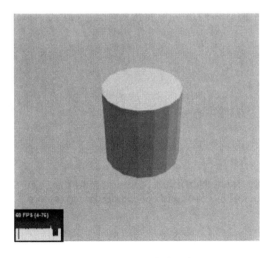

Figure 7-11. *Cylinder modelled with tQuery*

Of course, the previous example above is fairly stock, and the amount of flexibility that tQuery offers to customize meshes and scene details is very important.

Summary

This chapter showed the great power that a framework like Three.js combined with existing WebGL API knowledge can provide and how quickly we can develop code by using one.

In the next chapter, we will survey other WebGL frameworks and physics libraries. We will also show how to find and use existing mesh, shader and texture resources.

CHAPTER 8

▪ ▪ ▪

Productivity Tools

In the previous chapter we looked at the excellent Three.js WebGL framework and showed how it abstracts lower-level WebGL API calls. This abstraction simplifies and expedites development. This chapter introduces additional tools that can help your development be productive and enjoyable. Topics that we will cover in this chapter are the following:

- The merits of using a WebGL framework and the benefits of learning core WebGL
- Currently available frameworks
- Basic "Hello World" philoGL and GLGE framework examples
- Loading existing meshes and models
- File formats and import/export tools
- Finding and modifying existing shaders and textures
- JavaScript physics frameworks
- A physics demo using the physi.js library with Three.js

Frameworks

A framework abstracts lower-level API calls and also extends built-in functionality. WebGL frameworks get you started with less initial setup and boilerplate code. This makes it quicker to start programming and easier to develop complex applications. Frameworks can abstract vertex buffer object (VBO) and shader handling, ease camera manipulation, perform matrix math operations, and load meshes—among other things.

The trade-off of using a framework is that the abstraction of the lower-level details can limit configurability and performance (without hacking the framework source code). Usually, though, the amount of time savings outweighs what is lost in configurability.

However, it is beneficial not to get attached to any one framework and learn the basic WebGL API first. The rationale for this is that knowing how core WebGL works should enable switching between frameworks fairly easily. *The opposite is not true.* If you learn a framework first (no matter how good it is) and then need to use the base WebGL API or switch frameworks, you could be quite lost. Furthermore, if you understand core WebGL and want to understand a particular frameworks' nuances, you can view the source code and see and understand the basic WebGL API calls.

Many Choices

There are many, many frameworks available for WebGL. At present there are twenty five frameworks available according to `http://www.khronos.org/webgl/wiki/User_Contributions`. Which one(s) should you use?

To stand out in the crowd, several frameworks are built to provide specific niche usage such as general usage, game development, data visualization, globes and maps, and high performance. Apart from different focuses, what other factors determine which framework to use? Well as with other software projects, here are some criteria to evaluate:

- **Power and function**: It works and allows you to quickly create scenes that use advanced techniques. The code is well written and extendable, crashes infrequently, and does not have many critical bugs.

- **Usability**: Clear API and good documentation, wiki, FAQ, and so on.

- **Support and activity**: The author(s) and community are actively involved. Bug fixes are fairly quick, and new feature requests are being made (the code base is not stalled indefinitely). Some questions to ask are these: How many commits have been made to the project? How many contributors? How long has the project been around? When was the last commit? Release? Stable release? Is there a forum or user group?

- **Popularity**: This applies more to the low and high end of the spectrum. If no one uses something, it is hard to get support for a library. There is also more of a chance that the framework will become defunct and abandoned. On the flip side, if something is widely popular, resources are easy to come by and you can be sure that the framework will have a bright future.

- **Personal preference**: You just like it better. When all other things are near equal, your own gut preference is important.

One place to compare some project metrics for activity is at `https://www.ohloh.net/p/compare`, where you can compare statistics for up to three projects at once.

Available Frameworks

Here I present a selection of several of the most promising-looking frameworks (to me), with a synopsis and website locations. Afterward, we will give a basic "Hello World!" example with two of the frameworks: GLGE and philoGL.

▓ **Note**   I do not see much value in listing all the current frameworks because many lack the necessary criteria specified previously (support, features, users) that are needed for longevity. Displaying them all will only muddy the waters when trying to choose one to use. This list contains some of the top frameworks at the time of writing. The list is somewhat subjective, so I do apologize if I have omitted a framework that you feel is worthy.

C3DL

C3DL stands for **C**anvas **3D** **L**ibrary. The library is intended for providing "a set of math, scene, and 3d object classes that makes WebGL more accessible for developers that want to develop 3D content in browser but do not want to have to deal in depth with the 3D math needed to make it work."

The C3DL webpage has several tutorials and good documentation. You can find it here: `http://www.c3dl.org/`

CopperLicht

CopperLicht can be used for 3D applications and games. Features include fast rendering, a world editor, and importing of many model formats. You can find out more about it here:
`http://www.ambiera.com/copperlicht/index.html`

GLGE

The main goal of GLGE is simplification. "WebGL for the lazy" and "The aim of GLGE is to mask the involved nature of WebGL from the web developer, who can then spend his/her time creating richer content for the web." We will show an example with GLGE later on in the chapter. You can find GLGE here: `http://www.glge.org/`

Jax

Jax is designed with rapid development in mind. It is "a one-stop shop for building robust, high-quality WebGL applications—fast." Jax uses the Ruby language and the model-view-controller (MVC) pattern to separate components. Some of the built-in functionality includes keyboard and mouse input handling, and unit testing capability. You can find the Jax website at `http://jaxgl.com/` and the source code on github at `https://github.com/sinisterchipmunk/jax`

KickJS

KickJS is focused on game development with WebGL. KickJS also features an online interactive GLSL editor as demonstrated in Chapter 2 and an online editor (currently in beta). You can find the KickJS website here: `http://www.kickjs.org/`, and the source code hosted on github here: `https://github.com/mortennobel/KickJS/`

PhiloGL

PhiloGL is focused for data visualizations and game development. An aim of the framework is to be written with best JavaScript practices in mind as well as to thinly abstract the basic WebGL calls. We will show an example with philoGL later on in the chapter. You can find out more about it here: `http://www.senchalabs.org/philogl/`

SceneJS

SceneJS specializes in rendering a large number of pickable objects such as those used in engineering and medical applications. This is possible because the framework (as its name suggests) provides a scene graph engine that uses an efficient optimized draw list internally and is JSON-based. You can find out more about it here: `http://www.scenejs.com/`

TDL

Threedlibrary (TDL) is focused on low-level usage and performance over ease of use. Google body and many high-performance demos use TDL. You can find out more about it here:
`http://code.google.com/p/threedlibrary/`

Three.js

As mentioned in the previous chapter, Three.js is a general-purpose 3D engine that abstracts away a lot of the details making it easier to develop WebGL. Three.js is currently the most popular WebGL framework, and some people think that WebGL and Three.js are one and the same. This is not the case, but it is a great framework to try out as the previous chapter has demonstrated. You can find the Three.js library on github here: `https://github.com/mrdoob/three.js`

In this chapter, we will show how to import meshes and use a physics engine with Three.js.

A philoGL "Hello World!" Example

philoGL is a framework from Sencha Labs, and the main developer on the project is Nicolas Garcia Belmonte. The framework website is at `http://www.senchalabs.org/philogl/`, and its source code is on github at: `https://github.com/senchalabs/philogl`.

To get started, download the library and include it either locally

`<script src="./build/PhiloGL.js"></script>`, or from a remote location such as
`<script src="https://raw.github.com/senchalabs/philogl/master/build/PhiloGL.cls.js"></script>`

The \examples folder of the philoGL library presents philoGL versions of the core WebGL lessons of the popular site "Learning WebGL" by Giles Thomas at `http://learningwebgl.com/blog/?page_id=1217`. The library is split into a core and modules. Documentation is available at `http://www.senchalabs.org/philogl/doc/index.html`

Listing 8-1 shows a modified version of the ported "Learning WebGL" Lesson 4 example that is included with the library, for us to further analyze. As you can see from the listing, philoGL uses a very object-oriented approach to JavaScript. Mesh data is omitted for brevity, but can be found in the full file online at `/08/01_philogl_cube.html`

Listing 8-1. Code to rotate a cube with philoGL

```
<!doctype html>
<html>
    <head>
        <title>PhiloGL Cube Test</title>
        <style>
            body{ background-color: grey; }
            canvas{ background-color: white; }
        </style>
        <script src="./PhiloGL-1.5.1/build/PhiloGL.js"></script>
        <script id="shader-vs" type="x-shader/x-vertex">
            attribute vec3 aVertexPosition;
            attribute vec4 aVertexColor;

            uniform mat4 uMVMatrix;
            uniform mat4 uPMatrix;

            varying vec4 vColor;

            void main(void) {
                gl_Position = uPMatrix * uMVMatrix * vec4(aVertexPosition, 1.0);
```

```
                vColor = aVertexColor;
        }
</script>
<script id="shader-fs" type="x-shader/x-fragment">
        varying highp vec4 vColor;

        void main(void) {
            gl_FragColor = vColor;
        }
</script>
<script>
        //modified from
        //https://github.com/senchalabs/philogl/blob/master/examples/lessons/4/

        function webGLStart() {
            //Load model
            var cube = new PhiloGL.O3D.Model({
            vertices: [-1, ...],
            colors: [1, ...],
            indices: [0, ...]
        });

        PhiloGL('my-canvas', {
            program: {
                from: 'ids',
                vs: 'shader-vs',
                fs: 'shader-fs'
            },
            onError: function() {
                alert("An error ocurred while loading the application");
            },
            onLoad: function(app) {
                var gl = app.gl,
                canvas = app.canvas,
                program = app.program,
                camera = app.camera,
                view = new PhiloGL.Mat4,
                rCube = 0;

                gl.viewport(0, 0, canvas.width, canvas.height);
                gl.clearColor(0, 0, 0, 1);
                gl.clearDepth(1);
                gl.enable(gl.DEPTH_TEST);
                gl.depthFunc(gl.LEQUAL);

                camera.view.id();

                function setupElement(elem) {
                    //update element matrix
                    elem.update();
                    //get new view matrix out of element and camera matrices
                    view.mulMat42(camera.view, elem.matrix);
                    //set buffers with element data
                    program.setBuffers({
```

```
                            'aVertexPosition': {
                                value: elem.vertices,
                                size: 3
                            },
                            'aVertexColor': {
                                value: elem.colors,
                                size: 4
                            }
                        });
                        //set uniforms
                        program.setUniform('uMVMatrix', view);
                        program.setUniform('uPMatrix', camera.projection);
                    }

                    function animate() {
                        rCube += 0.01;
                    }

                    function tick() {
                        drawScene();
                        animate();
                        PhiloGL.Fx.requestAnimationFrame(tick);
                    }

                    function drawScene() {
                        gl.clear(gl.COLOR_BUFFER_BIT | gl.DEPTH_BUFFER_BIT);

                        //Draw Cube
                        cube.position.set(1.5, 0, -8);
                        cube.rotation.set(rCube, rCube, rCube);
                        setupElement(cube);
                        program.setBuffer('indices', {
                            value: cube.indices,
                            bufferType: gl.ELEMENT_ARRAY_BUFFER,
                            size: 1
                        });
                        gl.drawElements(gl.TRIANGLES, cube.indices.length,
                                        gl.UNSIGNED_SHORT, 0);
                    }
                    tick();
                }
            });
        }
    </script>
</head>
<body onload="webGLStart();">
    <canvas id="my-canvas" width="400" height="300">
        Your browser does not support the HTML5 canvas element.
    </canvas>
</body>
</html>
```

In Listing 8-1, the first thing to notice is that the shader programs are not abstracted away by default as in other frameworks such as ThreeJS (this was shown in the previous chapter and will later be shown for GLGE). On page load, the function `webGLStart` is called, which loads our mesh data and initializes our shaders. As you can see, philoGL does have its own matrix functionality, `requestAnimationFrame` defined, and partial abstraction of the view and VBOs built in. philoGL has a nice mix of core WebGL abstraction and visibility. The output of the program is shown in Figure 8-1.

Figure 8-1. *A cube rendered with philoGL*

A GLGE "Hello World!" Example

GLGE was written by Paul Brunt. The project's web page is `http://www.glge.org`, and the source code is on github at `https://github.com/supereggbert/GLGE`. Obtain the sources Zip file and unzip the archive. Add the main library file to your code with either

`<script src="./glge-compiled.js"></script>` for a local file or from an online source such as `<script src="https://raw.github.com/supereggbert/GLGE/master/glge-compiled-min.js"></script>`.

The API for GLGE has documentation at `http://www.glge.org/api-docs/`, but not much for quick start tips or tutorials. There are several examples in the `/examples` folder to inspect the code and build from.

Unlike core WebGL, the Three.js or philoGL frameworks, GLGE uses XML to represent the scene objects. Listing 8-2 shows a minimal example using GLGE. Later in the chapter, we will show that loading complex meshes with GLGE is very easy.

Listing 8-2. GLGE code to render a cube

```
<!doctype html>
<html>
    <head>
        <title>GLGE Cube Test</title>
        <style>
            body{ background-color: grey; }
            canvas{ background-color: white; }
        </style>
        <script src="./GLGEv0.9/glge-compiled-min.js"></script>
        <script src="./raf_polyfill.js"></script>
        <script>
            //create a GLGE document
```

```
        var doc = new GLGE.Document();
        var angle = 0.0;
        //load scene data from XML file. This scene file is modified from the demo at:
        //http://www.rozengain.com/blog/2010/06/23/hands-on-//webgl-basic-glge-tutorial/
        doc.load("02_glge_scene.xml");

        //callback when the scene is finished loading
        doc.onLoad = function() {
            //get a reference to the canvas element
            var canvas = document.getElementById("my-canvas");

            //create a GLGE renderer
            var renderer = new GLGE.Renderer(canvas);

            //set the scene for the renderer from the <scene> element of the XML file
            renderer.setScene( doc.getElement("mainscene") );

            //get the box object, not the box mesh
            var box = doc.getElement("box");

            //the rendering loop
            (function animLoop(){
                box.setRotX(angle);
                box.setRotY(angle);
                box.setRotZ(angle);
                angle += 0.005;

                renderer.render();
                requestAnimationFrame(animLoop, canvas);
            })();
        }
    </script>
</head>
<body>
    <canvas id="my-canvas" width="400" height="300">
        Your browser does not support the HTML5 canvas element.
    </canvas>
</body>
</html>
```

The scene file is shown in Listing 8-3 (mesh data has been omitted for brevity) and can be found in the file
/08/02_glge_scene.xml.

Listing 8-3. GLGE Scene file with a custom mesh

```
<?xml version="1.0" ?>
<glge>
    <mesh id="box-mesh">
        <positions>1.00000, ...</positions>
        <normals>0.00000, ...</normals>
        <uv1>0.33333, ...</uv1>
        <faces>0, ...</faces>
    </mesh>

    <camera id="maincamera" loc_z="20" />
    <material id="boxmaterial" color="#900" />
```

```
<scene id="mainscene" camera="#maincamera" ambient_color="#fff">
    <light id="mainlight" loc_y="5" type="L_POINT" />
    <object id="box" mesh="#box-mesh" rot_x="-.8" rot_y=".5" material="#boxmaterial" />
</scene>
</glge>
```

Listing 8-3 has a custom mesh defined inline. The output of this code that uses a cube mesh is shown in Figure 8-2.

Figure 8-2. *A spinning cube rendered with GLGE*

In Listing 8-2, we did not have to write code for the shader program or bind the VBO data. We specify the mesh data in our scene file, and the framework takes care of the rest. The nice part of the scene being represented with XML is that it is easy to traverse elements and has a well-formed hierarchy.

Going into details of advanced usage of philoGL or GLGE is beyond the scope of this book, but if you like the object-oriented partial abstraction of philoGL or the XML scene-based GLGE style, I urge you to follow up with these WebGL frameworks on your own or any other framework(s) that you are interested in.

Meshes

As you have no doubt noticed, defining even a trivial mesh in WebGL takes effort. For complex objects such as the classic teapot, an animal, a building, or anything else, we'll most likely want to load in our data from a rendering program such as Blender or Mesa, or an open-source online repository. Models can come in many formats with two of the most popular being OBJ (Wavefront) and DAE (Collada).

Loading Existing Meshes

As developers, we may or may not also be artistically talented. Even if you are, you probably do not want to spend hours creating a model that someone else has already made and is readily available for usage. If possible, we can download existing models and use them in WebGL.

▓ **Note** There are several places to download free or variably priced meshes such as the following:

http://sketchup.google.com/3dwarehouse/

http://www.blender-models.com/

http://artist-3d.com/

http://thefree3dmodels.com/

http://www.oyonale.com/modeles.php

http://www.3dvia.com/

http://www.3dcadbrowser.com/

http://www.3d02.com/

http://www.turbosquid.com/

Modeling Resources

In addition to downloading existing meshes, we may want to create our own, though defining vertex points by hand is error prone and not ideal. Instead, there are many existing modeling programs available for us:

- Trimble, available at http://ww2.trimble.com/3d/, used to be called SketchUp and was recently purchased from Google. As of June 1, 2012 on its FAQ section, Trimble says it will continue to support SketchUp customers and offer free and professional versions of its software. At the moment, the SketchUp modeling program is available at http://sketchup.google.com/.

- Blender, available at http://www.blender.org/, is an open-source 3D modeling and rendering program.

- Many other commercial programs such as Maya, Unity, Shade 3D, and 3DS Max.

File Formats

There are many different file formats that represent meshes. Whatever format a mesh is originally represented as, our ultimate goal is to convert the existing mesh format to something readable by our application. Because WebGL uses JavaScript, an obvious choice for this is JavaScript Object Notation (JSON). Some frameworks can convert models to JSON on the fly. However, best performance will be achieved by converting the mesh to a stored JSON formatted file first and then using the static file data.

We will discuss a couple of popular file formats to store mesh data and how to import these formats for usage with WebGL.

Wavefront Format (.obj)

The .obj 3D format was developed by Wavefront technologies more than 20 years ago. It is a fairly simple format that stores vertex, normal, texture coordinates, and polygon faces. By default, each face has counterclockwise winding.

The faces in a wavefront file do not need to be only triangles; they can contain polygons with more than three vertices. We must make sure that all faces are triangles when importing/exporting a wavefront model. Otherwise, we need to triangulate the mesh, which involves splitting up a single polygon into multiple triangle pieces. A very simple .obj file might look like this:

```
#lines with "#" are comments
#vertex lines    start    with "v". 4th homogeneous coordinate component is optional
v       0.5      1.0      0.25     1.0
v       0.25     1.5      0.25
v       0.5      0.0      0.25
v       0.25     1.0      0.25     1.0
v       0.75     1.5      0.25
v       0.75     0.0      0.25
#texture coordinates start with "vt"
vt      0.25     0.5
vt      0.125    0.75
vt      0.25     0.0
#normal coordinates start with "vn"
vn      0.0      0.0      1.0
#simple face - only vertex coordinates
f       1 2 3
#more complex face - vertex/texture coord/normal
f       4/1/1 5/2/1 6/3/1
```

The obj format can get a little more complex, but we don't need to worry about that because obj importers, exporters and converters already exist for us as we will show later in the chapter. The obj format also supports material property files that can use different illumination models from simple color and no ambient light to full lighting components of the form Ka, Kd, Ks for ambient, diffuse, and specular, respectively, and whether it casts shadows, or uses transparencies or reflections.

Collada Format (.dae)

Collada stands for **COLLA**borative **D**esign **A**ctivity and was introduced in 2004. It is an XML schema to transport 3D assets such as models and shaders between different authoring applications without losing data in the exchange. The XML files that describe the assets have a *.dae* extension, which stands for Digital Asset Exchange. Many formats can be interchanged, and as such the schema is large and beyond the scope of this book. Collada is overseen by the Khronos group, the same consortium that oversees WebGL.

JSON

A JSON object of arrays is perfect for loading data into VBOs. The exact object properties can vary. For example, we could have an object with attribute data separated, as follows:

```
var our_data={
    "positions": [],
    "normals": [],
    "texture_coords":[],
    "indices": []
}
```

You could load the preceding data into four separate VBOs or into an interleaved array for the first three sets of data and another VBO for the indices. The data passed in could also be preinterleaved; for example:

```
var our_data2 = {
    "interleaved_data": [],
    "indices": []
}
```

Interleaved arrays are discussed in Chapter 9.

With the first JSON data above, we can assign our data to a VBO like:

```
gl.bufferData(gl.ARRAY_BUFFER, new Float32Array(our_data.positions), gl.STATIC_DRAW);
...
gl.bufferData(gl.ARRAY_BUFFER, new Float32Array(our_data.normals), gl.STATIC_DRAW);
...
gl.bufferData(gl.ARRAY_BUFFER, new Float32Array(our_data.texture_coords), gl.STATIC_DRAW);
...
gl.bufferData(gl.ELEMENT_ARRAY_BUFFER, new Uint16Array(our_data.indices), gl.STATIC_DRAW);
```

■ **Note** There is a limit to the size of meshes that WebGL buffers can hold. The current limit is $2^{16} = 65{,}536$ indices per mesh. To get around these limits, a large mesh could be split into smaller meshes. There are also programs that can reduce the number of polygons in a mesh (by combining smaller triangles into larger triangles), which may not be that noticeable depending on the amount of reduction, the shape of the mesh, and the lighting model used.

Importing, Exporting, and Format Conversion

Regardless of the format initially used, remember that WebGL renders with triangle primitives. So if a model uses polygons, they will need to be broken down into triangles. And although WebGL refers to texture coordinates as st, a lot of programs refer to them as uv coordinates.

If you do a web search for convertors to JSON format, you will come across a few scripts. One of these scripts is http://code.google.com/p/blender-machete/, which aims to add JSON export capability to Blender. Maya users can use Inka available at http://www.inka3d.com/ to export data directly to a WebGL useable format.

There is no built-in way of loading mesh data with WebGL. We will show how to load meshes, starting with a multiple-step process using Blender to loading in model data directly if the framework supports it.

Using the Three.js Blender Import/Export Addon

We will use a Blender module that Three.js provides to export mesh data into a JSON format that the Three.js framework uses.

■ **Note** With some adjustment, you can use the Three.js–specific JSON format outside of the Three.js framework.

The Three.js library has a Python add-on module for Blender in this folder:
\three.js\utils\exporters\blender\2.63\scripts\addons\io_mesh_threejs. If you do not already have Blender, download and install it. Then copy the entire io_mesh_threejs folder into your Blender Python script add-on directory. The path of this folder will vary by operating system, version of Blender and your chosen installation directory. Using Blender 2.63 on a Windows 7 machine, the folder could be C:\Program Files (x86)\Blender Foundation\Blender\2.63\scripts\addons\. If you need

help finding the folder location for your installation, search the user forum at http://www.blender.org/forum/ for steps to find this information. To load the plugin, start Blender and go to the File >> User Preferences menu item, as shown in Figure 8-3.

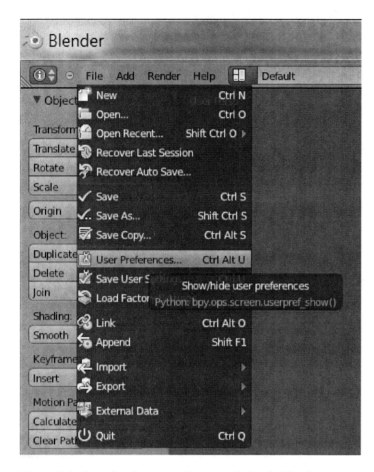

Figure 8-3. Accessing the user preferences window in Blender

Next, locate the Addons tab and search for "three", as shown in Figure 8-4. Click the checkbox to the right of the search result to enable it.

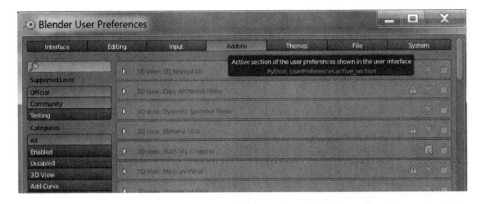

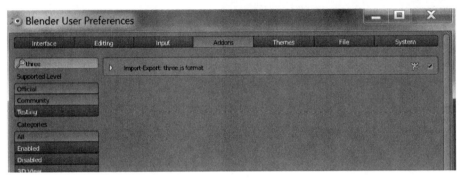

Figure 8-4. *Top: Addons tab within User Preferences window of Blender; bottom: finding the Three.js addon*

Now that we have enabled the three.js Blender module, after we import meshes using the File >> Import menu item (as shown on the left of Figure 8-5) we can now export the mesh at the File >> Export menu item into a Three.js JSON-formatted file.

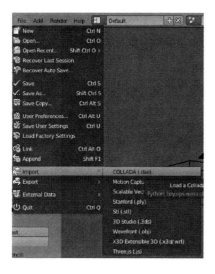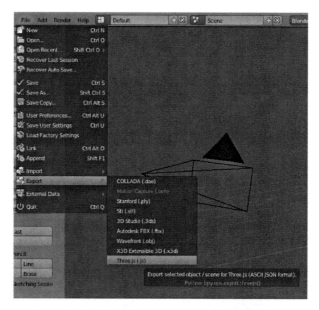

Figure 8-5. *Left: importing a model such as a dae or obj file; right: exporting as a Three.js JSON-formatted file*

We will now show how to export a mesh with this plugin and load it into a Three.js program.

Exporting a Mesh into the Three.JS JSON Format

Obtain some meshes of anything you desire. For these examples, I have obtained Collada models of the Taj Mahal by Kevin Girard and various animals by a user named mandun from the sketchup warehouse. I have also downloaded a duck model from `http://ourbricks.com/khronos/colladarepository`.

I then import each mesh into Blender one at a time and export into Three.js format.

■ **Note**   If a mesh is not working with a script, but others load and display properly with the same code, there could be indice, vertex, or normal data wrong within the model. The mesh could also be too large.

Loading the Mesh with Three.JS

To load a mesh in Three.js JSON format, we use the `THREE.JSONLoader` object as shown in Listing 8-4.

Listing 8-4. Loading a Three.js JSON format mesh

```
function addDuckMesh()
{
    var loader = new THREE.JSONLoader();
    loader.load("./meshes/duck_three.js", function(geometry){
        mesh = new THREE.Mesh(
```

```
            geometry,
            geometry.materials[0]
        );

        //mesh transforms if necessary
        scene.add(mesh);

        //make sure mesh is loaded before renderering
        loadRestOfScene()
    });
}

function loadRestOfScene()
{
    addLight();
    setupCamera();

    (function animLoop(){
        mesh.rotation.z = angle;
        angle += 0.005;

        renderer.render(scene, camera);
        requestAnimationFrame( animLoop );
    })();
}
...
```

In Listing 8-4, we make sure that the mesh has loaded before rendering the scene. Loading the mesh object is done asynchronously, so we are not otherwise guaranteed that the mesh will finish loading before the scene is rendered. The first parameter of the loader.load function is the mesh filename, and the second is a callback function when the mesh has loaded. The loaded mesh object is passed in and we have the materials and textures of the original mesh available in the geometry.materials[0] property. After we have added the mesh, we load the rest of our scene and render. The output of this is shown on the left of Figure 8-6.

Figure 8-6. *Left: rendering of a rubber duck; right: wireframe overlayed on image, showing hundreds of triangles that comprise it*

We showed last chapter how to generate a wireframe with Three.js. The duck on the right of Figure 8-6 is a wireframe on top of the regular material. To generate this image, we use multiple materials with the function THREE.SceneUtils.createMultiMaterialObject, as shown here:

```
var materials = [
            geometry.materials[0],
            new THREE.MeshBasicMaterial(
```

```
            {
                color: 0x000000,
                wireframe: true
            }
        )
    ];
mesh = new THREE.SceneUtils.createMultiMaterialObject(
            geometry,
            materials
        );
```

We could also vary the transparency of each material by adding the properties to our material:

```
transparency: true,
opacity: 0.5     //or other value between 0 and 1
```

Using a Three.js JSON Model with Core WebGL

What if you don't want to use the Three.js framework, but do find their JSON mesh generation Blender plugin useful? How can we use the exported file in regular old WebGL. Well, open up a file output with the Blender addon and examine it. Listing 8-5 shows the essentials of the file with the really important information in bold text.

Listing 8-5. Three.js JSON mesh File

```
{
    "metadata" :
    {
        //format, what generated this file
        //counts for vertices, faces, normals, uvs, materials, colors
    },

    "scale" : 1.000000,

    "materials": [        {
            //material color, blending, depth tests, textures, etc.
        ...
        "blending" : "NormalBlending",
        "colorAmbient" : [0.0, 0.0, 0.0],
        "colorDiffuse" : [0.6400000190734865, 0.6400000190734865, 0.6400000190734865],
        "colorSpecular" : [0.0, 0.0, 0.0],
        "depthTest" : true,
        "depthWrite" : true,
        "mapDiffuse" : "duckCM_fix.jpg",
        "mapDiffuseWrap" : ["repeat", "repeat"],
        ...
    }],

    "vertices": [35.022598,...],
    "morphTargets": [],
    "normals": [-0.194006,...],
    "colors": [],
```

```
    "uvs": [[0.866606,...]],
    "faces": [42,...]
}
```

■ **Note** The format of the file is liable to change and is currently in its third incarnation. Refer to the companion website at http://www.beginningwebgl.com for an updated specification and usage with core WebGL.

The properties that we are interested in here are the vertices, normal, uvs (texture coordinates), and faces arrays; and also colorDiffuse and mapDiffuse, which tell us the material color and texture file to load.

Now the vertices, normal, and uvs arrays are straightforward, and we can pass them directly into vertex buffer objects, but the faces array does not correspond to the indices array, as you might expect. For the duck model, the first items of the array are these:

```
"faces": [42, 89,243,6, 0,0,1,2,0,1,2,42...]
```

With a simple cube mesh exported from Blender to the Three.js JSON format, the first few items are the following:

```
"faces": [35,0,1,2,3,0,0,1,2,3,35,...]
```

A cube only has six faces, so why is 35 an index value? To understand what is going on, you need to take a look at the three.js JSONLoader.js source:

```
. . .
        isQuad              = isBitSet( type, 0 );
        hasMaterial         = isBitSet( type, 1 );
        hasFaceUv           = isBitSet( type, 2 );
        hasFaceVertexUv     = isBitSet( type, 3 );
        hasFaceNormal       = isBitSet( type, 4 );
        hasFaceVertexNormal = isBitSet( type, 5 );
        hasFaceColor        = isBitSet( type, 6 );
        hasFaceVertexColor  = isBitSet( type, 7 );
. . .
```

The first item of the face array gives information about the type of data contained in the next array elements by using binary bit checks. For example, 42 = 0010 1010 in binary, so it has a vertex normal, vertex uvs, and a material. Then the next numbers in the sequence 89,243,6, 0,0,1,2,0,1,2 point to appropriate array indices in the JSON object. A new number is checked for format information—in this case, 42 again—and this process repeats for each item in the array. As such, while it is possible to program handling of the face array data to determine indices, it is not a straightforward process. The full format used by Three.js is explained at https://github.com/mrdoob/three.js/wiki/JSON-Model-format-3.0.

Loading a Collada File Directly with GLGE

With GLGE, we can load Collada files directly by adding them to our XML scene file, as shown in Listing 8-6. Very simple!

Listing 8-6. *Loading Collada files with GLGE*

```
<?xml version="1.0" ?>
<glge>
    <camera id="maincamera" loc_z="20" />
    <scene id="mainscene" camera="#maincamera" ambient_color="#fff">
        <light id="mainlight" loc_y="5" type="L_POINT" />
        <collada document="./meshes/Gorilla/models/Gorilla.dae" loc_x="0.8"
                        loc_y="-3.0" rot_x="0.0" rot_y="0.9" scale=".0012" />
        <collada document="./meshes/Elephant/models/Elephant.dae"
                        loc_x="11.0" loc_y="-4.0" rot_x="0.0" rot_y="0.0" scale="0.8" />
    </scene>
</glge>
```

The output of Listing 8-6 is shown on the left of Figure 8-7.

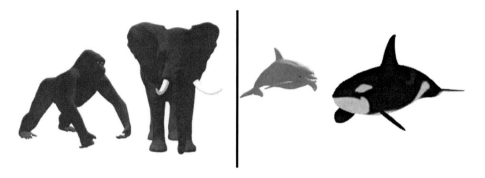

Figure 8-7. *Left: gorilla and elephant meshes loaded with GLGE; right: dolphin and orca meshes*

We can also load Collada meshes with Three.js using the THREE.ColladaLoader object:

```
var loader = new THREE.ColladaLoader();
loader.load("./meshes/Orca/models/Orca.dae", function(collada){
    dae = collada.scene;
    scene.add(dae);
```

Figure 8-8. *The Taj Mahal, loaded with Three.js*

A model of the Taj Mahal loaded with Three.js is shown in Figure 8-8.

As you can see, we can use elaborate meshes easily with these frameworks. Now we will look at finding existing shader and texture resources.

Shaders

We don't always want to reinvent the wheel creating a new shader if someone has already figured out one that is similar. Rather, we can reuse existing (uncopyrighted) vertex and fragment shaders and modify them to fit our program needs.

You are free to find inspiration from existing shaders that you come across, such as the ones at `http://code.google.com/p/glslang-library/source/browse/trunk/trunk/glslang/shaders`. Keep in mind that the shading language used might be a version of GLSL that is higher than the version that WebGL uses and could have features that WebGL does not support or be in a different shading language such as Cg (Nvidia) or HLSL (Microsoft) and need some conversion.

Nvidia also offers their excellent GPU Gems books online such as the third book which is available at `http://developer.nvidia.com/content/gpu-gems-3`.

Textures

There are a lot of places online to browse and download free high-quality textures, including these:

- `http://texturez.com/`
- `http://www.textureking.com`
- `http://www.texturelovers.com`

- `http://cgtextures.com/`
- `http://freestocktextures.com/`
- `http:/psd.tutsplus.com/category/freebies/texture/`

Physics Engines

In Chapter 5, we showed how to model some simple physical interactions such as gravity, velocity, and collisions. There are existing physics engines that can perform much more complex calculations. While these libraries are not necessarily geared exclusively to WebGL, they are written in JavaScript and can be used with WebGL.

The popular physics libraries Box2D (`http://box2d.org/`) and Bullet (`http://bulletphysics.org/`), which were originally written in C++ are available in JavaScript as the ports shown in Table 8-1.

Table 8-1. *Relevant Ports for Box2D and Bullet*

Library	Port
Box2D based	`http://code.google.com/p/box2dweb/`
	`https://github.com/kripken/box2d.js`
Bullet based	`https://github.com/kripken/ammo.js/`

Box2D is a 2D physics engine; Bullet is a 3D physics engine. Box2D has been used by games such as *Angry Birds*; Bullet has been used in games such as *Toy Story 3* and movies such as *Megamind* and *Sherlock Holmes*. Other physics engines include cannon.js and physi.js. cannon.js is inspired by ammo.js and three.js and available at `https://github.com/schteppe/cannon.js`. The physi.js library, available at `http://chandlerprall.github.com/Physijs/`, is a plugin for three.js, which uses the ammo.js physics library. A demo of the game *Jenga* is at `http://chandlerprall.github.com/Physijs/examples/jenga.html`. There is a nice wiki for getting started with physi.js at `https://github.com/chandlerprall/Physijs/wiki`.

Revisiting Old Code with physi.js and Three.js

We will look at coding the colliding and bouncing spheres demo from Chapter 5, this time using the physi.js library for physics together with Three.js. I choose to use physi.js, which is a newcomer to the physics scene, because it is very, very easy to use. It really does a nice job in letting you quickly get started simulating physics. Download the physi.js library and include it in the source:

```
...
<script src="https://raw.github.com/mrdoob/three.js/master/build/Three.js"></script>
<script src="./physi.js/physi.js"></script>
<script>
    Physijs.scripts.worker = './physi.js/physijs_worker.js';
    Physijs.scripts.ammo = '/08/ammo.js/builds/ammo.js';
...
```

Here we also set the path to the ammo.js library (which you will also need to download) and the `physijs_worker.js` file. The main difference in setup is using `Physijs` versions of the Scene object and Mesh objects:

```
scene = new Physijs.Scene;
...
var geometry = new THREE.SphereGeometry(Math.random() + .25);
var material = Physijs.createMaterial(new THREE.MeshLambertMaterial(
            {
                color:  new THREE.Color().setRGB(Math.random(), Math.random(),
                        Math.random()).getHex()
            }),
            0.1,    //friction
            0.9     //bounce
    );
var mesh = new Physijs.SphereMesh(
    geometry,
    material
);
```

The material is a `Physijs` material, which is a normal material along with friction and bounce properties. The SphereMesh is one of a few mesh shapes available, such as boxes, cylinders, cones, and convex geometry (generic to match custom meshes). In our render loop, we call `scene.simulate()` each time through:

```
(function animLoop(){
            if(!paused)
            {
                    scene.simulate();       //run the physics
                    renderer.render(scene, camera);
                    requestAnimationFrame( animLoop );
            }
    })();
```

The `simulate` call is what calculates the physical interactions of our objects. If we run the program at this point, the spheres will all fall. We need to add a ground and some walls as bounds. Once these are added, collision detection against them will be automatic. We did not have to specify any rules for the velocity—the effects of gravity are modeled for us. When we add the ground, we set the mass of it to 0. This means that other objects have no effect on it and it will not fall from gravity:

```
function addGround()
{
    var material = Physijs.createMaterial(
                        new THREE.MeshLambertMaterial({ "color": "0xffdddd" }),
                        .1, // low friction
                        .9  // high restitution
                );

    var ground = new Physijs.BoxMesh(
                        new THREE.CubeGeometry(ROOM_SIZE, 1, ROOM_SIZE),
                        material,
                        0 // mass
```

```
                );
    ground.position.y=-HALF_ROOM_SIZE/2.0;
    ground.receiveShadow=true;
    scene.add( ground );
}
```

We also add walls, which are shown in the output of the demo in Figure 8-9.

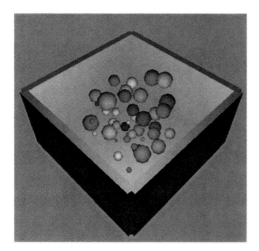

Figure 8-9. *Sphere collisions using Three.js and physi.js*

The full code that is shown in Listing 8-7 is very small compared with our home-brewed example of Chapter 5. However, the simulation is slower and less responsive than our Chapter 5 example. As this is a new library, I expect that some performance improvements will be made for it.

Listing 8-7. *Full code of Three.js and physi.js sphere collision demo*

```html
<!doctype html>
<html>
<head>
<title>Three.js and Physi.js Test</title>
<style>
        body{ background-color: grey; }
        canvas{ background-color: white; }
</style>
<script src="http://code.jquery.com/jquery-1.7.2.min.js"></script>
<script src="https://raw.github.com/mrdoob/three.js/master/build/Three.js"></script>
<script src="./physi.js/physi.js"></script>
<script>
    Physijs.scripts.worker = './physi.js/physijs_worker.js';
    Physijs.scripts.ammo = '/08/ammo.js/builds/ammo.js';

    var CANVAS_WIDTH = 500,
        CANVAS_HEIGHT= 500,
        ROOM_SIZE = 20.0,
        HALF_ROOM_SIZE = ROOM_SIZE * 0.5,
```

```
    NUM_SPHERES = 50,
    paused = false;

var renderer = null,          //WebGL or 2D
    scene = null,             //scene object
    camera = null;            //camera object

$(document).keyup(function(evt){
    switch(evt.keyCode){
        case 80: //'p'
            paused =!paused;
            break;
        default:
            break;
    }
});

function initWebGL()
{
    setupRenderer();
    setupScene();
    setupCamera();

    (function animLoop(){
        if(!paused)
        {
            scene.simulate();    //run the physics
            renderer.render(scene, camera);
            requestAnimationFrame( animLoop );
        }
    })();
}

function setupRenderer()
{
renderer = new THREE.WebGLRenderer( {clearColor: 0x007700, clearAlpha: 1} );
renderer.setSize( CANVAS_WIDTH, CANVAS_HEIGHT );
document.body.appendChild(  renderer.domElement );
}

function setupScene()
{
    scene = new Physijs.Scene();
    addMeshes();
    addLight();
}

function setupCamera()
{
    camera = new THREE.PerspectiveCamera(
                45,                             // Field of view
                CANVAS_WIDTH / CANVAS_HEIGHT,   // Aspect ratio
                .1,                             // Near clip plane
```

```
                  10000                        // Far clip plane
        );

    camera.position.set( ROOM_SIZE, ROOM_SIZE*1.5, ROOM_SIZE );
    camera.lookAt( scene.position );
    scene.add( camera );
}

function addMeshes()
{
    addGround();
    addWalls();

    for(var i=1; i<=NUM_SPHERES;++i)
    {
        var geometry = new THREE.SphereGeometry(Math.random() + .25);
        var material = Physijs.createMaterial(
                        new THREE.MeshLambertMaterial(
                            {
                                color:  new THREE.Color().setRGB(
                                                        Math.random(),
                                                        Math.random(),
                                                        Math.random()
                                                    ).getHex()
                            }
                        ),
                        0.1,    //friction
                        0.9     //bounce
                    );
        var mesh = new Physijs.SphereMesh(
                        geometry,
                        material
        );
        mesh.position.x = HALF_ROOM_SIZE*Math.random()-HALF_ROOM_SIZE*.5;
        mesh.position.y = HALF_ROOM_SIZE*Math.random()-HALF_ROOM_SIZE*.5;
        mesh.position.z = HALF_ROOM_SIZE*Math.random()-HALF_ROOM_SIZE*.5;
        mesh.castShadow = true;
        scene.add(mesh);
    }
}

function addGround()
{
    var material = Physijs.createMaterial(
                    new THREE.MeshLambertMaterial({ "color": "0xffdddd" }),
                    .1, // low friction
                    .9  // high restitution
                );

    var ground = new Physijs.BoxMesh(
                    new THREE.CubeGeometry(ROOM_SIZE, 1, ROOM_SIZE),
```

```
                            material,
                            0 // mass
                    );
        ground.position.y = -HALF_ROOM_SIZE/2.0;
        ground.receiveShadow = true;
        scene.add( ground );
    }

    function addWalls()
    {
        var material = Physijs.createMaterial(
                        new THREE.MeshLambertMaterial({ "color": "0xaaaaff" }),
                        .1, // low friction
                        .9  // high restitution
                    );

        var wall = new Physijs.BoxMesh(
                        new THREE.CubeGeometry(ROOM_SIZE, HALF_ROOM_SIZE, 1),
                        material,
                        0 // mass
                    );
        wall.position.z = -HALF_ROOM_SIZE;
        scene.add( wall );

        wall = new Physijs.BoxMesh(
                        new THREE.CubeGeometry(ROOM_SIZE, HALF_ROOM_SIZE, 1),
                        material,
                        0 // mass
                    );
        wall.position.z = HALF_ROOM_SIZE;
        wall.receiveShadow = true;
        scene.add( wall );

        wall = new Physijs.BoxMesh(
                        new THREE.CubeGeometry(1, HALF_ROOM_SIZE, ROOM_SIZE),
                        material,
                        0 // mass
                    );
        wall.position.x = -HALF_ROOM_SIZE;
        scene.add( wall );

        wall = new Physijs.BoxMesh(
                        new THREE.CubeGeometry(1, HALF_ROOM_SIZE, ROOM_SIZE),
                        material,
                        0 // mass
                    );
        wall.position.x = HALF_ROOM_SIZE;
        wall.receiveShadow = true;
        scene.add( wall );
    }
```

```
    function addLight()
    {
        var light = new THREE.PointLight( 0xFFFFFF );
        light.position.set( 10, 10, 10 );
        scene.add(light);
    }
</script>
</head>
<body onload="initWebGL()"></body>
</html>
```

Summary

This chapter introduced several more frameworks available for WebGL and showed basic usage examples for GLGE and philoGL. We showed how to import complex meshes into our scene and listed shader and texture resources. Finally we showed how to use Three.js and physi.js to recode an example from the physics chapter.

Chapter 9 will show what to do when things go wrong and how to debug WebGL code. We also show performance best practices. Even with a framework, if we are not following best practices, complex scenes can grind to a halt. As such, it is important to know how to improve rendering performance.

CHAPTER 9

■ ■ ■

Debugging and Performance

In this chapter we will show how to troubleshoot errors and improve application performance. We will:

- present helpful tools for debugging WebGL code and shaders
- go over some common errors and their solutions
- show ways to get more performance out of WebGL by optimizing our code to remove common bottlenecks
- identify WebGL best practices

Debugging

When our program is producing erroneous results, as computer programmers we say that the program has *bugs* in it or is acting *buggy*. The process of identifying the source of the bug(s)/error(s) and fixing them is known as *debugging*.

Why should we aim to be proficient at debugging code? Although debugging is often the most time-consuming and frustrating part of programming, it is also a natural part of development. Using tools and techniques that can pinpoint the source of error, and a knowledge of common errors, are essential to minimizing the time we spend debugging.

Integrated Development Environment (IDE)

The first place that we should look for assistance is where we code. Although we could use a plain text editor with no syntax highlighting or code intelligence, why would we want to? Most modern IDEs will give near-immediate feedback through coloring and/or other syntax highlighting, and display warnings or notices. There are many, many IDEs and text editors available, each with a variety of features. Some are lightweight, while others are memory-intensive, some are robust out of the box, while others have plugins or modules to add functionality. IDEs also range in price from free to very expensive. Some suitable text editors and IDEs for JavaScript and web development include Sublime, Notepad++, Netbeans, Eclipse, WebStorm, Zend Studio, Aptana, Cloud9, and Komodo. Of these, it is interesting to note that Cloud9, as its name suggests, is hosted in the cloud. There is no local installation, which of course has advantages and disadvantages.

Minimally, your IDE or text editor should be able to detect JavaScript and HTML syntax, have some color coding, visually match up braces and parentheses, have line numbering, and search/replace support. On the other end of the spectrum, IDEs can have built-in version control and remote file support, unit testing, refactoring, code completion, API intelligence, and much more. You can see an example of an IDE in action in Figure 9-1.

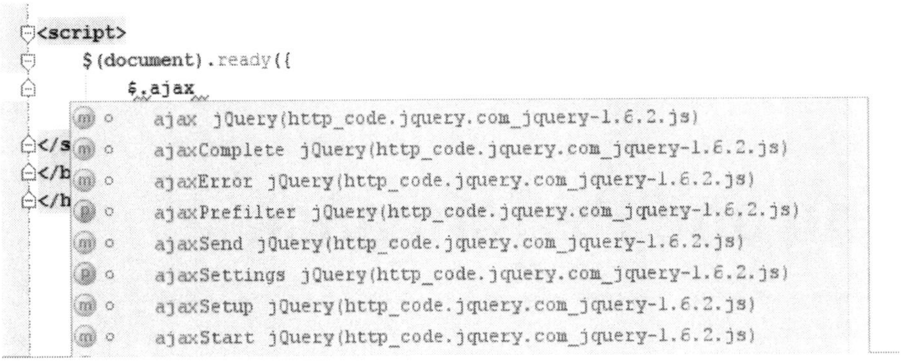

```
<script>
    $(document).ready({
        $.ajax
            ajax  jQuery(http_code.jquery.com_jquery-1.6.2.js)
    </s     ajaxComplete  jQuery(http_code.jquery.com_jquery-1.6.2.js)
    </b     ajaxError  jQuery(http_code.jquery.com_jquery-1.6.2.js)
    </h     ajaxPrefilter  jQuery(http_code.jquery.com_jquery-1.6.2.js)
            ajaxSend  jQuery(http_code.jquery.com_jquery-1.6.2.js)
            ajaxSettings  jQuery(http_code.jquery.com_jquery-1.6.2.js)
            ajaxSetup  jQuery(http_code.jquery.com_jquery-1.6.2.js)
            ajaxStart  jQuery(http_code.jquery.com_jquery-1.6.2.js)
```

Figure 9-1. jQuery library autocompletion inside of the Webstorm IDE

I won't try to convince you to use a particular IDE or text editor. The choice is yours and ultimately should be what you feel most comfortable and productive using. Some factors to consider are:

- Active development and community base: Don't invest the time to learn something that will soon be a relic or that no one else uses.

- Power and productivity: Can you do amazing things with a few keystrokes/macros or does the vastness of the IDE actually hinder your productivity? Remember that the purpose of an IDE is to increase your productivity and ease of use by offering tools that assist your development.

- Extendibility: Does the IDE have plugins, modules, and third-party integration support?

- Intuitiveness: Is the IDE well designed and easy to navigate?

- Configurability: If the initial settings are not to your liking, how much of the editor/IDE is customizable?

- Resource usage and stability: Does it take seconds or minutes to load up the IDE; is it responsive; does it take too much RAM; does it crash often?

- Focus: Is the IDE tailored toward one language or many? To a specific task or many? There are pros and cons of each of these. Often if an IDE is tailored to one language it will be sleeker and more optimal than software designed for use by a plethora of languages and may also have advanced tools. However, the tradeoff of an IDE geared toward several languages means that if you regularly code in many languages, you have to learn only one GUI.

Browser Developer Tools

WebGL is run inside a browser, and the API used is written with JavaScript. The next place that we should look for assistance when debugging is within the browser, as each of the major browsers has its own built-in developer tools. These developer tools have a varying level of usability and features, but do share the common functionality of: the ability to view and manipulate the Document Object Model (DOM), resources, network traffic, and an interactive console that outputs JavaScript debug and error information.

Chrome/Safari both offer *developer tools*. Firefox has the Firebug and Developer extensions, Internet Explorer has the developer toolbar, and Opera has Dragonfly. Internet Explorer developer tools have improved quite a lot between versions 8 and 9 in terms of baked-in support. However, in my opinion Chrome and Firefox remain the most feature-rich of the browser tools.

Safari by default has their developer tools disabled. To enable them, you need to go to the Preferences >>Advanced tab and click the "Show Develop menu in menu bar" check box. The Firefox extensions are available at http://getfirebug.com/ and https://addons.mozilla.org/en-US/firefox/addon/web-developer/.

In Figure 9-2 we demonstrate how to find a DOM element interactively through the Chrome Developer Tools console tab.

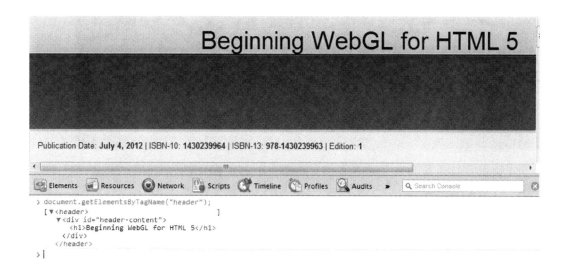

Figure 9-2. Using the console in Chrome Developer Tools to search for the < header > tag

In Figure 9-3 we show the Network traffic tab of Opera's Dragonfly developer tools. This tab shows a timeline of the loaded and loading resources for a webpage.

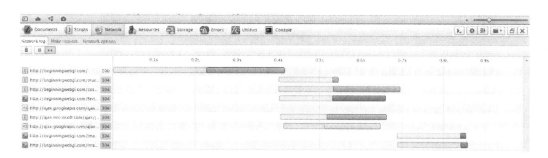

Figure 9-3. Viewing network statistics with Opera Dragonfly

In Figure 9-4, we show a rather cool new feature of Firefox: the ability to visualize the DOM in three dimensions. This tool is made possible by WebGL.

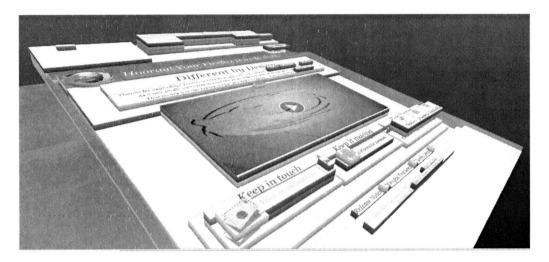

Figure 9-4. *3D visualization of DOM elements in Firefox, made possible by WebGL*

Two other specific browser tools are: Typing 'about:config' into the address bar in Firefox and searching for 'webgl' lets you adjust Firefox's webgl settings. Typing the address 'about:tracing' in Chrome lets you profile WebGL applications in that browser.

Debug Messages to the Console

To output information to ourselves or other developers about the state of our program or if there are warnings or errors that we should know about, instead of displaying potentially annoying alert boxes for nonsevere errors or muddying up the DOM document with our status updates we can print messages to the JavaScript console screen. As mentioned, all the browsers have developer tools that include a console screen for the input and output of commands and messages. There is also a `console` object in JavaScript that has methods to output messages to the developer console.

For instance, we can write log messages and error messages to the developer console with JavaScript code like this:

```
var myVar = 42;
console.log("just some helpful information");          //just some helpful information
console.error("something more severe: " + myVar);     //something more severe: 42
```

The main difference displayed in the console for these two messages will be that error messages usually have a red font color while log messages are black. There are many more methods of the `console` object, and the application programming interface (API) for the Firebug console is available at http://getfirebug.com/wiki/index. php/Console_API. Although the exact implementation of the `console` object is browser-dependent, others (such as those based on WebKit) support most of the implementation that Firebug uses.

View Other People's Code

Because WebGL uses a client-side API written in JavaScript, we can view other people's code easily. Doing so can give insight into techniques that we may not have previously considered. There are a couple of ways to view JavaScript code: right-clicking and accessing the menu item "View Page Source" or "View Source", or looking at the Resources tab of Developer Tools. For a shader source, we can also view the raw source. However, as we showed in Chapter 7, frameworks can modify the final shader source. As such, using a tool such as WebGL inspector, which we will cover later on in the chapter, can prove to be more useful.

Online Sandboxes

A *sandbox* is a safe environment that children are known to play within and toy around with their imagination. In development terms, a sandbox is an isolated testing environment that we can play around with our code without harming production code.

There are many places online that we can quickly and safely tinker around with our JavaScript code. jsFiddle at http://jsfiddle.net/ lets you run JavaScript code (optionally with HTML and CSS) and view the output. It offers toggling of the inclusion of common JavaScript libraries with a simple select box and has integrated JSLint support to check the validity of your code. A similar site to jsFiddle is JS Bin and its site at http://jsbin.com.

Shaders can be modified at several sites online, such as KickJS (which you can find at http://www.kickjs.org/example/shader_editor/shader_editor.html). We covered online shader tools in Chapter 2, and some additional sites are listed in Appendix D.

The main usefulness of online sandboxes is the ability to quickly test a small amount of code with much of the environment configured for you and the ability to safely share your code as a link for other developers to view, tweak, and collaborate with.

Generic WebGL Error Codes

An issue with WebGL that makes it fairly tough to debug is that there are only five major error codes (including the code to signal no error). These codes are numeric constants. An example from the WebGL specification is:
```
const GLenum INVALID_ENUM = 0x0500;
```
The main error codes are:

> `NO_ERROR` - *we are good to go*
>
> `INVALID_ENUM` - *an unacceptable value is specified for an enumerated argument*
>
> `INVALID_VALUE` - *a numeric argument is out of range (such as trying to specify a shader location of -1)*
>
> `INVALID_OPERATION` - *the specified operation is not allowed in the current state (such as trying to generate a mipmap with no bound texture)*
>
> `OUT_OF_MEMORY` - *application has exhausted memory*

The main errors are shared for the many function calls of WebGL. This makes it essential that we can trigger and detect exactly where and when an error occurs. Refer to the WebGL specification for a complete list of which error code(s) each function can throw.

There are also many WebGL states that we can check for, such as when we check the framebuffer status with:

```
GLenum checkFramebufferStatus(GLenum target);
```

We may receive the following among other possible return values:
FRAMEBUFFER_INCOMPLETE_ATTACHMENT //0x8CD6

Context Errors

The WebGL rendering context associated with a `HTMLCanvasElement` can have errors when created or throughout the life of the application. We will now show how to check for these errors and handle them appropriately when encountered.

Context Creation

If the request fails when we attempt to obtain a WebGL context, the browser is required to fire a WebGL context event named "webglcontextcreationerror" to the canvas. To listen for this event we can add a listener as demonstrated in the WebGL specification Example VII and shown in Listing 9-1.

Listing 9-1. Checking for a context-creation error

```
var errorInfo = "";
function onContextCreationError(event) {

 canvas.removeEventListener(
   "webglcontextcreationerror",
   onContextCreationError, false);

 errorInfo = e.statusMessage || "Unknown";
}
canvas.addEventListener(
  "webglcontextcreationerror",
  onContextCreationError, false);

var gl = canvas.getContext("experimental-webgl");
if(!gl) {
  alert("A WebGL context could not be created.\nReason: " +
    errorInfo);
}
```

The code in Listing 9-1 creates an error listener, attempts to get a WebGL context, and if there is an error will display the reason and then remove the error event listener. The benefit of adding the listener is that we can gain insight into the reason why the context could not be created.

Context Loss and Restoration

If the browser loses context with WebGL, we can detect this and restore it. However, any resources such as textures or buffers will need to be re-created. Context can be lost because of a mobile power event, GPU reset, a client dropping a background tab or being low on resources. Part of Example VI from the WebGL specification is shown in Listing 9-2 and demonstrates how to listen for the "webglcontextlost" and "webglcontextrestored"events.

Listing 9-2. Listening for context lost and restoring context

```
canvas.addEventListener(
  "webglcontextlost", function (event) {

 // inform WebGL that we handle context restoration
 event.preventDefault();

 // Stop rendering
 window.cancelAnimationFrame(requestId);
}, false);

canvas.addEventListener(
  "webglcontextrestored", function (event) {

 initializeResources();
}, false);
```

238

In Listing 9-2, we register context lost and restored listeners. If the context is lost, we stop animating. On restoration, we reload our resources.

▓ **Note:** The loss of context is one of the main security concerns with WebGL and the `OpessnGL GL_ARB_robustness` extension aims to add the ability for applications to detect lost contexts. This will help graphics cards "watchdog" malicious intentions such as denial of service attacks.

Continuously Checking For Errors

While developing we can use the `webgl-debug.js` library that was created by the Khronos group (the consortium that oversees WebGL) and is available at https://cvs.khronos.org/svn/repos/registry/trunk/public/webgl/sdk/debug/webgl-debug.js. Usage is outlined at http://www.khronos.org/webgl/wiki/Debugging. This library will make a call to `getError` between every WebGL call and output error results to the console. We can convert the error numbers to more readable strings with the call:

```
WebGLDebugUtils.glEnumToString( gl.getError() );
```

Calling `getError` is expensive because it polls the GPU, effectively blocking further communication between the WebGL API and GPU until a result is returned. As such, this library should not be used in production code.

Download the `webgl-debug.js` file locally. Starting with the `03/texture_and_lighting.html` file of Chapter 3, we will slightly modify the code to make use of this library. First we include the new script file:

```
<script src ="webgl-debug.js"></script>
```

Now let's cause an error so that we can demonstrate the library. In the `setupWebGL` function, change the enabling of the depth test from `gl.enable(gl.DEPTH_TEST)` to `gl.enable(gl.DEPTH_TEST_FOOBAR)`. If we run the program, it looks strange, but we get no indication in our console that there is a WebGL error as shown in Figure 9-5.

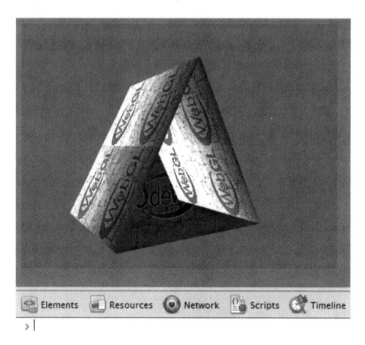

Figure 9-5. No error produced in our console

Now we will wrap our WebGL context in the `webgl-debug.js` library in our `initWebGL` function:

```
if(gl)
{ gl = WebGLDebugUtils.makeDebugContext(gl);
```

The result (found in the `09/texture_and_lighting_debug.html` file) is that no image is produced, but useful debug information is output to the console. It tells us exactly what function and line are erroneous—line 132 in the `setupWebGL` function—as shown in Figure 9-6.

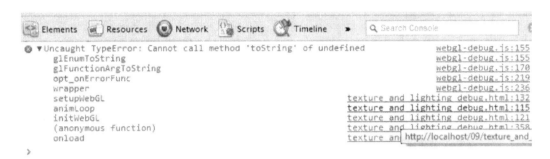

Figure 9-6. *The debug information from webgl-debug.js*

WebGL Inspector

By far the best in-browser debug tool currently available is WebGL Inspector, which is a useful tool to see view shader program information, loaded textures, the current states of our application, the contents of our buffers, capture a snapshot along with thorough trace data of a frame and much more. WebGL inspector was written by Ben Vanik and James Darpinian and is available from http://benvanik.github.com/WebGL-Inspector/. It is billed as

"An advanced WebGL debugging toolkit...inspired by gDEBugger and PIX with the goal of making the development of advanced WebGL applications easier. What Firebug and Developer Tools are to HTML/JS, WebGL Inspector is to WebGL."

WebGL inspector can be used by embedding a script into a web page or by installing the Chrome extension. Once it is installed, pages with WebGL content will have a GL icon show up in the address bar and two buttons on the web page, "Capture" and "UI" as shown in Figure 9-7.

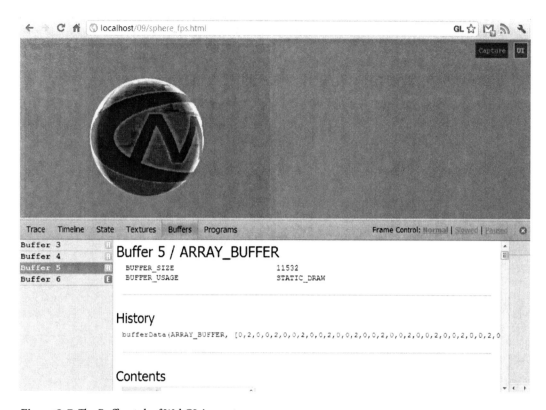

Figure 9-7. *The Buffers tab of WebGL inspector*

In Figure 9-7, the Buffers tab is displayed that shows the contents of our vertex buffer objects (VBOs). We can use the Textures tab to ensure that our textures have properly loaded, view filter and clamping parameters, and other information about the textures (see Figure 9-8).

Figure 9-8. *Texture data of WebGL inspector*

The Programs tab will show us the status of our program along with the attributes and uniforms and our vertex and fragment shader source code, as seen in Figure 9-9.

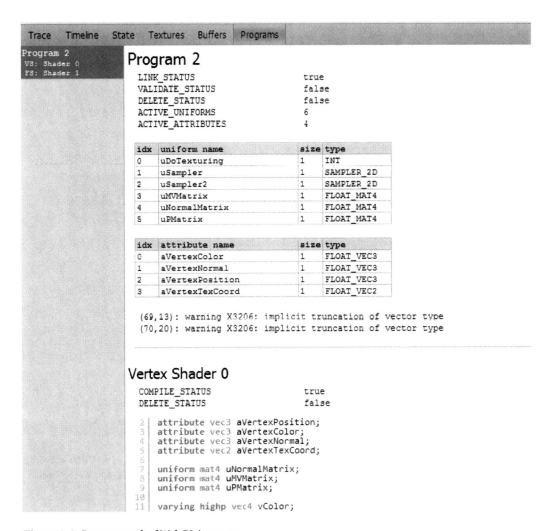

Figure 9-9. Programs tab of WebGL inspector

The State tab shows us all our adjustable state settings such as if blending is enabled, the blend color, the clear color, which orientation is used for front faces of our polygons, and so on, as shown in Figure 9-10.

The Timeline tab will display real-time data on various metrics such as frame time, primitives/frame, and buffer memory. The timeline is one area of this otherwise very useful program that could use some work in producing more scalable and readable results (see Figure 9-11).

Until now we have not discussed the Capture button. In my opinion, this is the most useful feature of WebGL inspector. When you click the button, WebGL inspector will capture the screen and a complete trace of the frame

Trace   Timeline   State   Textures   Buffers   Programs

State Snapshot

ACTIVE_TEXTURE	TEXTURE0
ALIASED_LINE_WIDTH_RANGE	1 - 1
ALIASED_POINT_SIZE_RANGE	1 - 64
ALPHA_BITS	8
ARRAY_BUFFER_BINDING	null
BLEND	false
BLEND_COLOR	rgba(0, 0, 0, 0)
BLEND_DST_ALPHA	ZERO
BLEND_DST_RGB	ZERO
BLEND_EQUATION_ALPHA	FUNC_ADD
BLEND_EQUATION_RGB	FUNC_ADD
BLEND_SRC_ALPHA	ONE
BLEND_SRC_RGB	ONE
BLUE_BITS	8
COLOR_CLEAR_VALUE	rgba(0, 0, 0, 0)
COLOR_WRITEMASK	true,true,true,true
CULL_FACE	false
CULL_FACE_MODE	BACK
CURRENT_PROGRAM	null
DEPTH_BITS	24
DEPTH_CLEAR_VALUE	1
DEPTH_FUNC	LESS
DEPTH_RANGE	0 - 1
DEPTH_TEST	false
DEPTH_WRITEMASK	true
DITHER	true
ELEMENT_ARRAY_BUFFER_BINDING	null
FRAGMENT_SHADER_DERIVATIVE_HINT_OES	undefined
FRAMEBUFFER_BINDING	null
FRONT_FACE	CCW
GENERATE_MIPMAP_HINT	DONT_CARE
GREEN_BITS	8
LINE_WIDTH	1
MAX_COMBINED_TEXTURE_IMAGE_UNITS	20
MAX_CUBE_MAP_TEXTURE_SIZE	16384
MAX_FRAGMENT_UNIFORM_VECTORS	221
MAX_RENDERBUFFER_SIZE	16384

Figure 9-10. WebGL state settings as displayed in the State tab of WebGL inspector

Figure 9-11. The timeline metrics of the WebGL inspector

will be generated as shown in the Trace tab in Figure 9-12 . Our sample program is small and has only 19 lines, but complex WebGL applications can have thousands of lines as we will later demonstrate. The lines highlighted yellow are redundant. This is great information to help improve performance as shown in the next section. You have the option to not highlight redundant calls, but will probably find the feedback useful. WebGL inspector also lets us slow or pause frame advancement.

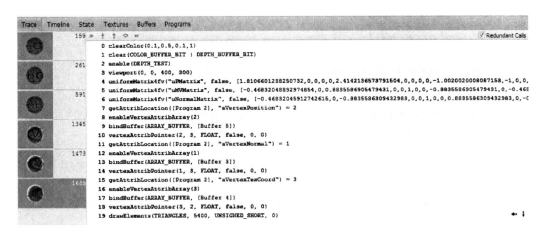

Figure 9-12. Trace tab shows frame captures with WebGL inspector

In line 19 of Figure 9-12 there are two icons on the right. The first, with a right-facing arrow, lets us run isolated output from a single draw command. In our sample application, this is the entire scene. However, in more complex applications with several draw calls, it can be quite useful to show what specific part of the scene was rendered. When the second link (that looks like an *i*) is clicked, a new window will pop up with complete draw information. The popup is extensive and first shows a mesh of the element drawn that can be zoomed in and out with the mouse wheel and rotated while holding down a mouse button. This mesh is useful to visually confirm that our vertices have rendered in the proper order and also so that we can ensure consistent winding of our polygon faces; the luminance of red in clockwise and counter-clockwise faces is different. We can also show a grid of texture coordinates used. Next, a list of program uniforms and current values are displayed followed by attributes. Finally we see the state of WebGL settings: vertex, fragment, depth/stencil and output. The first part of this popup is shown in Figure 9-13.

If we click a pixel of the image displayed to the right of the trace log (not shown in Figure 9-12), we get all the information about the color components and how the final pixel color is obtained in a new popup window. There is no blending for our example, so the final color calculation is straightforward, as shown in Figure 9-14. However, when blending with nonopaque alpha values, this information can be quite useful.

Lastly, WebGL inspector is also useful for indicating errors. Re-adding the gl.enable(gl.DEPTH_TEST_FOOBAR) line makes an erroneous line of the trace show up highlighted red, as displayed in Figure 9-15.

If we try to obtain an attribute location that does not exist (for example, by trying to get the mistyped attribute aVertexPosition2 instead of aVertexPosition), getAttribLocation returns (-1), which is an invalid value (see Figure 9-16).

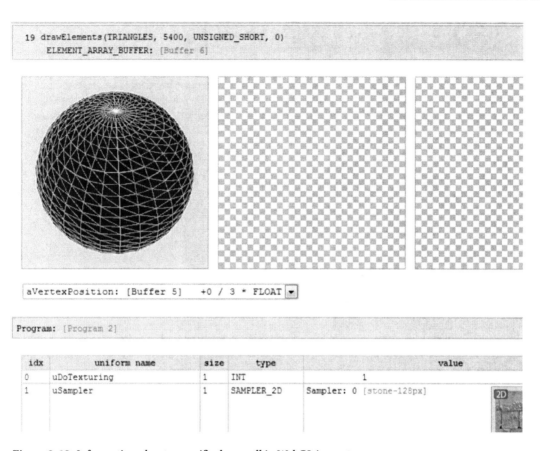

```
19 drawElements(TRIANGLES, 5400, UNSIGNED_SHORT, 0)
    ELEMENT_ARRAY_BUFFER: [Buffer 6]
```

```
aVertexPosition: [Buffer 5]    +0 / 3 * FLOAT ▼
```

Program: [Program 2]

idx	uniform name	size	type	value
0	uDoTexturing	1	INT	1
1	uSampler	1	SAMPLER_2D	Sampler: 0 [stone-128px]

Figure 9-13. Information about a specific draw call in WebGL inspector

---

■ **Note** If a variable does exist in your vertex shader but you never use it, the compiler will mark it as not used and remove it when compiling and linking your program. If you try to get its location later, you will receive (-1) and produce the same error.

Lastly, suppose we have called gl.bindBuffer with a null value binded to the WebGLBuffer parameter. This can easily happen, for instance, by writing data to a variable when generating or reading in data from a file, but using a different variable when binding that has been initialized to null and is never written to. The highlighted error is shown in Figure 9-17.

As you have seen, WebGL inspector is a tool with multiple uses, and I urge the reader to become familiar with it—you will thank yourself.

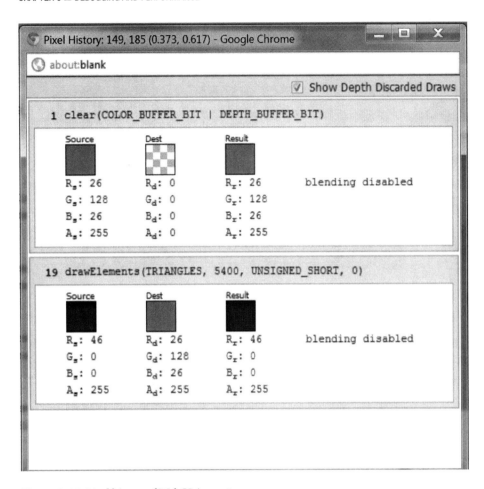

Figure 9-14. Pixel history of WebGL inspector

Figure 9-15. WebGL inspector error caused by invalid keyword

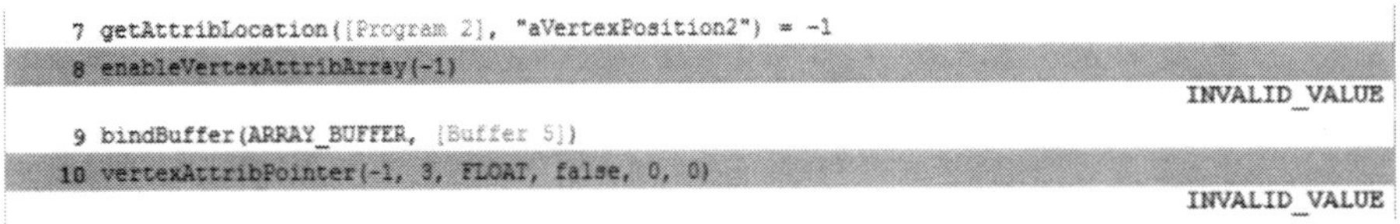

Figure 9-16. WebGL inspector error caused by invalid attribute location value

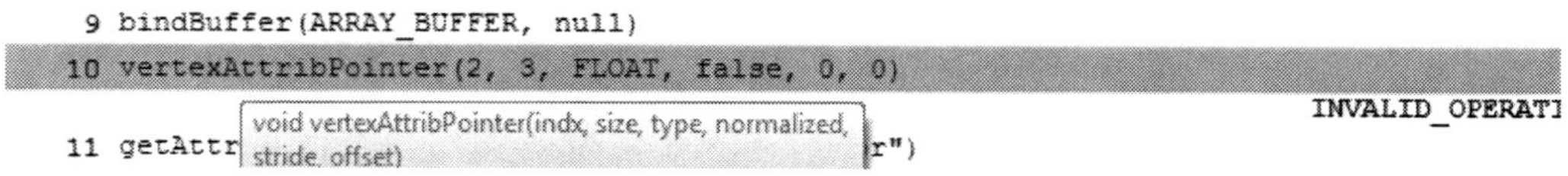

```
 9 bindBuffer(ARRAY_BUFFER, null)
10 vertexAttribPointer(2, 3, FLOAT, false, 0, 0)                    INVALID_OPERATI
     void vertexAttribPointer(indx, size, type, normalized,
11 getAttr  stride, offset)                                    r")
```

Figure 9-17. WebGL inspector error caused by binding a VBO to null

Testing with glsl-unit

Unit testing code—isolating parts of a program into small units and running automated tests on each unit—is a valuable way to ensure that a program functions the way that is expected and to detect errors brought on to code when refactoring (making structural but not behavioral changes to the code, to improve code design and quality).

There is a fairly new unit testing framework for the GLSL available at http://code.google.com/p/glsl-unit/. To clone the git repository you can use this:

```
git clone
https://code.google.com/p/glsl-unit/
```

Common Pitfalls

There are certain errors when programming with WebGL that are more commonly encountered than others. Here are some pitfalls to avoid.

Cached Content

File changes are not being used. The browser is instead still using an old version. Do a hard browser refresh with Shift-F5 or make the browser notice by renaming the resource file or purposely adding an error (temporarily) to your shader program or javascript file.

Reusing a Canvas for Incompatible Contexts

"2D" and "webgl" contexts are incompatible. Trying to use one and then call canvas.getContext with the other will return null instead of obtaining a valid context.

Mobile Device Fragment Precision Support

WebGL only requires that fragment shader floating values support mediump. Many phones and mobile devices only support this precision. If you are targeting mobile users, do not use highp. We can also poll the supported precision of a device with a call to the function getShaderPrecisionFormat. This can allow you to serve different shaders based on the device capabilities.

Camera View Is Facing a Wrong Way

Make sure that the virtual camera is pointed in the right direction of the scene and also that vertice points lie within the clipspace and the viewport.

Texture Issues

Using non power of two (NPOT) textures when trying to generate a mipmap is a fatal error. There is also a limit of the number of texture units that are available. If you run the webglreport shown in Figure 9-18, you can easily see the exact number supported on your current browser and GPU.

Performance Varies by GPU

GPUs have different hardware setups and optimizations. What is optimal on one GPU may be very slow on another GPU.

Loading the Wrong Resource

Check that you are loading the correct file, whether it be a texture image, mesh, or shader file. Also ensure that you are not violating cross-original resource sharing rules.

Browser Differences

It is advisable to try your code in different browsers when debugging because results may vary or work only in some browsers. The reason for this is that some of the WebGL specification is client-dependent. There are minimum requirements, but not all implementations are the same. Not all extensions are supported, either. To poll the list of available extensions supported in a browser, you can use these functions:

```
DOMString[] getSupportedExtensions()
object getExtension(DOMString name)
```

The getSupportedExtensions function returns an array of supported extension names. Every string in the returned array will return a valid object from getExtension, while any string name not in the supported array will return null. The objects that are returned signal that the extension has been properly enabled but are not required to contain any functions or constants.

We can also use the function getParameter(GLenum pname) to find other browser support information, such as checking the maximum supported texture size with:

```
gl.getParameter(gl.MAX_TEXTURE_SIZE).
```

Even without WebGL browser differences, there are JavaScript browser differences that need to be tested. For example, a trailing comma in a JavaScript object or array is fine in most browsers, but will be erroneous in Internet Explorer.

ie) [1,2,3,] is bad in IE while [1,2,3] is good in all browsers.

And {"a":"1","b":"2",} is bad in IE while {"a":"1","b":"2"} is good in all browsers.

A nice utility to view the WebGL constants of your browser is available at http://analyticalgraphicsinc.github.com/webglreport/, and example Chrome output is shown in Figure 9-18.

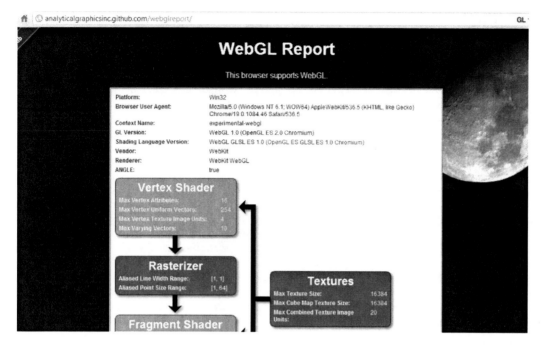

Figure 9-18. *Using webglreport to see your browser WebGL support*

External Shader Parse Errors

When loading in a shader from an external file, you might notice a statement that seems to be valid, such as either of the following:

```
if ( a<b ){ ; }

if( a && b ){ ; }
```

Each line will cause the shader to not load because the XML entities " < " and "&" need escaping. To correct this, try use the entities < and & directly in the shader source files:

```
if ( a &lt; b ){ ; }
if( a &amp;&amp; b ){ ; }
```

Alternatively, you can adjust the dataType returned from the Ajax call to HTML and then parse out the script tag with jQuery:

```
$.ajax({
        async: false,
        url: './my_shader.fs',
        success: function (data) {
                fs_source = $(data).html();
        },
        dataType: 'html'
});
```

Performance

For simple applications, following WebGL best practices for optimization will not be that important. Browsers and the GPU can perform calculations extremely quickly, so a small number of draw calls will render fast and appear at a good framerate, regardless of whether our code is optimized or not. However, as our applications become more complex and involve more WebGL and GPU interaction, they will quickly slow down, and the effect can range from slightly noticeable to debilitating usage. Luckily for us, there are known ways to take existing code and optimize it.

Measuring Framerate

In order to see whether what we are doing is actually improving processing, we need to measure the *framerate* (the number of frames per second) that we are rendering. A lower framerate will appear choppy, while a higher framerate will appear smooth and natural. The framerate is usually measured in frames per second (fps). Silent films had variable framerates of around 14–26 fps as the cameras were hand-cranked. Early projectors set the fps at a constant 24 fps that of course appears much smoother. Some newer films are using 48 fps, and a computer monitor refresh rate is typically 60 Hz (Hz, Hertz, is the number of cycles per second), though larger digital displays now are over 100 Hz. So the higher the framerate you can achieve, the better.

To measure framerate, we will use the `stats.js` library available on Github at https://github.com/mrdoob/stats.js. This library is written by the author of the `three.js` framework that was covered in Chapter 7. Download the `stats.js` file and include it in the code using this:

```
<script src="stats.js"></script>
```

Next we need to attach the stats `<div>` to our document and call its update method every time through the `requestAnimationFrame` loop. Note that the update method is not called if our scene is paused. This is a personal preference, as otherwise the fps will just fluctuate to a much higher, but irrelevant value when the application is paused. Code that uses the `stats.js` library is shown in Listing 9-3.

Listing 9-3. Adding the Stats calculator to our application

```
var stats = new Stats();
...
function initWebGL()
{
        ...
        ...
                attachStats();

                (function animLoop(){
                        if( !paused ){
                                setupWebGL();
                                setMatrixUniforms();

                                drawScene();
                                stats.update();
                        }
                        requestAnimationFrame(animLoop, canvas);
                })();
}else{
                alert( "Error: Your browser does not appear to support WebGL.");
        }
}
```

```
function attachStats()
{
        stats.getDomElement().style.position = 'absolute';
        stats.getDomElement().style.left = '0px';
        stats.getDomElement().style.top = '0px';

        document.body.appendChild( stats.getDomElement() );
}
```

Note: You can view the milliseconds it took to render the frame instead of fps by using the setMode method: stats.setMode(1); // 0: fps, 1: ms

The stats widget is shown in the top-left corner of Figure 9-19.

Figure 9-19. Displaying the fps metric of stats.js

When we use stats.js and have multiple browser tabs open, if we switch to a different tab and then back, the framerate decreases dramatically when we return. This is good, as it shows that requestAnimationFrame is working as promised, and unnecessary animations are not being performed.

Complexity in Optimizations

It is very hard to determine how to optimize GPUs because there are many different hardware implementations, and some optimizations that help certain GPUs will actually hinder performance on others.

Bottlenecks

In order to optimize code, you generally need to find the bottleneck(s)—the places where the performance of a system is being most restricted—and fix them.

An example that will be familiar to many people is washing and drying clothes. Suppose you have three clothes washers and one dryer. Each washer takes 30 minutes per load and the dryer takes twice as long: 60 minutes per load. The capacity of the washer and dryer are the same. We need to wait for the dryer to finish and are limited by the time it takes; it is the bottleneck of our system.

Suppose that we have three loads of clothes to launder. The total time to do 3 loads is 210 minutes (30 minutes for the concurrent washes + 60*3 for each dry). We can improve the performance of the system by limiting or removing the bottleneck in these ways:

- decreasing the drying time

- increasing the capacity of the machine

- buying more dryers

With the first improvement, suppose that you can fiddle around with the machine and get the drying time down to 45 minutes. The total time of 3 loads will then be 165 minutes (30 + 45*3).

For the second improvement (but no speed improvement), suppose that you can modify the dryer to take two full loads instead of one. You still need to do 2 full dryer cycles (1 at half capacity = 1 washer load and then 1 at full capacity = 2 washer loads), but the total time is decreased to 150 minutes (30 + 60*2).

For the third option, if you can buy two extra machines, your total time is reduced to just 90 minutes (30 + 60).

In the washer/dryer example, buying more hardware (analogous to having more computing power or RAM) leads to the most improvement. However, in other cases a bottleneck can be improved upon most by a more efficient algorithm.

For example, if you have a computation that takes 1,000 numbers, and the current complexity of the computation increases in the order n^3, it will take 1,000,000,000 computing units to finish. If you buy 4 machines and distribute the calculation among them, it will still take 250,000,000 calculations per machine. However, if you can reduce the complexity of the algorithm to n^2 without buying anything new, you reduce the computing cost by 1,000 to 1,000,000.

WebGL Bottlenecks

While optimizations are not absolute, there are some general best practice guidelines for maximum performance and to limit bottlenecks. Expensive operations include things that block communication of the browser and GPU and unnecessary calculations and lookups. The fragment shader has the most calculations to perform as it operates on every pixel in a scene. For this reason, the fragment shader can also often be the bottleneck in an application.

Fragment Shader

The fragment shader works on every pixel. As such, it is a possible source of computational bottlenecks and performance loss. One way to judge whether the fragment shader is in fact a bottleneck is to reduce the size of your canvas and compare the framerate. If there is significant performance improvement, it is because there are fewer pixels that need to be computed on, so you should try to optimize the fragment shader.

One tip is to do the reverse: After the fragment shader is done, stretch the canvas to a larger size. This will not require any more GPU computation and should be a relatively inexpensive client-side operation. Of course, this is viable only if stretching produces an acceptable number of artifacts or aliasing marks (that is, it still looks good).

Browser Resources

Even before we start rendering our scene, we need to load resources. There are several ways to reduce the physical size of resources that will improve the initial loading time of our web page.

Minify JavaScript Files

When our code is ready for production, we can combine multiple files and minify them into a compressed file. There are a number of tools available for this, from direct cutting/pasting of the source or uploading of files:

http://www.minifyjavascript.com/
http://jscompress.com/

To command line usage:

http://html5boilerplate.com/docs/Build-script/
http://developer.yahoo.com/yui/compressor/

Textures

We should keep texture sizes as small as possible. If a smaller 128 x 128 texture looks nearly identical to a larger 512 x 512 one, we should use it instead. It will be 16 times smaller in memory. Second we should choose an appropriate image format. BMP images are usually larger than PNGs, which are larger than JPEGs, which are larger than WEBPs. Which format you choose also depends on whether you need an alpha channel and how much image data you can afford to lose and still obtain a satisfactory level of image quality.

Browser vs. GPU Power

The GPU can calculate orders of magnitude faster than JavaScript in the client. On the GPU, many, many operations can be done in parallel and using compiled native code. As such, any "heavy lifting" should be offset to the GPU if possible.

Blocking the GPU

The GPU takes stream(s) of data from the application associated with vertex attributes. These streams then go to the vertex processor and then the fragment processor. The GPU computes in parallel but the communication between the JavaScript API and the GPU is more serial. Naturally we do not want to block this browser to GPU communication as much as possible. Doing so will lead to our program appearing to stall and the framerate decrease. So what can we do to limit unnecessary browser to GPU communication?

Batch Draw Calls

We should limit draw calls as much as possible (`drawArrays, drawElements`) by batching them together. The GPU can easily handle hundreds or thousands of triangles at once. However, there is also an upper limit to how large a single VBO can be.

> ■ **Note:** Three.js has a utility to merge disjoint geometries in order to reduce the number of separate draw calls needed. Details are in the `/src/extras/GeometryUtils.js` file and the function `THREE.GeometryUtils.merge`.

Reduce Buffer Switching

Instead of having separate VBOs for vertex attributes such as color, normal, and position we should combine them into interleaved arrays. We will discuss interleaved arrays later on in the chapter.

Reduce Shader Program Switching

If we have a few shader programs in use and several objects, we want to group the elements that use each shader if possible so that we can limit how often we need to change our active shader program.

Cache State Changes (gl.getX/gl.readX)

Every time you need to poll a state component of WebGL, the browser needs to interrupt the GPU and obtain information. Some calls to avoid as much as possible are `getAttachedShaders`, `getProgramParameter`, `getProgramInfoLog`, `getShaderParameter`, `getShaderInfoLog`, `getShaderSource`, `getTexParameter`, `getParameter`, `getError`, `getActiveAttrib`, `getActiveUniform`, `getAttribLocation`, `getUniform`, `getUniformLocation`, `getVertexAttrib`, `getVertexAttribOffset`, `getTexParameter`, `getRenderbufferParameter`, `getFramebufferAttachmentParameter`, `getBufferParameter`, and associated set X calls. If possible we should store cached versions of this information in JavaScript instead. We also want to limit `uniform` changes because they require interactions to the GPU. Additional WebGL calls to limit are `readPixel` and `finish`.

Do Not Use getError in Production

As mentioned above, using `getError` queries the GPU which is expensive. Use it continuously while developing but not once your code is in a production environment.

Remove Redundant Calls

We have showed how WebGL inspector is very helpful at showing you unnecessary API calls. An example of an unnecessary call is setting a state every frame when nothing changes it. This can be remedied by moving the particular state setting code into an initialization function outside of the rendering loop.

Another example of needless redundancy is generating 1,000 spheres by recalculating the vertice points for each one and then transposing them in the scene. Instead, calculate the vertices once for a unit length $(1 = x^2 + y^2 + z^2)$ sphere and store them. Then for the other spheres, scale and transform all the generated points to produce variance. This greatly reduces the number of trigonometric operations required and replaces them with the much less expensive elementary operations of multiplication and addition.

Limit Active Texture Changes

We can reduce how often we need to change the active texture by combining small textures into a single larger texture. This resultant image is known as a *texture atlas*. A texture atlas of some planets, the sun, and the moon is shown in Figure 9-20.

Figure 9-20. *Texture atlas of the moon, sun, and some planets*

We will use this texture atlas for performance optimization later in the chapter. For performance, also ensure that you generate mipmaps as outlined in Chapter 3.

Use it or Lose it

If you are not using features such as blending or the depth test, disable them. For example, if you are only rendering to two dimensions with no MVP transform or if you are rendering 2D objects that you know are being drawn in order from furthest away to nearest, you can safely disable depth testing.

Faster Arrays

WebGL arrays are naturally faster than traditional JavaScript arrays because they make use of new JavaScript typed arrays. Combining this with the use of interleaved arrays will improve VBO and attribute performance, as we will now explain.

Typed Arrays

Traditionally raw data transferred in JavaScript is treated as a string. As WebGL passes data to the GPU in large quantities, typed arrays are used to increase performance. Typed arrays use raw binary data and have a fixed byte size and type, which increases streaming efficiency.

WebGL uses the primitive sizes:

gl.BYTE - 1 byte
gl.SHORT - 2 bytes
gl.FLOAT - 4 bytes

The kinds of typed arrays available in JavaScript are these:

```
ArrayBuffer, ArrayBufferView, DataView
Float32Array, Float64Array
Int16Array, Int32Array, Int8Array
Uint16Array, Uint32Array, Uint8Array
```

Typed arrays are required in WebGL. You can view more information about them at https://developer.mozilla.org/en/JavaScript_typed_arrays.

Interleaved arrays

Switching VBOs is expensive. Often attribute data is separated for simplicity. However, instead of using a separate array for color, texture, position and normals, we can combine some or all of this data into an interleaved array. This will be much better performance-wise because it is not the size of data passed to our GPU at one time, but the number of separate draw calls required that hinders performance.

Interleaved arrays simply mix data together per vertex. In Figure 9-21 each row of array data has the RGBA color data followed by the XYZ position data (W is omitted). The total number of elements per row is seven:

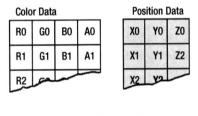

Figure 9-21. *Using separate data arrays versus an interleaved array*

RGBAXYZ. The size and order will be needed when we tell WebGL how to interpret our data. WebGL is not concerned by the actual contents of the data, and it is up to us to provide the proper context of our data. We could just as validly interleave the array in XYZRGBA order instead.

Let's look at the actual code we need in order to use an interleaved array. In Listing 9-4 we show the array declaration for two attribute arrays and then that of an interleaved array below it.

Listing 9-4. Separate position and color arrays and an interleaved array

```
//a square with separated arrays
var vertexPositionArray = [
```

```
            10.0,  10.0,  0.0,
            10.0, -10.0,  0.0,
           -10.0, -10.0,  0.0,
           -10.0,  10.0,  0.0
];
var vertexColorArray = [
            1.0, 0.0, 0.0,
            0.0, 1.0, 0.0,
            0.0, 1.0, 1.0,
            0.0, 0.0, 1.0
];
//a square with interleaved array data
var vertexInterleavedArray = [
            //x,   y,   z,   r,   g,   b
            10.0,  10.0,  0.0, 1.0, 0.0, 0.0,
            10.0, -10.0,  0.0, 0.0, 1.0, 0.0,
           -10.0, -10.0,  0.0, 0.0, 1.0, 1.0,
           -10.0,  10.0,  0.0, 0.0, 0.0, 1.0
];
```

Now that we have data, we can bind it to a buffer(s) and then point our attributes to the buffer(s) when we later draw our scene. Separate buffers are shown in Listing 9-5.

Listing 9-5. Binding separate buffers and later pointing attributes to

```
//two buffers for position and color data
var vertexPositionBuffer = gl.createBuffer();
gl.bindBuffer(gl.ARRAY_BUFFER, vertexPositionBuffer);
gl.bufferData(gl.ARRAY_BUFFER, new Float32Array(vertexPositionArray), gl.STATIC_DRAW);

var vertexColorBuffer = gl.createBuffer();
gl.bindBuffer(gl.ARRAY_BUFFER, vertexColorBuffer);
gl.bufferData(gl.ARRAY_BUFFER, new Float32Array(vertexColorArray), gl.STATIC_DRAW);

...
gl.bindBuffer(gl.ARRAY_BUFFER, vertexPositionBuffer);
gl.vertexAttribPointer(vertexPositionAttribute, 3, gl.FLOAT, false, 0, 0);

gl.bindBuffer(gl.ARRAY_BUFFER, vertexColorBuffer);
gl.vertexAttribPointer(vertexColorAttribute, 3, gl.FLOAT, false, 0, 0);
```

The last two parameters of vertexAttribPointer are the *stride* and *offset*. These are measured in bytes and the defaults are both 0.

Stride

The stride lets WebGL know how far apart each row of vertex data is in the array. So for vertexPositionArray, this is 3 * Float32Array.BYTES_PER_ELEMENT = 12. The following statement would produce the same result as using the default stride of 0.

```
gl.vertexAttribPointer(vertexPositionAttribute, 3, gl.FLOAT, false, 12, 0);
```

For our interleaved array, we have a stride of 6 * Float32Array.BYTES_PER_ELEMENT = 24. Note that we could also use an array with "garbage data" that we are not using or later using in each row such as://[r, g, b, x, y, z, some_extra_value]In this case, the stride would be 7 * Float32Array.BYTES_PER_ELEMENT = 28 even though we are still only using 24 of the bytes per row.

Offset

The offset tells WebGL what byte to start reading data from. With the vertexPositionArray in Listing 9-4, if we wanted to discard the first two numbers and start with the third, we would use an offset of 2 * Float32Array. BYTES_PER_ELEMENT = 8. Our first three vertices would then be:

```
(0.0,10.0,-10.0)
(0.0,-10.0,-10.0)
(0.0,-10.0,10.0)
```

Where stride and offset really come in handy is when we need to point to the specific data attributes in an interleaved array. Using the same buffer, we can set the offsets of our attributes to varying appropriate values. With the interleaved data of Listing 9-4 the position data has no offset, while the color data comes 3 * Float32Array.BYTES_PER_ELEMENT = 12 bytes later so we set its offset to this value as shown in Listing 9-6.

Listing 9-6. Using a single buffer with interleaved data

```
//interleaved data using a single buffer
var vertexInterleavedBuffer = gl.createBuffer();
gl.bindBuffer(gl.ARRAY_BUFFER, vertexInterleavedBuffer);
gl.bufferData(gl.ARRAY_BUFFER, new Float32Array(vertexInterleavedArray), gl.STATIC_DRAW);

...

gl.bindBuffer(gl.ARRAY_BUFFER, vertexInterleavedBuffer);
gl.vertexAttribPointer(vertexPositionAttribute, 3, gl.FLOAT, false, 24, 0);
gl.vertexAttribPointer(vertexColorAttribute, 3, gl.FLOAT, false, 24, 12);
```

Index Buffers

When possible, use index buffers as the GPU is optimized for their usage. Index buffers allow us to reuse vertices, so require less data to be transferred between the CPU and GPU.

Estimating Calculations Early

You would not calculate the value of PI to 100 decimal places every time you needed to use it—you would use a precomputed value instead. Further, the precision of PI to 100 decimals is most likely not necessary and would not produce any difference in the final result. This demonstrates two important concepts in computing:

- The fastest calculation is the one that does not have to be made.

- Estimates and simplifications are often better than accuracy if the (visual) results are approximately equal.

Reusing a precomputed value is better than performing the calculation many times. For example, if each vertice calculates the cos(time), it is much better to compute this value once per frame in our JavaScript and pass in to the vertex shader as a uniform value than compute it every single vertex.

In order from least- to most-expensive:

- External calculations done that are set as constants inside of the code

- Calculations done during application setup

- Calculations redone each frame of the application

- Calculations done every vertex in the vertex shader
- Calculations done every single pixel in the fragment shader

Of course we must also consider that the GPU is much more powerful than JavaScript, so there are situations where doing a complex calculation in JavaScript early will be just as bad if not worse than doing it more than once in the GPU.

Best Practice Summary

The following are techniques that are widely regarded as best practice usage for WebGL:

- Batch as much as possible, reduce the number of draw calls
- Interleave attribute data
- Reduce state change queries
- Do not call getError in production
- Keep texture sizes as small as possible; use mipmaps and batch textures
- Offload as much calculation from the browser to the GPU as it is magnitudes faster
- Ensure that the fragment shader is optimized as it is used most frequently
- Use requestAnimationFrame

Further resources can be found in Appendix D.

A Cooked-up Example

We tend to forget (or not fully understand) what we learn unless we dig in and try it for ourselves. So we will now cook up an example that has many objects moving randomly around in the scene in order to get WebGL to be slow enough to notice optimization improvements. We will increase the number of objects until we obtain a poor framerate and then we will use the debug and performance knowledge that we have obtained to optimize it.

I have created an example, 09/spheres_original.html, that uses six textures (of the Sun, Earth, Moon, Mars, Jupiter, and Saturn) with a basic lighting model and random movement. Initially there will be a separate draw call per spherical object and non-interleaved data used. By adjusting the number of objects rendered, we can lower the framerate. On my machine, 6 objects runs at 60 fps, 50 runs at around 35 fps, 100 is at around 30 fps which is still ok. A thousand objects reduces the framerate to a crawl at around 4 fps. I attempted 10,000, but my browser just hung for a while. You can see 50 objects on the left of Figure 9-22 and 1,000 on the right. You

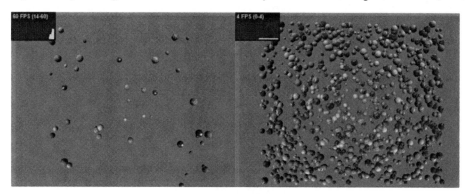

Figure 9-22. Fifty objects on the left; 1,000 on the right

can adjust the number of objects rendered on your machine by changing the following line and can observe the framerate by using the stats.js widget displayed in the top-left corner of the canvas:

```
var num_spheres = 1000;
```

A low-4 fps is a great starting point to see performance improvements in action. Opening up WebGL Inspector, we can capture a frame and see in the Trace tab that there are more than 18,000 lines executed per frame; and 1,000 total draw calls as shown in Figure 9-23; 4,000 separate buffers in the Buffers tab; and more than 40 MB of buffer data being used.

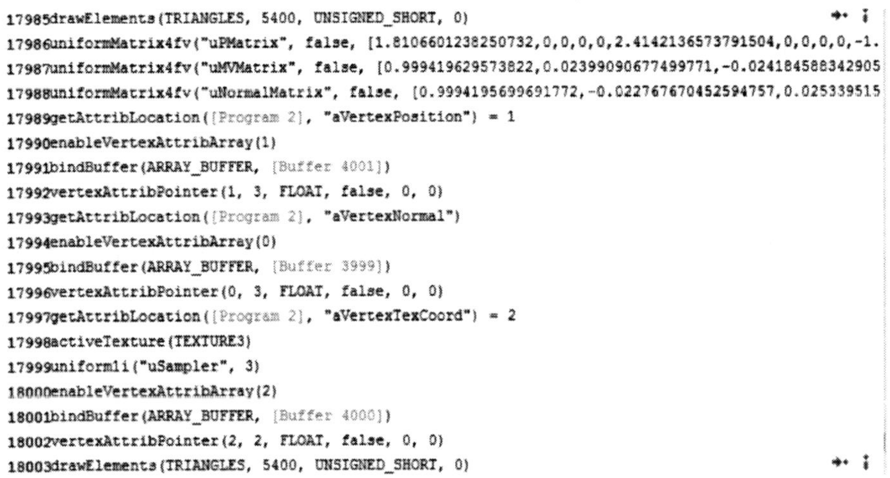

```
17985drawElements(TRIANGLES, 5400, UNSIGNED_SHORT, 0)                              ← i
17986uniformMatrix4fv("uPMatrix", false, [1.8106601238250732,0,0,0,0,2.4142136573791504,0,0,0,0,-1.
17987uniformMatrix4fv("uMVMatrix", false, [0.999419629573822,0.02399090677499771,-0.024184588342905
17988uniformMatrix4fv("uNormalMatrix", false, [0.9994195699691772,-0.022767670452594757,0.025339515
17989getAttribLocation([Program 2], "aVertexPosition") = 1
17990enableVertexAttribArray(1)
17991bindBuffer(ARRAY_BUFFER, [Buffer 4001])
17992vertexAttribPointer(1, 3, FLOAT, false, 0, 0)
17993getAttribLocation([Program 2], "aVertexNormal")
17994enableVertexAttribArray(0)
17995bindBuffer(ARRAY_BUFFER, [Buffer 3999])
17996vertexAttribPointer(0, 3, FLOAT, false, 0, 0)
17997getAttribLocation([Program 2], "aVertexTexCoord") = 2
17998activeTexture(TEXTURE3)
17999uniform1i("uSampler", 3)
18000enableVertexAttribArray(2)
18001bindBuffer(ARRAY_BUFFER, [Buffer 4000])
18002vertexAttribPointer(2, 2, FLOAT, false, 0, 0)
18003drawElements(TRIANGLES, 5400, UNSIGNED_SHORT, 0)                               ← i
```

Figure 9-23. Trace capture showing more than 18,000 lines and redundant calls highlighted

Capturing a frame and using the trace to identify redundancies for us, we can see that the viewport is being set and the perspective matrix is being recalculated every frame. Our view does not change and our camera does not move, so this is a waste. We can move the following lines to be placed before our render loop:

```
gl.viewport(0, 0, canvas.width, canvas.height);
mat4.perspective(45, canvas.width / canvas.height, 0.1, 100.0, pMatrix);
gl.uniformMatrix4fv(glProgram.pMatrixUniform, false, pMatrix);
```

This change improves the fps slightly. We will work through the trace until we get rid of as many redundancies as possible. Next we can see that we are reenabling vertex array attributes every time that we render an object. We can move these lines to be placed before our render loop as well.

```
vertexPositionAttribute = gl.getAttribLocation(glProgram, "aVertexPosition");
vertexNormalAttribute1 = gl.getAttribLocation(glProgram, "aVertexNormal");
vertexTexCoordAttribute1 = gl.getAttribLocation(glProgram, "aVertexTexCoord");

gl.enableVertexAttribArray(vertexPositionAttribute);
gl.enableVertexAttribArray(vertexNormalAttribute);
gl.enableVertexAttribArray(vertexTexCoordAttribute);
```

Amazingly, this code increases the framerate all the way to 50 fps! There are no more redundancies marked in the trace, with the total number of calls being reduced from 18,000 to 11,000. Now let's see how many objects we can push this application to display. Increase the number of objects rendered until your framerate lowers to a number below 15. The full code with redundancies removed is in the `09/optimized_1_removed_redundancies.html` file, and output is shown in Figure 9-24.

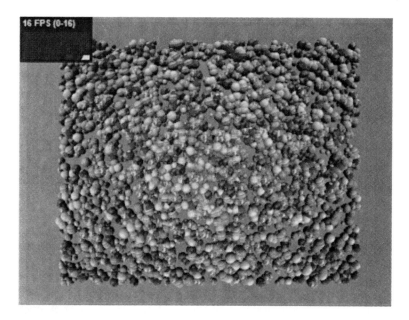

Figure 9-24. Three thousand objects at 16 fps

▓ **Note:** With too many buffers you may experience misleading results. With 100,000 objects I got a high framerate, but after looking in the WebGL inspector, there were only 12,000 VBOs not the 400,000 that there should have been. There were also only 33,000 lines in the trace; we would need at least 100,000 for the separate draw calls. The biggest evidence that we did not actually have 100,000 objects was that the result of 3,000 objects looked identical to 100,000.

Later after interleaving my vertex attributes, I could see 20,000 VBOs and the much fuller image shown in Figure 9-25.

In addition to limits for the number of total VBOs, there is also a limit to the number of elements per single VBO. The maximum number of indices is $2\wedge 16 = 66536$.

When optimizing, if a result seems too good to be true use your intuition and determine whether an upper browser limit has been reached or results have been cached somewhere.

Our next optimization is interleaving the vertex position, texture coordinate, and normal arrays into 1 array, so this should enable us to draw more elements as the number of buffers we use per object is reduced from 4 to 2 (1 buffer is for the index array). Interleaving the arrays cleans up the `drawScene` function nicely. Listing 9-7 shows our code to use our interleaved data (the generation is not shown but is viewable in the `09/optimized_2_interleaved.html` file) and send it on to the GPU.

Listing 9-7. Interleaved array attribute pointing

```
function drawScene()
{
        for( var i=0; i<num_spheres;++i ){
                setMvMatrix(spherePositions[i])
                setMatrixUniforms();
                var active_num = i%textures.length;

                gl.activeTexture(gl.TEXTURE0 + active_num);
                gl.uniform1i(glProgram.samplerUniform, active_num);

                gl.bindBuffer(gl.ARRAY_BUFFER, trianglesInterleavedBuffers[i]);
                gl.vertexAttribPointer(vertexPositionAttribute, 3, gl.FLOAT, false,
                                8 * Float32Array.BYTES_PER_ELEMENT, 0);
                gl.vertexAttribPointer(vertexNormalAttribute, 3, gl.FLOAT, false,
                                8 * Float32Array.BYTES_PER_ELEMENT,
                                3 * Float32Array.BYTES_PER_ELEMENT);
                gl.vertexAttribPointer(vertexTexCoordAttribute, 2, gl.FLOAT, false,
                                8 * Float32Array.BYTES_PER_ELEMENT,
                                6 * Float32Array.BYTES_PER_ELEMENT);

                gl.drawElements(gl.TRIANGLES, vertexIndexBuffers[i].numItems,
                                gl.UNSIGNED_SHORT, 0);
        }
}
```

Now if you put in the wrong stride, such as just 8 instead of 8 * `Float32Array.BYTES_PER_ELEMENT` (the total number of bytes) in the preceding code, you will get unexpected results, as shown in Figure 9-25.

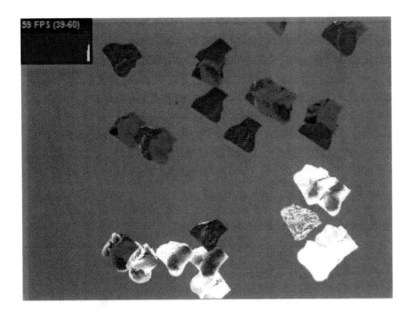

Figure 9-25. *Interleaved arrays gone wrong. These objects are not very spherical*

However, using the correct stride values produces the expected result shown in Figure 9-26.

Figure 9-26. Interleaved arrays gone right; 10,000 objects but at a low framerate

Next we will combine our six 256 x 256 textures into a single 512 x 512 texture atlas. You will remember that the texture atlas image was shown earlier, in Figure 9-20. Using the texture atlas will mean that instead of changing the active texture every object, we will never need to change the uniform sampler value!

The hardest part of using a texture atlas is generating the coordinates. This is actually fairly easy for a texture atlas with each inner image also having dimensions a power of 2, though the width and height do not have to be equal. We keep track of the x and y offset of each image and the scale (from 0 to 1) that the image lengths will be relative to the overall texture atlas dimensions as shown here:

```
//x_offset, y_offset, x_scale, y_scale
var textureAtlasAreas = [
        [0.0, 0.0, 0.5, 0.5],           //moon
        [0.5, 0.0, 0.5, 0.5],           //sun
        [0.0, 0.5, 0.25, 0.25],         //saturn
        [0.0, 0.75, 0.25, 0.25],        //jupiter
        [0.5, 0.5, 0.25, 0.25],         //earth
        [0.5, 0.75, 0.25, 0.25]         //mars
];
```

Then when we set up our sphere data, we can access this information like so:

```
var num_textures = textureAtlasAreas.length;
for(var i=0; i<num_spheres;++i){
        var active_num  = i%num_textures;
        var      tex_start_x = textureAtlasAreas[active_num][0],
                tex_start_y      = textureAtlasAreas[active_num][1],
```

```
                 tex_scale_x    = textureAtlasAreas[active_num][2],
                 tex_scale_y    = textureAtlasAreas[active_num][3];
      ...
      //texture coordinates
      interleavedData.push(u * tex_scale_x + tex_start_x);
      interleavedData.push(v * tex_scale_y + tex_start_y);
...
}
```

■ **Note**   A potential drawback of texture atlases is the possibility of color bleeds at texture boundaries.

We will generate a mipmap with a call to gl.generateMipmap(gl.TEXTURE_2D); The final optimization we will make and the most important is to batch draw calls.

Instead of looping through all the spheres we are to draw, we will perform a double loop of batches and spheres per batch when we generate our meshes in the setupSphereData method of our example and then use the number of batches in our drawScene method.

However, there is at least one issue we face now. Previously, we changed the model view matrix per sphere object. However, now we are batching several object draws together and still only adjusting the modelview matrix once per batch. That means that every sphere in a batch will be drawn at the same location. We will only see the largest sphere per batch, and the smaller ones will be hidden inside of it. For example, with 10,000 spheres batched at 40 at once, we will render all 10,000 but see only 250. We need to be able to set the model view per sphere. We also do not want to update uniforms unnecessarily. Instead of calculating the model view for every object in JavaScript we can offset this calculation to the GPU. This will actually be a performance improvement as the GPU is much faster. We will also have to update a uniform of translation and rotation amounts once per draw instead of for every object. Our original JavaScript code to calculate the per object model view matrix is shown in Listing 9-8.

Listing 9-8. JavaScript code for calculating per object model view matrix values

```
function setMvMatrix(sp)
{
        mat4.identity(mvMatrix);
        mat4.identity(normalMatrix);
        mat4.translate(mvMatrix, [sp.x_offset, sp.y_offset, sp.z_offset]);
        mat4.rotate(mvMatrix, sp.angle, [sp.x_angle, sp.y_angle, sp.z_angle]);
        mat4.inverse(mvMatrix, normalMatrix);

        sp.x_angle += Math.random();
        sp.y_angle += Math.random();
        sp.z_angle += Math.random();
        sp.x_offset = (Math.cos(sp.angle) * sp.x_offset_orig);
        sp.y_offset = (Math.sin(sp.angle) * sp.y_offset_orig);
        sp.z_offset = -25.0 + 12.0 * Math.sin(sp.angle);
        sp.angle += 0.005;
}
```

Instead of recalculating cosine and sine values which are constant across all the spheres, we can create uniform variables to store these values and use them in our vertex shader:

```
uniform float uCosTime;
uniform float uSinTime;
```

We will now also calculate the sphere geometry only once and store it as shown in Listing 9-9.

Listing 9-9. Calculating the points on a unit sphere

```
var unit_sphere = null;
...
function calculateUnitSpherePoints(latitudeBands, longitudeBands)
{
        //O(n^2) trig operations - costly!
        unit_sphere = {
                "vertices": [],
                "uvs": []
        };

        for (var latNumber = 0; latNumber <= latitudeBands; latNumber++) {
          var theta = latNumber * Math.PI / latitudeBands;
          var sinTheta = Math.sin(theta);
          var cosTheta = Math.cos(theta);

          for (var longNumber = 0; longNumber <= longitudeBands; longNumber++) {
           var phi = longNumber * 2 * Math.PI / longitudeBands;
           var sinPhi = Math.sin(phi);
           var cosPhi = Math.cos(phi);

           var x = cosPhi * sinTheta;
           var y = cosTheta;
           var z = sinPhi * sinTheta;
           var u = 1- (longNumber / longitudeBands);
           var v = latNumber / latitudeBands;

                //position
           unit_sphere.vertices.push({"x": x, "y": y, "z": z});
           //texture coordinates
           unit_sphere.uvs.push({"u": u, "v": v});
         }
       }
}
```

And we can use the stored coordinates to generate all the other spheres in our scene:

```
//position
interleavedData.push(radius * vertex.x + spherePositions[mesh_number].x_offset_orig);
interleavedData.push(radius * vertex.y + spherePositions[mesh_number].y_offset_orig);
interleavedData.push(radius * vertex.z + spherePositions[mesh_number].z_offset_orig);

//normal
interleavedData.push(vertex.x);
interleavedData.push(vertex.y);
interleavedData.push(vertex.z);

//texture coordinates
interleavedData.push(uv.u * tex_scale_x + tex_start_x);
interleavedData.push(uv.v * tex_scale_y + tex_start_y);
```

This allows us to not change the MVP matrices or need to use the spherePositions array data after generation. We can now draw our objects in batches with the code of Listing 9-10.

Listing 9-10. Drawing our objects in batches

```
var num_spheres = 15000;
var num_per_batch = 250;
var batches = num_spheres/num_per_batch;

...

function drawScene()
{
        gl.uniform1f(glProgram.cosTimeUniform, Math.cos(currentTime) );
        gl.uniform1f(glProgram.sinTimeUniform, Math.sin(currentTime) );
        for(var i=0; i<batches;++i){
                gl.bindBuffer(gl.ARRAY_BUFFER, trianglesInterleavedBuffers[i]);
                gl.vertexAttribPointer(vertexPositionAttribute, 3, gl.FLOAT, false,
                            8 * Float32Array.BYTES_PER_ELEMENT, 0);
                gl.vertexAttribPointer(vertexNormalAttribute, 3, gl.FLOAT, false,
                            8 * Float32Array.BYTES_PER_ELEMENT,
                            3 * Float32Array.BYTES_PER_ELEMENT);
                gl.vertexAttribPointer(vertexTexCoordAttribute, 2, gl.FLOAT, false,
                            8 * Float32Array.BYTES_PER_ELEMENT,
                            6 * Float32Array.BYTES_PER_ELEMENT);
                gl.drawElements(gl.TRIANGLES, vertexIndexBuffers[i].numItems,
                            gl.UNSIGNED_SHORT, 0);
        }
        currentTime += 0.01;
}
```

As we are limited in how big a single VBO can be, we will use spheres of 10 divisions (600 indices per sphere) instead of 30 (5,400 indices per sphere) to demonstrate the speedup by batching. Rendering 15,000 of these spheres one at a time results in 3 fps. Rendering 15,000 but batching 250 at a time produces a much better 45 fps as shown in Figure 9-27.

Figure 9-27. *Left: a batch size of 1 renders at 3 fps; right:- a batch size of 250 renders at 47 fps*

Summary

This chapter discussed how to debug WebGL applications and improve performance. These are two important topics that will benefit your WebGL development and the user's enjoyment of your application. The difference between a complex scene crawling at 3 fps and one moving nicely along at 40 fps is remarkable and could be the difference between a user enjoying your application or abandoning it. WebGL can be difficult to debug as many elements are at play: the specific browser, computer, and GPU used; the JavaScript API; shader programs; and resources such as textures. Each one of these can be the source of error. Luckily for us, there are powerful tools to assist us, starting from the IDE we use, to browser developer tools, and using WebGL inspector.

In the next and final chapter, we will present a diverse range of effects, tips and tricks—image processing, non-photorealistic shaders, and using framebuffer objects to both determine which element in our scene is currently picked by the mouse and to implement a shadowmap.

■ ■ ■

Effects, Tips, and Tricks

In this chapter, we will introduce a variety of WebGL effects, tips, and tricks such as these:

- Basic image processing
- Image processing using convolution filters
- Antialiasing
- Nonphotorealistic shaders
- Framebuffers and renderbuffers
- Picking objects from the canvas
- Shadow map implementation

Effects

A wide variety of effects can be achieved through image-processing and convolution filters such as sharpening, blurring, grayscale, sepia tone, color adjustments, and edge detection.

To apply these effects, we will start by loading a texture image. Then we will alter the raw color values at each pixel in the texture within the fragment shader. For these examples, the setup is similar to some of the Chapter 6 examples in which algorithms were used to create images purely within the fragment shader. This time around, we have a starting texture image to alter. In practice, the texture image could be from a HTMLVideoElement object, so we could alter streaming video on the fly using these same techniques. We will concentrate on static image processing.

Basic Image Manipulation

Our first example of image manipulation will show grayscale, inverted color values and a green tinted image next to the original texture image. We do this by first setting some effect constants and a variable to store a uniform value that will inform our shader which effect to use:

```
var    NO_EFFECT = 0,
       GRAYSCALE_EFFECT = 1,
       NEGATIVE_EFFECT = 2,
       GREEN_TINT_EFFECT = 3;
var    effectUniform = null;
```

When we render to the canvas, we will actually draw our scene four times, using a quarter of the viewport and changing the effect each time. The rendering is shown in Figure 10-1. Unfortunately, it is hard to see any difference in black and white print, so please visit the site http://www.beginningwebgl.com/ for a full colour version.

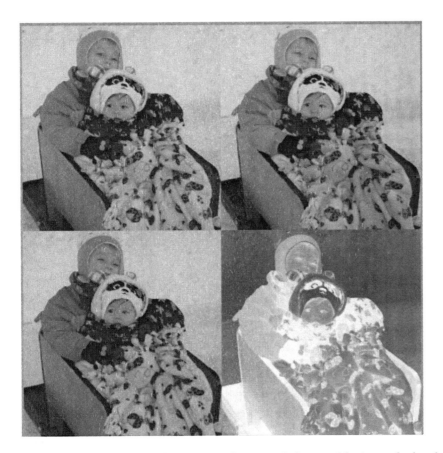

Figure 10-1. *Top left: original image; top right: grayscale; bottom right: inverted colors; bottom left: tinted more green*

Adjusting the viewport and rerendering allows us to easily view several variations at once and is an application of using multiple viewports in the same scene as discussed in Chapter 1. The code for the viewport setup is shown in Listing 10-1. In it, we draw four times to different areas of the viewport and inform the fragment shader which effect to apply each time by changing the uniform value.

Listing 10-1. Code for the viewport setup

```
...
//top left
gl.uniform1i(effectUniform, NO_EFFECT);
gl.viewport(0, canvas.height/2.0, canvas.height/2.0, canvas.height/2.0);
drawScene();

//bottom left
gl.uniform1i(effectUniform, GREEN_TINT_EFFECT);
gl.viewport(0, 0, canvas.height/2.0, canvas.height/2.0);
drawScene();
```

```
//top right
gl.uniform1i(effectUniform, GRAYSCALE_EFFECT);
gl.viewport(canvas.height/2.0, 0, canvas.height/2.0, canvas.height/2.0);
drawScene();

//bottom right
gl.uniform1i(effectUniform, NEGATIVE_EFFECT);
gl.viewport(canvas.height/2.0, canvas.height/2.0, canvas.height/2.0, canvas.height/2.0);
drawScene();
...
```

The full code can be found in the 10/01_image_processing.html file. The vertex shader is very simple and passes only the original x and y coordinates onto the fragment shader:

```
<script type = "x-shader/x-vertex">
        attribute vec3 aVertexPosition;

        varying vec2 position;
        void main(void) {
                position = vec2(aVertexPosition.xy);
                gl_Position = vec4(position, 0.0, 1.0);
        }
</script>
```

The fragment shader is also simple, but may appear complex due to the if/else if branches. It is shown in Listing 10-2.

Listing 10-2. Fragment shader to apply no effect or one of three different image modifications

```
<script id="shader-fs" type="x-shader/x-fragment">
    varying highp vec2 position;
    uniform sampler2D uSampler;
    uniform int uEffect;

    void main(void) {
        //convert texture coordinates from [-1, 1] clipspace to [0, 1]
        highp vec2 texCoords = position * 0.5 + .5;

        highp vec4 texColor = texture2D( uSampler, vec2(texCoords.s, texCoords.t) );
        highp vec4 finalColor;

        if(uEffect == 0){ //no effect
                finalColor = texColor;
        }else if(uEffect == 1){ //inverted colors
                finalColor = vec4( vec3(1.0, 1.0, 1.0) - texColor.rgb, 1.0 );
        }else if(uEffect == 2){ //grayscale
                highp float gray = (texColor.r  + texColor.g + texColor.b)/3.0;
                finalColor = vec4( gray, gray, gray, 1.0);
        }else if(uEffect == 3){ //reduced red, blue
                texColor.rb *= 0.8;
                finalColor = texColor;
        }

        gl_FragColor = finalColor;
    }
</script>
```

In Listing 10-2, we take in the varying position from the vertex shader, which we then convert from the clipspace coordinate range [−1,1] to the texture range [0,1] and store in texCoords. No matter what effect is being applied, we first perform a texture lookup and store the result in texColor. Now we check the value of uEffect that was passed in and determine a final color value accordingly. If uEffect is 0 (no effect), we simply set the final color, finalColor, to the texColor value. If uEffect is 1 (inverted color), we compute the color as (1 – RGB). If uEffect is 2 (grayscale), we take the average of the sum of the individual RGB components. Finally, if uEffect is 3, we lower the red and blue channel values. This increases the green tint of the image.

■ **Note**   In Chapter 6, when we loaded in a texture image that was used as a height map, only one of the channels was read from to find the grayscale color. This worked because the image was grayscale to begin with. Here, though, the image is full color. While using only one input color channel such as red may still produce a grayscale image, we can sample more input data by using a summed average of all three RGB channels. This can produce an image with more detail. For example, consider an input image that always has a red component of 0.0 and only the green and blue channels vary in value. In this case, the grayscale image produced using only the red channel will be completely black.

There are many other advanced methods to convert an image to grayscale. For instance, it is said that the human eye does not weigh the three color channels evenly, so RGB weights of (0.3, 0.59, 0.11), respectively, are better. GrayValue = dot(vec3(0.3, 0.59, 0.11), color.rgb);

We will perform two more direct pixel adjustments before moving on to convolution filters. The first direct adjustment will swap color channels, and the second direct adjustment will create a sepia-toned image. Our application is nearly the same, with the following modifications:

```
var     COLORS_SWAPPED_EFFECT = 0,
        SEPIA_EFFECT = 1;
...
//rendering to just the bottom half of the viewport
//bottom left
gl.viewport(0, 0, canvas.height/2.0, canvas.height/2.0);
gl.uniform1i(effectUniform, COLORS_SWAPPED_EFFECT);
drawScene();


//bottom right
gl.viewport(canvas.height/2.0, 0, canvas.height/2.0, canvas.height/2.0);
gl.uniform1i(effectUniform, SEPIA_EFFECT);
drawScene();
...
```

And our fragment shader code for these operations now contains the following:

```
...
if(uEffect == 0){
        finalColor = texColor.gbra;
}else if(uEffect == 1){
        highp vec3 sepia = vec3(
                min( (texColor.r * .393)+(texColor.g *.769)+(texColor.b * .189), 1.0),
```

```
                min( (texColor.r * .349)+(texColor.g *.686)+(texColor.b * .168), 1.0),
                min( (texColor.r * .272)+(texColor.g *.534)+(texColor.b * .131), 1.0)
            );
        finalColor = vec4(sepia, 1.0);
}
...
```

If uEffect is 0 (colors swapped), we map the RGB channels around to GBR, producing the image on the left of Figure 10-2. If uEffect is 1(sepia tone), we use the Microsoft recommended color values to multiply the original RGB values with to create the sepia tone, as shown on the right of Figure 10-2.

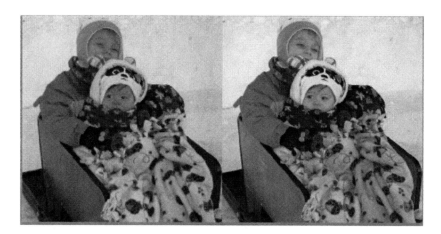

Figure 10-2. *Left: color channels swapped; right: sepia tone*

We could also adjust the brightness of the image simply by multiplying all channels by a factor:

```
finalColor = color.rgb * brightnessFactor
```

Setting the brightnessFactor to 1.0 maintains the same brightness; above this value brightens the image, and below it darkens the image.

The preceding direct pixel adjustments are pretty cool, but also simple as they affect pixel data looked up from a texture directly. To produce more-complex effects, we need to look at the surrounding pixel area around each pixel as we will do next.

Convolution Filters

For more-complex effects, we need to look at the region around each pixel in the original image. This region will be an n x n matrix, where n is odd, typically of sizes 3 x 3 or 5 x 5. This smaller image region consisting of a weighted matrix of neighboring pixel values is known as a convolution kernel or filter.

The weighted values of the matrix will determine the final value of the pixel. We may include the original pixel in the calculation or omit it completely and use only neighboring values. In Figure 10-3, the latter is the case, and we take an equal average of neighboring pixels, which blurs the image.

For example, the highlighted pixel in row 2 and column 2 has its final value computed as follows:

```
FinalColor2,2 = (      1 * color₁,₁+1 * color₁,₂+1 * color₁,₃ +
                       1 * color₂,₁+0 * color₂,₂+1 * color₂,₃ +
                       1 * color₃,₁+1 * color₃,₂+1 * color₃,₃
                )/8
```

271

Figure 10-3. *Top left: original image; top right: convolution filter around a single pixel; bottom left: the final color value of a target pixel; bottom right: the final image after each pixel has been processed*

For a pixel near the edge, we compute the pixels in the neighborhood and average appropriately. For instance, the value of the top left pixel is this:

FinalColor1,1 = (color$_{1,2}$+color$_{2,1}$+color$_{2,2}$)/3

In the preceding example, the original values are black or white, so the computation is easy. For color values, the RGB channels need to be computed separately. Above, each pixel's value is from neighboring pixels in the original image. There are also filters in which neighboring values are not from the original image, but from the modified results. In these cases, the order of traversal is important.

To compute the final value of each pixel that a convolution matrix is applied to we also have to factor in the total weight of the matrix values: the sum of each individual (w1, w2.., w9). Then we multiply the final result by the reciprocal of the total weight if it is nonzero or 1 if it is zero:

w1	w2	w3
w4	w5	w6
w7	w8	w9

x (1/[max(1, total_weight)])

Multiplying the matrix by the reciprocal of the total weight keeps the output values within an appropriate range. The matrix used to compute the final image of Figure 10-3 can be represented as follows:

1	1	1
1	0	1
1	1	1

x (1/[max(1,8)]) =

1/8	1/8	1/8
1/8	0	1/8
1/8	1/8	1/8

As another example (shown in Figure 10-4), consider the following 4 x 5 matrix of input values shown on the left, the 3 x 3 kernel shown in the center, and the final value produced for one example cell shown on the right. The kernel only keeps the factor from the top-left corner of the neighboring matrix.

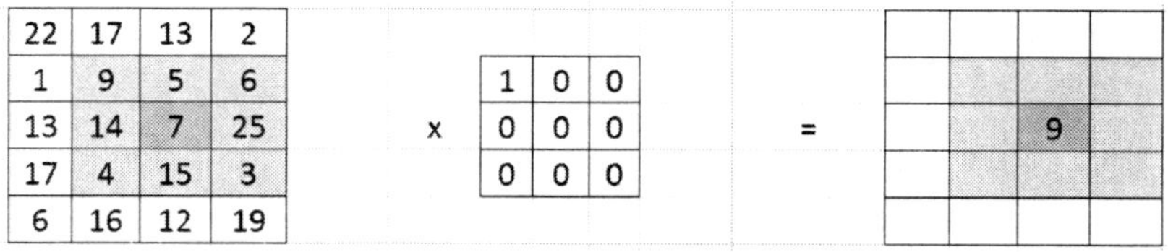

22	17	13	2
1	9	5	6
13	14	7	25
17	4	15	3
6	16	12	19

x

1	0	0
0	0	0
0	0	0

=

	9		

Figure 10-4. *A convolution filter that only keeps the top-left value*

We have enough theory now that we can start to experiment with different convolution kernels.

Sharpen

To sharpen an image, we want to increase the contrast between bordering colors. One filter that accomplishes this is the following:

```
[  0, -1,  0,
  -1,  4, -1,
   0, -1,  0 ]
```

We need to know the total weight of the kernel which is the sum of its, elements. Above the total weight is calculated as $(0 - 1 + 0 - 1 + 4 - 1 + 0 - 1 + 0) = 0$. Usually the total weight equals 1, so we do not need to do anything further.

This sharpening mask works by putting more weight on the center pixel and negative weight on edge values. When the center and edge values are the same color, the calculation will cancel each other out, while edges that differ from the center pixel will have their differences highlighted.

An even sharper kernel is this:

```
[ -1, -1, -1,
  -1,  8, -1,
  -1, -1, -1 ]
```

Here the total weight is also 0. If you output the image produced from this kernel, with the input image on the left of Figure 10-6 you get the mostly black image of Figure 10-5.

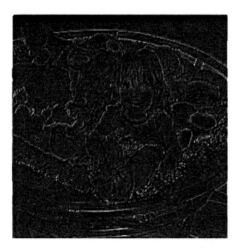

Figure 10-5. *Image produced from sharpen kernel*

To apply the sharpened output, we need to add this result to our original image by adding this result to our input image. This can be achieved directly as follows:

```
[ -1, -1, -1,            [ 0,  0, 0,              [ -1, -1, -1,
  -1,  8, -1,     +        0,  1, 0,       =        -1,  9, -1,
  -1, -1, -1 ]             0,  0, 0 ]               -1, -1, -1 ]
```

A fairly blurry image is shown on the left of Figure 10-6 along with applying both sharpen kernels to the original image.

Figure 10-6. *Left: original; center: sharpened; right: second sharper kernel*

The matrices used to produce Figure 10-5 and the right of Figure 10-6 illustrate how a small kernel modification that changes the total weight can produce vastly different results.

Blur

When we blur an image, we are essentially losing contrast. An easy way to do this is to average all the neighboring values for each pixel, which is known as a "box" blur. First, we set our matrix to factor in all neighboring pixels evenly:

```
var blurKernel = [
                    1, 1, 1,
                    1, 1, 1,
                    1, 1, 1
                  ];
```

Then we calculate the total weight, which is 9 for this matrix, and use it to produce our final matrix:

```
var blurKernel = [
                    1/9, 1/9, 1/9,
                    1/9, 1/9, 1/9,
                    1/9, 1/9, 1/9
                  ];
```

Now the total weight of this matrix is 1. A box blur will produce quick results. Another kind of blur that produces better results uses a Gaussian statistical distribution and is known as a Gaussian blur. The 3 x 3 kernel is this:

```
[0.045, 0.122, 0.045,
 0.122, 0.332, 0.122,
 0.045, 0.122, 0.045]
```

A very interesting blur filter is the Kuwahara filter, which reduces noise while preserving edges. This filter produces an image that looks painted.

We will now look at some filters that detect edges.

Sobel Edge Detection

A well-known filter, known as the Sobel operator, detects horizontal or vertical images (you can view the theory behind it at http://en.wikipedia.org/wiki/Sobel_operator). To find horizontal edges, we can use this kernel:

```
[ -1, 0, 1,
  -2, 0, 2,
  -1, 0, 1 ]
```

And to find vertical edges we can use this:

```
[ -1, -2, -1,
   0,  0,  0,
   1,  2,  1 ]
```

Notice that both these kernels do not factor in the original (central) pixel value. In Figure 10-7, we apply the horizontal, vertical, and combined Sobel edge detectors to the input image that is shown on the right of Figure 10-6.

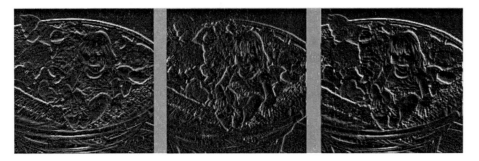

Figure 10-7. *Sobel edge detectors—left: horizontal; center: vertical; right: both*

Lastly, we will demonstrate the emboss kernel before we show how to implement these filters within WebGL and build a small application to switch filters.

Emboss

Embossing can make an image look raised like bump mapping by replacing each source pixel with either a highlight or shadow. Embossing is often used in printing and metal work to produce raised highlights of a graphic. An embossed image is shown in Figure 10-8.

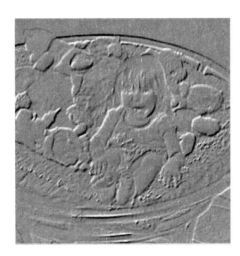

Figure 10-8. *An embossed image*

To achieve this effect, we first take both the Sobel horizontal and vertical kernels and add them together:

```
var embossKernel = [
                -2, -2, 0,
                -2,  0, 2,
                 0,  2, 2
            ];
```

We can adjust the intensity of the edge detection effect by multiplying this matrix. There are four different effects that we can achieve by swapping the direction of the 0 diagonal and the side of this diagonal in which the positive/negative signs reside. The four possibilities are these:

```
[                              [
    -1, -1,  0,                     1,  1,  0,
    -1,  0,  1,                     1,  0, -1,
     0,  1,  1                      0, -1, -1,
],                             ],
[                              [
     0,  1,  1,                     0, -1, -1,
    -1,  0,  1,                     1,  0, -1,
    -1, -1,  0                      1,  1,  0,
],                             ]
```

Each of these kernels will alter the direction that shadows and highlights face—either out from the surface or into the surface. Once we apply the kernel to our image, we then convert it to grayscale and add 0.5 to each RGB value. This makes the image mainly gray except for where the shadows and highlights occur.

A demo that allows you to toggle these various emboss settings is in the file 10/emboss.html.

Other common convolution filter values can be found at http://www.codeproject.com/Articles/6534/Convolution-of-Bitmaps. Another cool interactive demo that lets you adjust many effects in real time is available to view at http://evanw.github.com/webgl-filter/.

In Figure 10-9, we show the simple graphical user interface (GUI) that shows an original image, effect in the middle, and final combined image on the right along with a select box of various effects. We will now show how to build this application.

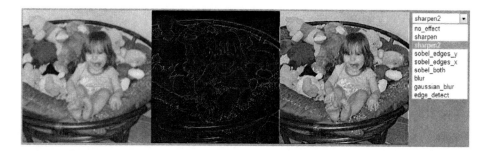

Figure 10-9. A simple GUI that we will build—left: original image; center: kernel matrix effect; right: the effect combined with the original image

We will now show how to build the application in Figure 10-9 that displays our original image on the left, an image kernel by itself in the middle, and after the image filter is combined with the original image on the right. It also has a drop-down select list that will change the filter. The first thing we will do is define a new variable to store the kernel weight, the current kernel and an object containing various kernel names and values. We will also add an initially empty <select> element:

```
var     kernelUniform = null,
        kernelWeightUniform = null,
        kernels = null,
        current_kernel = "no_effect";
...
<select id = "filters"></select>
```

We attach an event listener to our `select` element that will store the filter value that has been selected:

```
$(document).ready(function(){
        $("#filters").on('change', function(evt){
                current_kernel = $(this).find(":selected").text();
        });
});
```

We will create a function called `setKernels` in which we can add properties that correspond to convolution arrays within our `kernels` JSON object (see Listing 10-3).

Listing 10-3. Declaring our kernel filters

```
function setKernels()
{
        kernels = {
                "no_effect": [
                        0, 0, 0,
                        0, 1, 0,
                        0, 0, 0
                ],
                "sharpen": [
                        0, -1, 0,
                        -1,  4,-1,
                        0, -1, 0
                ],
                "sharpen2":  [
                        -1, -1, -1,
                        -1,  8, -1,
                        -1, -1, -1
                ],
                "sobel_edges_y":  [
                        -1, 0, 1,
                        -2, 0, 2,
                        -1, 0, 1
                ],
                "sobel_edges_x": [
                        -1, -2, -1,
                         0,  0,  0,
                         1,  2,  1
                ],
                "sobel_both": [
                        -2, -2, 0,
                        -2,  0, 2,
                         0,  2, 2
                ],
                "blur": [
                        1, 1, 1,
                        1, 1, 1,
                        1, 1, 1
                ],
```

```
                "gaussian_blur":[
                        0.045, 0.122, 0.045,
                        0.122, 0.332, 0.122,
                        0.045, 0.122, 0.045
                ],
                "edge_detect":[
                        0,  1, 0,
                        1, -4, 1,
                        0,  1, 0
                ]
        };

        var sel = $("#filters").get(0);
        sel.options.length = 0;
        $.each(kernels, function (x) {
                sel.options[sel.options.length] = new Option(x, x);
        });
}
```

In Listing 10-3, we add properties that correspond to filters. Each property name is added as an option in our select drop-down. The core of our application now displays three viewports. The first one is constant, while the second one displays the result of the selected kernel, and the third one displays the sum of these two images.

When we initialize our texture, we pass its dimensions to the fragment shader :

```
function loadTexture()
{
        textureImage = new Image();
        textureImage.src = "./textures/sample.jpg";
}
...

gl.uniform2f(
        gl.getUniformLocation(glProgram, "uTexDimensions"),
        textureImage.width,
        textureImage.height
);
```

We shall see later in Listing 10-5 that the dimension information is needed to calculate the size of each texel within the [0, 1] range that it should be.

We pass the kernel array to our shader as a 1fv type: a one-dimensional float vector. Lastly, we change the dimensions of our canvas for this example to 768px by 256px as shown in Listing 10-4.

Listing 10-4. Passing kernels to our fragment shader

```
...
kernelUniform = gl.getUniformLocation(glProgram, "uKernel");
kernelWeightUniform = gl.getUniformLocation(glProgram, "uKernelWeight");

loadTexture();
textureImage.onload = function() {
        setupTexture();
        setKernels();

        (function animLoop(){
                setupWebGL();
```

```
        //left
        gl.uniform1fv(kernelUniform, kernels.no_effect);
        gl.uniform1f(kernelWeightUniform, sum_array(kernels.no_effect) ) ;
        gl.viewport(0, 0, canvas.width/3.0, canvas.height);
        drawScene();

        var currentKernel = kernels[current_kernel].slice();
        var currentKernelWeight = sum_array(currentKernel);

        //center
        gl.uniform1fv(kernelUniform, currentKernel);
        gl.uniform1f(kernelWeightUniform, currentKernelWeight ) ;
        gl.viewport(canvas.width/3.0, 0, canvas.width/3.0, canvas.height);
        drawScene();

        //right
        //kernel result added to our original image (central pixel)
        if(current_kernel ! = "no_effect")
        {
                currentKernel[4]+= 1;
        }

        gl.uniform1fv(kernelUniform, currentKernel);
        gl.uniform1f(kernelWeightUniform, currentKernelWeight+1 );
        gl.viewport(2.0 * canvas.width/3.0, 0, canvas.width/3.0, canvas.height);
        drawScene();

        requestAnimationFrame(animLoop, canvas);
      })();
}
...
      <body onload = "initWebGL()">
              <canvas id = "my-canvas" width = "768" height = "256">
              Your browser does not support the HTML5 canvas element.
              </canvas>
              <select id = "filters"></select>
      </body>
</html>
```

The sum_array function is:

```
function sum_array(a)
{
      var key, sum = 0;
      for (key in a) {
              sum+= a[key];
      }
      return sum;
}
```

Last but not least, let us look at our fragment shader code that takes 3 x 3 kernels and returns a final color value (shown in Listing 10-5):

Listing 10-5. Fragment shader code

```
<script id="shader-fs" type="x-shader/x-fragment">
        varying highp vec2 position;
        uniform sampler2D uSampler;
        uniform highp vec2 uTexDimensions;
        uniform highp float uKernel[9];
        uniform highp float uKernelWeight;

        void main(void) {
                //convert texture coordinates from [-1, 1] to [0, 1]
                highp vec2 texCoords = position * 0.5 + .5;

                //find the size of each pixel relative to the [0, 1] range
                highp vec2 texelSize = vec2(1.0, 1.0) / uTexDimensions;

                //modified from http://games.greggman.com/game/webgl-image-processing/
                highp vec4 colorSum =
                texture2D(uSampler, texCoords + texelSize * vec2(-1, -1)) * uKernel[0] +
                texture2D(uSampler, texCoords + texelSize * vec2( 0, -1)) * uKernel[1] +
                texture2D(uSampler, texCoords + texelSize * vec2( 1, -1)) * uKernel[2] +

                texture2D(uSampler, texCoords + texelSize * vec2(-1,  0)) * uKernel[3] +
                //current pixel, central in the kernel
                texture2D(uSampler, texCoords) * uKernel[4] +
                texture2D(uSampler, texCoords + texelSize * vec2( 1,  0)) * uKernel[5] +

                texture2D(uSampler, texCoords + texelSize * vec2(-1,  1)) * uKernel[6] +
                texture2D(uSampler, texCoords + texelSize * vec2( 0,  1)) * uKernel[7] +
                texture2D(uSampler, texCoords + texelSize * vec2( 1,  1)) * uKernel[8];

                highp float weight;
                weight = uKernelWeight;
                if (0.01 > weight) {
                        weight = 1.0;
                }

                gl_FragColor = vec4( (colorSum / weight).rgb, 1.0 );
        }
</script>
```

The fragment shader in Listing 10-5 computes the size of each texel based on the dimensions of the texture that we passed in. Then it looks up the nine locations corresponding to the kernel matrix within our texture. If the total kernel weight that we pass in is close to zero, we set it to 1. Finally, the fragment color is set to the weighted sum of the kernel values.

Combining Filters

You could very easily create a fragment shader that chains or combines operations. For example, you could sharpen an image and then set it to sepia tone. Or you could find edges with the Sobel filter and then add the results to the original image.

The emboss filter in the `10/emboss.html` example with output shown in Figure 10-8 is similar to Listing 10-5, but also does a grayscale operation and bias:

```
//to grayscale and bias
highp float gray = dot( (colorSum/weight).rgb, vec3(.3,.59,.11) )  + .5;
highp vec3 finalColor = vec3( gray, gray, gray );
gl_FragColor = vec4( finalColor, 1.0 );
```

As a final example of image filtering, we will set an image to grayscale except for hues that are close to a certain value. You have probably seen this effect before on TV or in photos. It makes the colored part of the image really stand out.

The first and third photos in Figure 10-9 are the original; the second and fourth are grayscale except for very red areas such as the chair material in the second image and the blue of the scarf, blanket pattern, parts of the sled and gloves. (see Figure 10-10). The contrast of the final image was adjusted in order to see the changes in a grayscale printing.

Figure 10-10. *Producing grayscale images except for certain colors*

The code to produce the effect in Figure 10-10 within the fragment shader is simply the following which tests color channel values:

```
...
//equivalent to dot( texColor.rgb, vec3(.3,.59,.11) )
highp float gray = texColor.r * .3 +  texColor.g * .59+texColor.b * .11;

finalColor = vec3( gray, gray, gray );

if( texColor.r>0.3 && texColor.g<0.2 && texColor.b>0.2 )
{

        finalColor = texColor.rgb;
}
...
```

We will now look at built-in antialiasing that blurs edges to be less jagged within WebGL.

Antialiasing

Aliasing refers to distortion or artifacts that result because sampling or resolution is too low. With visual images, this is most often caused because we are limited in the number of pixels that monitors display, and the result is the appearance of jagged edges. In addition to our hardware limitations, the human eye is extremely good at picking out edges—look away from the text in this book for a minute at the objects surrounding you and pay attention to how quickly and accurately you can discern the edges of these objects. When you combine these two factors (image limitations and the acuity of our vision), aliasing will always be an issue with graphics.

Methods that we have at our disposal in WebGL to antialias include multisampling/supersampling, which take the average of multiple rendering passes with slightly different coordinate offsets. When we do this to a texture, it is analogous to using a blur kernel. We can also use more gradual function variations when possible; for instance, using `smoothstep` instead of `step`. Most antialiasing involves blurring of edges in one form or another.

By default, antialiasing is performed in the drawing buffer with the implementation dictated by the particular browser client. To override the defaults and set antialiasing to `false`, you can provide a second argument when obtaining a canvas context with this:

```
gl =    canvas.getContext("webgl", {"antialias":false}) ||
        canvas.getContext("experimental-webgl", {"antialias":false});
```

Of course, you would probably not want to do this unless you had a very intensive application in which framerate was very important or you wanted to perform your own aliasing implementation. The difference between turning antialiasing on and off is shown on the left of Figure 10-11 and with antialiasing turned off on the right.

Figure 10-11. *Left: an image rendered with WebGL; right: an image rendered with WebGL and antialiasing disabled*

The above uses the file `04/11_all_techniques.html`, and a highlighted region of the image is zoomed to show jagged edges.

Nonphotorealistic Rendering

Usually, when we render graphics we are attempting to produce highly realistic scenes that accurately model the world. These types of renderings attempt to be indistinguishable from a photograph and are thus known as photorealistic rendering.

However, there are times when we do not want this at all, and simpler is better. Two such applications of nonphotorealistic rendering (NPR) are when we are trying to produce a high-contrast, cartoon-like effect and when we are trying to convey technical diagrams in which the details are not important, but the shapes of the objects are. We will discuss these two techniques now.

Cartoon Shading

Cartoon shading, also known as *cel-shading*, is used to mimic the look of a hand-drawn image. It is prevalent in many current cartoons, such as Futurama, and in films as well. To shade something with a cartoon appearance, we select a limited number of tones that an object can have and then pick the tone based upon the diffuse light angle. There is a good interactive demo of toon-shading at http://webglsamples.googlecode.com/hg/toon-shading/toon-shading.html.

Implementation of cartoon shading is straightforward once we have the diffuse term calculated. If we start with the shaders of the the 04/04_gouraud_phong.html example as our basis, we already have the diffuse term calculated in our vertex shader and passed along to our fragment shader. Now we can set the final color based on discrete diffuse values, as shown in the fragment shader of Listing 10-6.

Listing 10-6. Fragment shader for toon shading

```
<script id="shader-fs" type="x-shader/x-fragment">
        varying highp vec3 vColor;
        varying highp float diffuseLambert;

        void main(void) {
                highp vec4 color = vec4( vColor * .1, 1.0);

                if (diffuseLambert > 0.9)
                {
                    color = vec4( vColor * .8, 1.0);
                }else if (diffuseLambert > 0.6){
                    color = vec4( vColor * .5, 1.0);
                }else if (diffuseLambert > 0.3){
                    color = vec4( vColor * .3, 1.0);
                }

                gl_FragColor = color;
                //gl_FragColor = vec4(vColor * floor(diffuseLambert*10.0)*.1, 1.0);
        }
</script>
```

In Listing 10-6, based on the diffuse light component that was passed into the fragment shader, we set the component to a percentage of the original color. This produces four distinct colors for each object. The result is shown in the center of Figure 10-12, and uncommenting the last line produces ten distinct bands (as shown on the right of the figure).

Figure 10-12. *Cartoon shading—left: two bands; center: four distinct colors; right: ten distinct colors*

> **Note** Listing 10-6 works only because each object is a constant color to begin with. If it were not, we need to explicitly set our constant colors between the conditions, such as the following:
>
> ```
> highp vec4 color = vec4( 0.1, 0.0, 0.0, 1.0);
>
>
> if (diffuseLambert>0.9)
> {
>     color = vec4(1.0, 0.0, 0.0, 1.0);
> }else if (diffuseLambert>0.6){
>     color = vec4(0.5, 0.0, 0.0, 1.0);
> }else if (diffuseLambert>0.3){
>     color = vec4(0.3, 0.0, 0.0, 1.0);
> }
> ```

Technical Diagrams

For technical drawings, such as those used in engineering and computer-aided design (CAD) software, details such as shadows and reflections are not important. In fact, they might distract from what we are trying to present. Instead, we want to convey a simple, consistent 3D shading. One way to accomplish this is to use the *Gooch shader*, which is named after Bruce and Amy Gooch.

The Gooch shader defines boundaries and edges in black, specular highlights in white and all other shades as varying from a "cold" to a "warm" color. The cold color can be blue, purple, or green; while the warm color can be yellow, orange, or red. The value of the color in the range can convey depth and curvature hints. Everything else in the scene is kept simple; there is one light which is usually above the objects.

We will use an existing implementation of the Phong lighting model, either `04/04_gouraud_phong.html` or `04/05_phong_phong.html` from Chapter 4 as our starting point. With this base, the Gooch shader is easy to implement because we already have all our lighting calculations in place and only need to set the final color to a value within our range of cold to warm hues. The only difference of these two Chapter 4 starting files is whether the lighting calculations occur per vertex or per fragment. A Gooch fragment shader with a per–vertex lighting calculation passed in is shown in Listing 10-7.

Listing 10-7. Gooch shading in the fragment shader

```
<script id="shader-fs" type="x-shader/x-fragment">
        varying highp vec3 vColor;
        varying highp float diffuseLambert;
        varying highp float specular;

        void main(void) {
                //below is modified from http://3dshaders.com/shaders/CH15-Gooch.frag.txt
                highp vec3  SurfaceColor = vec3(0.75, 0.75, 0.75);
                highp vec3  WarmColor = vec3(0.6, 0.6, 0.0);
                highp vec3  CoolColor = vec3(0.0, 0.0, 0.6);
                highp float DiffuseWarm = 0.45;
                highp float DiffuseCool = 0.45;
```

```
highp vec3 kcool     = min(CoolColor + DiffuseCool * SurfaceColor, 1.0);
highp vec3 kwarm     = min(WarmColor + DiffuseWarm * SurfaceColor, 1.0);
highp vec3 kfinal    = mix( kcool, kwarm, diffuseLambert );

gl_FragColor = vec4 ( min(kfinal + specular, 1.0), 1.0 );
    }
</script>
```

The per-fragment light version is similar, and full code for both can be found in the files
`10/06_gooch_vs.html` and `10/07_gooch_fs.html`.

The amount of cool and warm color used at each pixel in the Gooch shader depends on the diffuse light component, which we have calculated in our vertex shader and passed in. We also apply the specular value that we have calculated for the light. You can see the outcome in Figure 10-13.

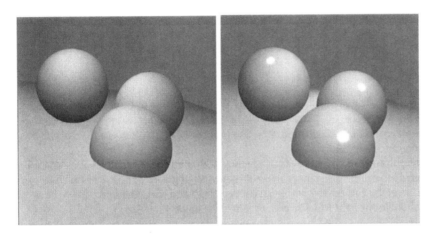

Figure 10-13. *Gooch shading of our Chapter 4 scene—left: vertex shader lighting; right: fragment shader*

We will shift gears now and talk about the framebuffer, which is memory that stores a full frame of image data that can be written to and read from.

Framebuffers

The *framebuffer* is a type of buffer—a region of physical memory in the GPU used to temporarily hold data—that stores an image for rendering. A framebuffer can also have attachments, such as a color buffer, depth buffer, and stencil buffer. In WebGL the drawing buffer of the canvas element uses the default framebuffer, but we can also have extra framebuffers that are rendered "off-screen." These alternate framebuffers are not shown to the user, but instead are used to store additional information such as depth or color information for later lookup. When we initialize our WebGL context, we can specify the depth or stencil attachments of the default framebuffer (see Appendix C).

To use a framebuffer, first we will create variables to store our data:

```
var     fbo = null,
        fboTexture = null,
        fboUniform = null;
```

Now we are ready to setup a `Framebuffer` object. We will show the steps to render to an alternate framebuffer and some applications of using an extra framebuffer.

Creating a Framebuffer Object

To create a `Framebuffer` object (FBO), we call the API methods `createFrameBuffer`:

```
WebGLFramebuffer createFramebuffer();
```

In practice, it will look like this:

```
//create a framebuffer object
fbo = gl.createFramebuffer();
```

If we are to save the framebuffer image for use as a texture, we need to make the dimensions a power of 2. We can either set the dimensions in variables or as object properties of our newly created `fbo` object:

```
fbo.width = 256;
fbo.height = 256;
```

The preceding two lines do nothing to the FBO by themselves; they are just a convenient place to set data for later retrieval. If we are working on a copy of the rendering, it is useful to set the dimensions of the framebuffer to the size of the canvas viewport. This way, we can look up values from the alternate framebuffer on a direct mapping with the size of the framebuffer of the canvas.

The framebuffer itself does not allocate memory. To do this, we attach a memory buffer to it, which can be in the form of a `WebGLTexture` object or `WebGLRenderbuffer` object.

Attaching a Texture to the Framebuffer

The initialization of using a texture with a framebuffer differs from regular usage in that the the data is set to `null` instead of actual values. This is because we do not have the data until we render the scene:

```
//create the texture
fboTexture = gl.createTexture();
gl.bindTexture(gl.TEXTURE_2D, fboTexture);
gl.texImage2D(
        gl.TEXTURE_2D, 0, gl.RGBA, fbo.width, fbo.height, 0,
        gl.RGBA, gl.UNSIGNED_BYTE, null);

//attach the texture to the framebuffer
gl.framebufferTexture2D(
        gl.FRAMEBUFFER, gl.COLOR_ATTACHMENT0, gl.TEXTURE_2D, fboTexture, 0);
```

The API call to attach the texture to the framebuffer has this signature:

```
void framebufferTexture2D(    GLenum target, GLenum attachment, GLenum textarget,
                              WebGLTexture texture, GLint level);
```

The target is `FRAMEBUFFER`, and the attachment can be `COLOR_ATTACHMENT0`, `DEPTH_ATTACHMENT`, `STENCIL_ATTACHMENT`, or `DEPTH_STENCIL_ATTACHMENT`. In the preceding code, we are storing color information in the texture and so use a `COLOR_ATTACHMENT0` attachment.

Binding the Framebuffer

We now have to tell WebGL which framebuffer to render output to by binding it with an API call to this:

```
void bindFramebuffer(GLenum target, WebGLFramebuffer framebuffer);
```

The `target` is `FRAMEBUFFER`. If the `framebuffer` object value is `null`, WebGL will use the default framebuffer of the canvas element.

To set rendering to our new framebuffer, we would use this:

```
gl.bindFramebuffer(gl.FRAMEBUFFER, fbo);
```

Using an alternate framebuffer has the effect that the current rendering is not visible on the screen. Our full code to set up an alternate framebuffer and render to it is shown in Listing 10-8.

Listing 10-8. Setting up and rendering to an alternate framebuffer object

```
var fbo = null,
    fboTexture = null;
    ...
    glProgram.fboUniform = gl.getUniformLocation(glProgram, "uFBO");
    createFBO();

    (function animLoop(){
            ...
    })();

    function createFBO()
    {
            //create frambuffer object
            fbo.width = 256;
            fbo.height = 256;
            gl.bindFramebuffer(gl.FRAMEBUFFER, fbo);

            //create the texture
            gl.bindTexture(gl.TEXTURE_2D, fboTexture);
            gl.texImage2D(
            gl.TEXTURE_2D, 0, gl.RGBA, fbo.width, fbo.height, 0,
                        gl.RGBA, gl.UNSIGNED_BYTE, null);
            gl.texParameteri(gl.TEXTURE_2D, gl.TEXTURE_WRAP_S, gl.CLAMP_TO_EDGE);
            gl.texParameteri(gl.TEXTURE_2D, gl.TEXTURE_WRAP_T, gl.CLAMP_TO_EDGE);
            gl.texParameteri(gl.TEXTURE_2D, gl.TEXTURE_MIN_FILTER, gl.NEAREST);
            gl.texParameteri(gl.TEXTURE_2D, gl.TEXTURE_MAG_FILTER, gl.NEAREST);

            //attach the texture
            gl.framebufferTexture2D(gl.FRAMEBUFFER, gl.COLOR_ATTACHMENT0,
                    gl.TEXTURE_2D, fboTexture, 0);

            //render the scene to the fbo
            setupWebGL();
            gl.uniform1i(glProgram[0].fboUniform, 1);
            gl.viewport(0, 0, fbo.width, fbo.height);
            drawScene();
```

```
            //attach the texture to the framebuffer object
            gl.bindTexture(gl.TEXTURE_2D, null);
            gl.bindFramebuffer(gl.FRAMEBUFFER, null);
    }
```

The `glProgram[0].fboUniform` variable in Listing 10-8 will be used to switch our fragment shader functionality, as we will now show.

░ **Note**   The `createFBO` call is outside of the render loop, but if we move our scene around, we need to rerender to the FBO each time the scene shifts positions in our view. If you place the `createFBO()` call inside of the render loop, make sure that you keep these lines outside or you will create a new `WebGLFramebuffer` and `WebGLTexture` object each time through:
`fbo = gl.createFramebuffer();`

`fboTexture = gl.createTexture();`

Changing Shader Functionality per Framebuffer

We can now render to either the regular drawing buffer or to extra framebuffers. We will have our fragment shader either perform Phong lighting or simply use the color passed in from the vertex shader, depending on the uFBO integer uniform:

```
<script id = "shader-fs" type = "x-shader/x-fragment">
        ...
        uniform int uFBO;
        varying highp vec4 vColor;

        void main(void) {
                //initialize the color to the varying value passed in
                highp vec4 color = vColor;

                if(uFBO == 0)
                {
                        //apply complex Phong lighting calculations
                        ...
                        color = phongBasedColor;
                }
                gl_FragColor = color;
}
</script>
```

We will render our scene twice. The first time it will be to the canvas framebuffer context and use the Phong lighting model. The second time we will render to the FBO that we have set up with basic color rendering.

We cannot actually see what is rendered to the alternate framebuffer. To demonstrate what it contains, we will render to the canvas a second time, as shown in Figure 10-14, this time using the framebuffer texture. However, the image does not look right because we can see only part of two of the spheres. This is occurring because a framebuffer by default does not perform depth testing as it does not have a depth component. The image on the right of Figure 10-14 is produced by reversing the order of rendering, which improves the viewed objects; but the front sphere is completely visible even though the bottom should be hidden. We will fix depth testing for the entire scene by adding a `DEPTH_ATTACHMENT` to the framebuffer which already has a `COLOR_ATTACHMENT0`.

289

Figure 10-14. *Left: Phong shading; center: basic color FBO with no depth buffer; right: basic color FBO with no depth buffer and object render order adjusted*

You can see in Figure 10-14 that there is aliasing going. We can limit the aliasing artifacts by performing better texture filtering with this:

```
gl.texParameteri(gl.TEXTURE_2D, gl.TEXTURE_MAG_FILTER, gl.LINEAR);
gl.texParameteri(gl.TEXTURE_2D, gl.TEXTURE_MIN_FILTER, gl.LINEAR_MIPMAP_NEAREST);
gl.generateMipmap(gl.TEXTURE_2D);
```

To render using the framebuffer texture, we have defined two programs and switch between them as you can see if you examine the full source code of the file 10/08_framebuffer_lookup.html.

Listing 10-9 shows the current render loop, which renders to the canvas twice and the alternate framebuffer once.

Listing 10-9. Rendering the same scene representing multiple FBOs by splitting the viewport

```
(function animLoop(){
        if( !paused ){
                setupWebGL();

                //draw to canvas twice
                gl.bindFramebuffer(gl.FRAMEBUFFER, null);
                gl.uniform1i(glProgram[0].fboUniform, 0);
                gl.viewport(0, 0, canvas.width/2.0, canvas.height);
                drawScene();

                //we will draw the framebuffer texture once to the regular canvas
                //as well, just so that we can see what is going on
                gl.useProgram(glProgram[1]);
                gl.bindTexture(gl.TEXTURE_2D, fboTexture);
                gl.viewport(canvas.width/2.0, 0, canvas.width/2.0, canvas.height);
                drawFBOContents();
                gl.bindTexture(gl.TEXTURE_2D, null);
                gl.useProgram(glProgram[0]);
        }
        requestAnimationFrame(animLoop, canvas);
})();
```

The example at this point can be found in the 10/08_framebuffer_lookup.html file. Now we will add a DEPTH_ATTACHMENT so that we can do depth testing in the framebuffer.

Adding a Depth Attachment

As mentioned, we can provide attachments to a framebuffer in the form of textures or a `WebGLRenderbuffer` object. We have shown how to store the color information in a texture. It could have alternatively been stored in a `WebGLRenderbuffer` object. For the depth information, we will use a `WebGLRenderbuffer` attachment to the framebuffer.

As with textures and framebuffers, you must bind a renderbuffer to override the default value. The API calls to create and bind a `WebGLRenderbuffer` are these:

```
WebGLRenderbuffer createRenderbuffer()
void bindRenderbuffer(GLenum target, WebGLRenderbuffer renderbuffer)
```

In our code, it will look like this:

```
var rbo = gl.createRenderbuffer();
gl.bindRenderbuffer(gl.RENDERBUFFER, rbo);
```

Setting the `renderbuffer` to `null` will unbound the current object from the `RENDERBUFFER` target. Next we have to tell WebGL how much size to allocate for the renderbuffer with the API call:

```
void renderbufferStorage(GLenum target, GLenum internalformat, GLsizei width, GLsizei height)
```

The target will be `RENDERBUFFER`, and the format we will use will be `DEPTH_COMPONENT16`. All possible `internalformat` values are listed in Appendix C. In our code, this declaration will look like this:

```
gl.renderbufferStorage(gl.RENDERBUFFER, gl.DEPTH_COMPONENT16, fbo.width, fbo.height);
```

The preceding code tells WebGL to allocate enough memory in the currently bound renderbuffer to hold (`fbo.width*fbo.height`) 16-bit depth values.

Analogously to how we set up our texture as an attachment to the framebuffer, we now set up the renderbuffer as an attachment of the framebuffer:

```
//setup attachments
gl.framebufferTexture2D(gl.FRAMEBUFFER, gl.COLOR_ATTACHMENT0, gl.TEXTURE_2D, fboTexture, 0);
gl.framebufferRenderbuffer(gl.FRAMEBUFFER, gl.DEPTH_ATTACHMENT, gl.RENDERBUFFER, rbo)
```

The API signature for the new method above is this:

```
void framebufferRenderbuffer(    GLenum target, GLenum attachment,
                                 GLenum renderbuffertarget,
                                 WebGLRenderbuffer renderbuffer );
```

Rerunning the code now, which is in the 10/09_framebuffer_with_depth.html file, produces the expected result on the right of Figure 10-15.

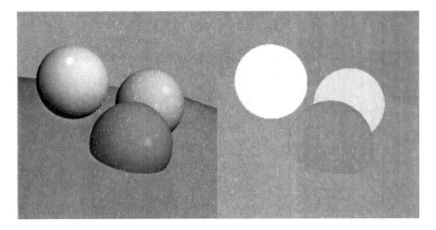

Figure 10-15. *Left: Phong shading; right: basic colored FBO with a depth attachment*

You might be thinking that this was quite a bit of work to produce an image less impressive than the original. Why bother? Well, remember that the offscreen framebuffer can be used to look up values. We will discuss two applications of this next.

Picking Objects

So far, we have discussed throughout the book how to project 3D coordinates onto 2D canvas space. But how do we find the 3D coordinates from a 2D canvas point? An application of this is "picking"—being able to grab the proper object associated with a point. But how do we do this? There could be several objects sharing the same (x,y) coordinate. One method for complex scenes is to use a scene graph that is basically a tree-like representation of objects that helps keep track of spatial relationships of objects. This is one of the features that the SceneJS framework (scenejs.org) is centered around.

Another technique is to assign (and keep track of) a distinct color for each object and render it to an off-screen buffer. Then when the user clicks the mouse in the scene, we can look up the color value of the pixel and immediately know what object was clicked. Pretty cool, eh? In the example that produced Figure 10-15, we already have a distinct color for each object, so do not need to add code for this part of the technique. In practice, you would just store an object mapping and pass in different uniform colors to the shader, such as these:

```
var myObjectColors = {
    0: {"name": "sphere1", "color": [0, 255, 0]},
    1: {"name": "cube", "color": [255, 0, 0], },
    2:...
};
```

This lets you have up to 255^3 unique colors that should be more than enough to use this technique especially if you can restrict selection to a particular region and subset of objects within your scene. The name property is mostly for the programmer/users benefit, while the numeric index could map to VBOs, and the color property would be passed in as a vec3 uniform to the fragment shader for the offscreen FBO rendering pass.

Looking Up a Value

To look up the current color of a location on the canvas, we can use the API call:

```
void readPixels( GLint x, GLint y, GLsizei width, GLsizei height,
                 GLenum format, GLenum type, ArrayBufferView pixels);
```

Note The value (0,0,0,0) is returned by readPixels for any pixel outside of the bound framebuffer.

The code to capture a click event and look up the pixel value of the mouse position is not that long and is shown in Listing 10-10. We just need to switch the active framebuffer and then restore it to the default canvas framebuffer after we are done with our readPixels call.

Listing 10-10. Code to look up the color value from an alternate framebuffer

```
$(this).on("click", "canvas", function(evt){
        gl.bindFramebuffer(gl.FRAMEBUFFER, fbo);
        var status = gl.checkFramebufferStatus(gl.FRAMEBUFFER);

        if (status == gl.FRAMEBUFFER_COMPLETE)
        {
                var pixelValues = new Uint8Array(4);
                gl.readPixels(evt.clientX, 255 - evt.clientY, 1, 1, gl.RGBA,
                        gl.UNSIGNED_BYTE, pixelValues);

                if(pixelValues[0] == 255 && pixelValues[1] == 0 && pixelValues[2] == 0)
                {
                        console.log(    "Location: ("+evt.clientX+", "+evt.clientY +
                                        ") is in the RED sphere!");
                }else if(       pixelValues[0] == 255 && pixelValues[1] == 255 &&
                                pixelValues[2] == 0)
                {
                        console.log(    "Location: ("+evt.clientX+", "+evt.clientY +
                                        ") is in the YELLOW sphere!");
                }else if(       pixelValues[0] == 0 && pixelValues[1] == 255 &&
                                pixelValues[2] == 0)
                {
                        console.log(    "Location: ("+evt.clientX+", "+evt.clientY +
                                        ") is in the GREEN sphere!");
                }
        }
        gl.bindFramebuffer(gl.FRAMEBUFFER, null);
});
```

Console log messages will look like those in Figure 10-16 when using the application.

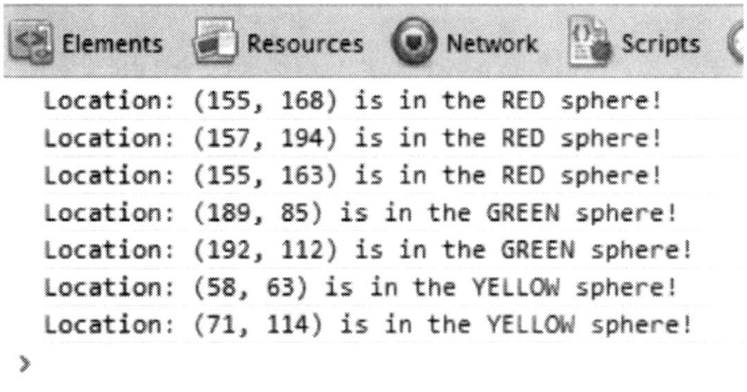

```
 Elements      Resources      Network      Scripts

    Location: (155, 168) is in the RED sphere!
    Location: (157, 194) is in the RED sphere!
    Location: (155, 163) is in the RED sphere!
    Location: (189, 85) is in the GREEN sphere!
    Location: (192, 112) is in the GREEN sphere!
    Location: (58, 63) is in the YELLOW sphere!
    Location: (71, 114) is in the YELLOW sphere!
 >
```

Figure 10-16. *Clicking a sphere now logs a message to the console*

The working program is in the 10/10_picking.html file. The 10/11_picking_moving.html file demonstrates the scene being animated and the FBO being regenerated in each frame. You can extend the example by changing the active sphere color while it is clicked or allowing the sphere to be moved or thrown when picked.

Shadow Map Implementation

To implement the shadow map that we discussed in Chapter 4, we look at the scene from the light's perspective and render to an off-screen framebuffer. The framebuffer setup is the same as it was for the picking example (see Listing 10-8), as outlined in the framebuffers section of the chapter. This involves using a separate MVP matrix for the light's perspective such as this:

```
var lightMVMatrix = mat4.lookAt([5, 0, 5], [0, 0, 0], [0, 1, 0]);
```

This function call will return the model view matrix representation obtained by setting the light's camera position to [5,0,5], telling it to look at the origin [0,0,0], and that the "up" direction of the camera is [0,1,0]. Our shader program for the first pass, which will calculate and store the nearest depth value of each (x,y) coordinate as seen from the light, is shown in Listing 10-11.

Listing 10-11. *Depth storage shader program*

```html
<script type="x-shader/x-vertex">
        uniform mat4 uLightMVMatrix;
        uniform mat4 uPMatrix;

        attribute vec3 aVertexPosition;

        void main(void) {
                gl_Position = uPMatrix * uLightMVMatrix * vec4(aVertexPosition, 1.0);
        }
</script>
```

```
<script id="shader-fs" type="x-shader/x-fragment">
        //http://spidergl.org/example.php?id=6
        highp vec4 pack_depth( const in highp float depth ) {
                const highp vec4 bit_shift = vec4( 256.0 * 256.0 * 256.0,
                                                   256.0 * 256.0,
                                                   256.0,
                                                   1.0 );
                const highp vec4 bit_mask  = vec4( 0.0,
                                                   1.0 / 256.0,
                                                   1.0 / 256.0,
                                                   1.0 / 256.0 );
                highp vec4 res = fract( depth * bit_shift );
                res -= res.xxyz * bit_mask;
                return res;
        }


        //http://www.nutty.ca/?page_id=352&amp;link=shadow_map
        highp vec4 pack_depth2 (highp float depth)
        {
                const highp vec4 bias = vec4(
                                             1.0 / 255.0,
                                             1.0 / 255.0,
                                             1.0 / 255.0,
                                             0.0
                                                );

                highp float r = depth;
                highp float g = fract(r * 255.0);
                highp float b = fract(g * 255.0);
                highp float a = fract(b * 255.0);
                highp vec4 colour = vec4(r, g, b, a);

                return colour - (colour.yzww * bias);
        }

        void main()
        {
            gl_FragColor = pack_depth( gl_FragCoord.z );
            //gl_FragColor = pack_depth2( gl_FragCoord.z );
        }
</script>
```

In Listing 10-11, the vertex shader is a basic MVP transform, but this time uses the light model view matrix. The fragment shader, although long, has one main line that takes the z coordinate after transformation and stores it as a color value. I have shown two similar packing functions that use the bits of each color channel to store a broader range of depth values. Since the packing functions use a different channel order, the colors of the image, if rendered to the canvas (as shown on the center and right of Figure 10-17), will vary. The first function results in green-blue values and the second results in white-red values.

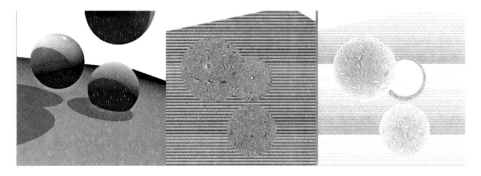

Figure 10-17. *Left: a rendered shadow map; center: first pack function depth map; right: second pack function depth map*

Next, we render the scene a second time and look up the stored depth value for each fragment. If the current fragment is closer than the value stored in the texture, we render it as normal; otherwise, we darken it or make it completely black to represent that it is shadowed. In our application we need to add one more matrix, which converts clipspace coordinates to texture coordinates:

```
shadowBiasMatrix = mat4.create();
mat4.identity(shadowBiasMatrix);
mat4.scale(shadowBiasMatrix, [0.5, 0.5, 0.5], shadowBiasMatrix);
mat4.translate(shadowBiasMatrix, [1.0, 1.0, 1.0, 1.0], shadowBiasMatrix);
```

The contents of the shadowBiasMatrix will be the following:

```
[    0.5, 0.0, 0.0, 0.5,
     0.0, 0.5, 0.0, 0.5,
     0.0, 0.0, 0.5, 0.5,
     0.0, 0.0, 0.0, 1.0
]
```

In the vertex shader, we calculate the shadow coordinate by transforming each input coordinate by the light model view matrix, projection matrix, and then light bias:

```
shadowPosition = uShadowBiasMatrix * uPMatrix * uLightMVMatrix * vec4(vertexShifted, 1.0);
```

This vector is passed on to the fragment shader, in which it is compared with the stored depth value that we pass in as a FBO texture attachment:

```
//////////////////////// shadowmap specific code ////////////////////////
highp vec3 shadowCoordZDivide = shadowPosition.xyz/shadowPosition.w;

highp vec4 rgba_depth = texture2D( uFBOTexture, shadowCoordZDivide.xy );
highp float depth = unpack_depth( rgba_depth );
//highp float depth = unpack_depth2( rgba_depth );

highp float visibility = 1.0;
highp float bias = 0.00005; //used to reduce self shadow, "shadow acne"

if( shadowCoordZDivide.z > (depth - bias) )
{
        visibility = 0.5;
}
```

296

```
////////////////////////   end shadowmap specific code   ////////////////////////
...
gl_FragColor = vec4(color.rgb * visibility, color.a);
```

The first thing we do here is divide the shadowPosition by the homogeneous w coordinate in order to get Cartesian coordinates in the clipspace range. Then we look up the stored depth value for this (x,y) coordinate from our texture uniform. As we packed the depth values in the first shader pass, we now need to unpack the values in order for comparisions to make sense. We will show the implementation of the unpack functions after explaining the rest of the preceding code. Finally, we compare the current fragment z-value, which has been converted to the light projection with the stored value minus a small bias amount. If the input fragment is greater than the stored value, it means that it lies behind a closer fragment that the light can see and so is in shadow.

You can use either pack/unpack function in combination but cannot mix them. The code for the unpack functions is this:

```
//http://spidergl.org/example.php?id=6
highp float unpack_depth( const in highp vec4 rgba_depth ) {
       const highp vec4 bit_shift = vec4(
                                          1.0 / ( 256.0 * 256.0 * 256.0 ),
                                          1.0 / ( 256.0 * 256.0 ),
                                          1.0 / 256.0,
                                          1.0
                                          );
       highp float depth = dot( rgba_depth, bit_shift );
       return depth;
}

//http://www.nutty.ca/?page_id=352&amp;link=shadow_map
highp float unpack_depth2 (highp vec4 colour)
{
       const highp vec4 bitShifts = vec4(
                                          1.0,
                                          1.0 / 255.0,
                                          1.0 / (255.0 * 255.0),
                                          1.0 / (255.0 * 255.0 * 255.0)
                                          );
       );
       return dot(colour, bitShifts);
}
```

The result of this program is displayed on the left of Figure 10-17. The full code is in the 10/12_shadow.html file. Applying a shadow map to the textured, blended, foggy image at the end of Chapter 4 has been demonstrated in the 10/13_all_techniques.html file and is shown in Figure 10-18.

Figure 10-18. *Left: semitransparent objects do not cast a shadow; right: all objects cast a shadow*

In Figure 10-18, the left image enables blending and disables the depth test during the depth pass. On the right, all objects produce shadows. Alternatively, you could pass in a uniform value that varies the shadow visibility based on the amount of transparency.

It is left to the reader to implement this and investigate further techniques such as percentage-closer filtering (PCF), which produces softer shadows and less aliasing.

Summary

This chapter demonstrated a variety of image-processing techniques that can be extended for real-time video processing and animation usage. We have also presented nonphotorealistic rendering and gone over framebuffer basics and setup. Finally, we have shown two applications of using an off-screen framebuffer: picking and a shadow map.

I sincerely hope that you have enjoyed the material presented in this book. There are many more advanced topics that you can now look forward to moving on to, and the knowledge that you gained here should help you on your quest.

Stop by the companion website at http://www.beginningwebgl.com if you have not already done so to give your feedback on the book, report errata, and request and view other tutorials and examples.

In the afterword, we will discuss the future of WebGL—at least as much as can be predicted at this point—based on current browser and mobile support and scheduled feature additions.

AFTERWORD

■ ■ ■

The Future of WebGL

What does the future hold for WebGL? In this afterword, we will discuss both what WebGL has going for it and some concerns, and speculate on its future.

In order for WebGL to have a bright future and not fail like other past 3D browser attempts such as the Virtual Reality Markup Language (VRML), it needs the following:

- Support

- Adoption from the development community, especially game developers

- Improvements and active development

Support

Here we will look at support from browsers and devices.

Browser support

As mentioned in the book introduction, Chrome and Firefox do a very good job of supporting WebGL. Safari and Opera are improving, and IE does not have plans to natively support WebGL anytime soon. While five years ago this could be a disaster, IE does not command the market share that it used to enjoy—Chrome has surpassed it and Firefox is not far behind.

Mobile Device support

The level of mobile devices that currently support WebGL is small but will improve with each new device released and should be much higher in 2013.

Right now, there are several mobile browsers that support WebGL: Firefox Mobile, Android Browser, Opera Mobile (Android only), BlackBerry Playbook, and iOS Mobile Safari (supported for only iAd at the moment).

The mobile market share is growing and is an important area in which to gain ground. As Adobe recently announced that it will be discontinuing mobile Flash support, WebGL has an even better opportunity to establish itself as the go-to technology for mobile 3D.

The site http://webglstats.com/ by Florian Boesch has some very interesting statistics on the current support of various WebGL metrics across browsers, devices, and operating systems.

Adoption

As mentioned in this book, Google has used WebGL for its Body, Map, and Earth applications.

We showed in Chapter 9 that Firefox is using WebGL for a new 3D debugging visualization of the Document Object Model (DOM). It is important to get support and usage from the big name companies, and this is happening with support from Google, Mozilla, Apple and Opera. It is also important to get well-written frameworks that lower the bar to 3D coding. Frameworks such as Three.js are already easy to use and will continue to get better.

What WebGL Has Going for It

- No plugin needed.

- The timing is right. 3D in the browser is more useful now than back when VRML tried. GPUs are more powerful. WebGL is part of the larger movement of HTML5 and related technologies, which adds many browser enhancements which are making it possible to create applications previously only possible on the desktop.

  "For a couple of decades, the web has been sipping that power through a straw but with WebGL, it's as if the straw had been replaced by a fire hose when it comes to graphic processing power..." http://www.tnl.net/blog/2011/10/23/webgl-and-the-future-of-the-web/

- Web applications do not have platform compatibility issues or need to be installed.

- WebGL frameworks are making it easier all the time to get started with WebGL.

- For the experienced graphics programmers, the ability to tweak WebGL at a low level is extremely useful.

- Many awe-inspiring demos.

- Transparent development of the specification.

- Experience and existing developers. Khronos is also in charge of OpenGL and Collada. There are many current OpenGL and OpenGL ES developers who can fairly easily pick up/transition to the WebGL API.

Concerns

WebGL is powerful and very promising. However it is a relatively new language and has some concerns which include these:

- Lack of Microsoft support. As mentioned previously, this is not as big a deal as it would have been when Microsoft dominated the browser demographic. Whether it is not supporting WebGL because of security concerns or because of interest in its own DirectX technology, only Microsoft can say for certain.

- Security concerns. GPU blacklists, and newer graphics cards with improved security will help with GPU concerns. Other web security measures such as cross-origin resource sharing will enable flexibility while maintaining security.

- Flash or other technology being used for 3D instead. As mentioned, Flash discontinuing mobile support helps alleviate this concern.

- Performance issues with JavaScript . JavaScript is slow. Improvements have been made such as typed arrays, and more optimizations are being investigated.

- Game developers need to get on board. This point will now be expanded upon.

Game Developers

An excellent blog entry at `http://codeflow.org/entries/2011/sep/11/webgl-and-html5-challenges-for-the-future/` by Florian Boesch explains how WebGL needs game developers to adopt it. In the entry several features that are needed by game developers are listed with those relating to WebGL specifically being: multiple render targets, geometry instancing, texture lookup in the vertex shader, and floating-point textures. Current support for these features by browser can be found at the webglstats.com link mentioned here.

Active Development

The WebGL specification, future extensions, and browser implementations are all under active development.

Extensions

The WebGL language has extensions to the core that are in development and can be viewed at `http://www.khronos.org/registry/webgl/extensions/`. Of the extensions currently listed, three in particular that will be useful are these:

- Anisotropic filtering, which improves the quality of textures that are viewed at an oblique angle

- Depth textures for shadow maps

- Compressed textures

Future features that could be added soon include these:

- More extensions, such as cross-context sharing or multiple render targets.

- Multithreading in web workers. This would allow uploading textures and data without blocking the main thread.

- Asynchronous context creation and resource sharing between contexts.

The Final Word

Nothing in technology is certain, but I firmly believe that WebGL is here to stay—or I wouldn't have taken the time and energy to write this book. WebGL is a very promising technology being developed at the right time when browsers are under rapid release cycles and are supporting more advanced features daily. It is also a time when more and more powerful computers are being crammed into mobile devices everywhere. WebGL is already a very useable technology. Framework improvements will help lower the bar for new developers, more debug and utility tools will be created, and performance will continue to improve.

■ ■ ■

Essential HTML5 and JavaScript

There are many, many improvements and features that are either part of HTML5 or associated with it: geolocation, new input types, form validation, local storage, and web sockets (to name a few). Covering everything new is both not feasible and not desired here—there are recent large books that do so in depth.

Essential HTML5

While you will not need to know everything new and great about HTML5 to follow along with this book, to maximize your understanding of the code samples we will present the relevant differences from HTML 4 that you need to be aware of.

Brevity

First, HTML5 allows more compact writing of a document by standardizing the opening tags and having shorthand for scripts and styles. In HTML 4, you would have something like code Listing A-1 below:

Listing A-1. A minimalistic HTML 4 document

```
<!DOCTYPE HTML PUBLIC "-//W3C//DTD HTML 4.01//EN" "http://www.w3.org/TR/html4/strict.dtd">
<html>
        <head>
                <TITLE>Example</TITLE>
                <META HTTP-EQUIV="Content-Type" CONTENT="text/html; charset=utf-8">
                <style type="text/css">
                        body{ color: #222222; }
                </style>
                <script type="text/javascript">
                        ...
                </script>
        </head>
        <body>
                <p>Some text</p>
        </body>
</html>
```

With HTML5, the equivalent document is shorter and clearer to write, as shown in Listing A-2. You do not have to declare transitional or strict in your doctype, just the simple and clean `<!doctype html>`. We can also leave out the `type` attribute for the `style` and `script` tags because JavaScript and CSS are the default.

Listing A-2. A minimalistic HTML5 document

```
<!doctype html>
<html>
       <head>
                <meta charset="UTF-8">
                <title>Example</title>
                <style>
                    body{ color: #222222; }
                </style>
                <script>
                        ...
                </script>
       </head>
       <body>
                <p>Some text</p>
       </body>
</html>
```

Semantic Areas

We just showed that HTML5 has some nice shorthand over HTML 4. HTML 5 also lets you outline your document in a more natural and expressive manner. In the past, if you wanted a header and footer area of your page, one way of styling would be to group the relevant content in a `<div>` with an appropriately expressive `id` attribute value such as that shown in Listing A-3.

Listing A-3. HTML 4 document with id used to mark major sections

```
<!DOCTYPE HTML PUBLIC "-//W3C//DTD HTML 4.01//EN" "http://www.w3.org/TR/html4/strict.dtd">
<html>
       <head>
                <META HTTP-EQUIV="Content-Type" CONTENT="text/html; charset=utf-8">
                <title>Example</title>
       </head>
       <body>
                <div id="header">
                        my header stuff
                </div>
                <div id="main-content">
                        <p>Some text</p>
                </div>
                <div id="footer">
                        my footer stuff
                </div>
       </body>
</html>
```

With HTML5, we have many new included tags such as `<header>` and `<footer>`, which make this markup cleaner and the sections more natural as shown in Listing A-4.

Listing A-4. HTML5 document with new semantic tags for major page sections

```
<!doctype html>
<html>
        <head>
                <meta charset="UTF-8">
                <title>Example</title>
        </head>
        <body>
                <header>
                        my header stuff
                </header>
                <div id="main-content">
                        <p>Some text</p>
                </div>
                <footer>
                        my footer stuff
                </footer>
        </body>
</html>
```

Other new structural elements are `article`, `aside`, `figcaption`, `figure`, `hgroup`, `nav`, and `section`. There are new non-structural elements as well—such as `audio`, `canvas`, `time`, and `video`—and new attributes for existing elements, but we will cover only the new `canvas` element in this book.

The `<canvas>` Element

For graphics programming within the browser, the most important difference between HTML 4 and 5 is the addition of the `<canvas>` element. This new element allows the scriptable rendering of graphics within the browser. The `canvas` element has `width`, `height`, and `id` attributes. The area within a canvas element can be manipulated with the JavaScript language. Most modern browsers support the `<canvas>` element, which has markup like this:

```
<canvas id="my-canvas" width="600" height="400">
    Your browser does not support the HTML5 canvas element.
</canvas>
```

The text within the tag is displayed only if the browser does not support the `<canvas>` tag.

`<canvas>` Context

Because canvas supports more than one graphics API, to start rendering in a canvas, we must first specify the API we wish to use. We do this with the `getContext(contextId, args...)` function, where the first argument is the context name such as '2d' or 'webgl,' and additional arguments are optional and dependent on which API is used.

```
<script>
        var canvas = document.getElementById("my-canvas");
        var context = canvas.getContext('webgl');
        //draw something awesome
</script>
```

```
<canvas id="my-canvas" width="600" height="400">
        Your browser does not support the HTML5 canvas element.
</canvas>
```

Essential JavaScript

Ideally the reader has some JavaScript experience. However, some readers will have zero JavaScript experience—possibly coming from the world of OpenGL. If this describes you, I highly recommend doing some independent JavaScript research on a site such as `https://developer.mozilla.org/en/JavaScript`, which presents many very good learning references. In this section, we recap a few basic JavaScript concepts, but it is not intended to be used as a thorough reference.

JavaScript variables are typeless. Variables are declared with `var`:

```
var name = "Brian";
var age = 30;
```

Although typeless, certain operations are dependent on the stored value. Here the "+"operator is used as either addition or string concatenation depending on the context:

```
var one = 1;
console.log(15 + one); //16
console.log("15" + one); //"151"
```

To declare an array:

```
var color = [1.0, 0.0, 0.0];     //or

var color = [];
color.push(1.0);
color.push(0.0);
color.push(0.0);
console.log(color); //[1, 0, 0]
```

To declare an JavaScript Object Notation (JSON) object:

```
var my_object = {};
my_object.name = "Brian";
my_object.age = 30;
my_object.color = [0.0, 0.2, 1.0]
```

or equivalently:

```
var my_object = {
        name: "Brian",
        age: 30,
        color:  [0.0, 0.2, 1.0]
};
```

Although JavaScript has objects, it does not have classes. Objects can simulate class behavior and contain functions:

```
var my_object = {
        name: "Brian",
        age: 30,
        color:  [0.0, 0.2, 1.0],
```

```
        getName: function (){
                return "My name is " + this.name;
        }
};


my_object.getName(); //"My name is Brian"
```

Self-invoking Anonymous Functions

We will sometimes make use of self-invoking anonymous functions, which look like this:

```
(function (){
        //executed immediately
        //not global scope for variables
})();
```

The previous function calls itself (self-invoking) and is nameless (anonymous). An advantage of this type of method is that the scope of all variables declared within it are not global. In this way, it is considered a best practice to wrap part or all of our JavaScript code in a self-invoking function.

A variation of the self-invoking anonymous function is a self-invoking function. For example, in the book we use a named function called animLoop and call it again within each loop—creating an endlessly running loop:

```
(function animLoop (){
        if ( !paused ){
                setupWebGL();
                setMatrixUniforms ();
                drawScene();
        }
        requestAnimationFrame(animLoop, canvas);
})();
```

▮ **Note** The applications in the book use many global variables. This is not a good practice, but easiest and most practical for the types of fairly small standalone applications presented in the book.

---

jQuery

jQuery is a hugely popular JavaScript library available at http://jquery.com/. There is nothing you can do with jQuery that you cannot do with core JavaScript, but you will probably be able to achieve the result quicker and using less but more-readable code.

First, we need to include the jQuery library in our code:

```
<script src="http://code.jquery.com/jquery-latest.js"></script>
```

jQuery enables easy Document Object Model (DOM) traversal. With regular JavaScript, to find an element with id value "super-dog" you would use this:

```
document.getElementById("super-dog");
```

With jQuery you would use one of the following:

```
 $ ("#super-dog");
```

or

```
jQuery("#super-dog");
```

To find the third td cell of the fifth row of an HTML `<table>` with an id of "super-dog" with jQuery you would use this:

```
$("#super-dog tr:5 td:3");
```

So, you can also use CSS selectors! To find all the links on an HTML page with class "menu" and store the href values with jQuery, you would use the following:

```
var links = [];
$ ("a.menu").each (function(){
      links.push ( $(this).attr("href") );
});
```

Both of these operations are not nearly as straightforward with regular JavaScript.

You need to ensure that the entire DOM has loaded before traversing it. Two ways to accomplish this are to place the jQuery code just before the closing `</body>` tag or to wrap code in a document ready block:

```
$(document).ready(function(){
      var links = [];
      $ ("a.menu").each (function(){
            links.push ( $(this).attr("href") );
      });
      consolc.log(links);
});
```

Two more features of jQuery that make it popular are its abstraction of Ajax calls, which we cover in the book, and also its chainability. We can call a function and then call a function on that function, and so on. For example:

```
$ ("#super-dog tr").each (function(){
      $(this).find("td span.new").
            addClass("old").
            removeClass("new").
            closest("tr").
            next().
            find("td span.old").
            addClass("dead").
            removeClass("old");
});
```

This is a contrived example, but it is valid and illustrates the power of jQuery. For each row in the table, we find spans with class "new" and switch them to "old". Then we find the closest tr parent element (we could have nested tables where we have multiple tr parents), find the next sibling row, and this time find spans with "old" classes and change them to "dead" classes.

■ ■ ■

Graphics Refresher

It is assumed throughout this book that the reader has a basic understanding of 3D graphics but we will refresh memories of some relevant topics in this appendix.

Pixels

When we digitally represent an image on a computer screen, it is composed of a rectangular grid of individual points of color known as *pixels*. This type of a representation is known as a *raster graphic* or *bitmap*. How true to the original image the displayed image appears depends on the number of pixels on the screen: the resolution. In Figure B-1, we show an input image on the left, a 4 × 4 pixel grid representation in the center and a 16 × 16 grid representation on the right. As the resolution increases, the difference between the original image to the rendered image decreases.

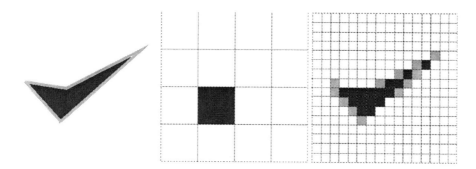

Figure B-1. *Left: an input image; center: 4 × 4 pixel output; Right: 16 × 16 pixel output*

Primitives

Graphics primitives are the smallest building blocks that we can compose images and scenes with. The primitives available to us depend on the language used and can be points, lines, polygons such as triangles and quadrilaterals, or solid shapes in some higher-level languages.

Colors

A color has several properties, including hue (tint), saturation (darkness), and value (intensity). In fact, colors can be represented by these three properties in the Hue-Saturation-Value (HSV) color model. There is more than one way to represent colors, though, depending on whether we are using additive or subtractive color theory, and the application usage such as printing an image or displaying it to a screen.

When we print images, the subtractive CMYK model is often used, which has four channels comprised of Cyan, Magenta, Yellow, and a darkness (K). This is why some printers have a color CMY cartridge and a black cartridge.

On computer monitors, color values are typically expressed using the additive RGBA scheme that has four channels that comprise Red, Green, Blue, and Alpha (transparency) values. Each channel value can range from 0.0 to 1.0 in floating point, 0 to 255 in integer values, or 0×000000 to 0×ffffff in hexadecimal values.

To convert from CMY to RGB we take [(1.0, 1.0, 1.0) - CMY]. So yellow in CMY is (0.0, 0.0, 1.0) and in RGB is (1.0, 1.0, 0.0). In this book, we will exclusively use the RGB(A) color model.

■ **Note**   More information on the RGBA color format can be found on Wikipedia at http://en.wikipedia.org/wiki/RGBA_color_space.

Coordinate Systems

The Cartesian coordinate system is named after the mathematician, philosopher, and writer Rene Descartes and uses (x,y) pairs in two dimensions and (x,y,z) triplets in three dimensions. The origin is the intersection of all the axes. In two dimensions, this is (0,0), and in three dimensions it is (0, 0, 0). For each axis, values increase on one side of the origin and decrease on the other. There are two separate 3D coordinate system orientations, as shown in Figure B-2. The difference between them is the z direction in relation to the x and y axes.

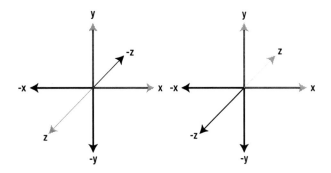

Figure B-2. *Two distinct 3D coordinate system orientations*

Transforms

Elementary or affine transforms alter the vertices of a figure. There are three elementary transforms: translation, rotation, and scaling, as shown in Figure B-3.

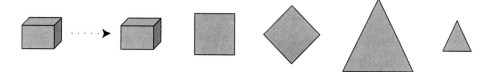

Figure B-3. *Transforms of a translation (left), a rotation (middle), and a scale (right)*

A translation of a painted region 3 positions to the right and 2 positions up is shown in Figure B-4.

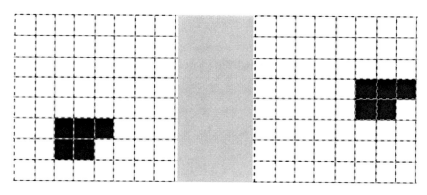

Figure B-4. *Translation of an image*

A rotation of an image subregion 90 degrees clockwise around its center pixel is shown in Figure B-5.

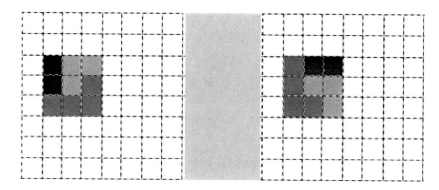

Figure B-5. *Rotation of an image*

A scaling of two times the original size of a painted subregion is shown in Figure B-6.

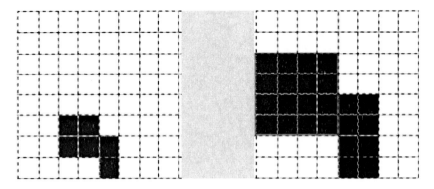

Figure B-6. *Scaling of an image*

Graphics programming uses a lot of mathematics, and although libraries can abstract away much of the calculations, it is good to know some essentials.

Math

The first things that we should know are angles, degrees, pi, and radians.

Angles

An angle is formed when two rays intersect, as shown on the left of Figure B-7. Technically, an angle is a measure of the quotient of the arc length of the two rays and the radius when inscribed inside of a circle, as shown on the right of Figure B-7. A circle has 360 degrees, so angles are sometimes measured in degrees.

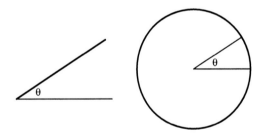

Figure B-7. *Left: two rays forming an inner angle; right: angle inside of a circle*

Pi

The constant number pi, represented as π, is approximately 3.14159 which is the ratio of a circle's circumference to its diameter. Pi is used extensively in trigonometry, geometry, and other branches of mathematics.

Radians

In addition to degrees, we have radians which are defined as 360 degrees = 2π radians. This means that 1 radian is about 57.3 degrees. Figure B-8, shows various angles and the radian values of the four quadrant right angles. Angle A looks to be about 45 degrees and E is about 150 degrees, which makes angle B about 30 degrees. Angle D looks like it is -60 degrees, which would make angle C about 30 degrees.

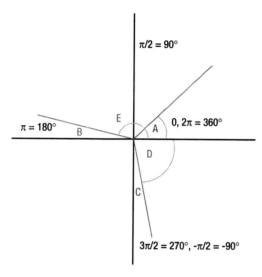

Figure B-8. *Various angles of rotation*

The relations of the angles and sides of a triangle are studied in the branch of mathematics known as trigonometry.

Trigonometry

For a right-angled triangle (one angle is exactly 90 degrees) and another angle θ in the triangle, we can know the ratio of the side lengths. Figure B-9 shows the hypotenuse (side opposite the right angle), opposite and adjacent sides in relation to the angle.

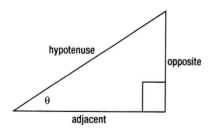

Figure B-9. *The sides of a right-angled triangle*

Given these sides and angle, θ, we can express the angle in terms of the sides as follows:

$\sin \theta$ = opposite/hypotenuse
$\cos \theta$ = adjacent/hypotenuse
$\tan \theta$ = opposite/adjacent

These relations are often memorized as *soh, cah,* and *toa,* which are the acronyms of the relation names and sides.

Rotations

In two dimensions, a rotation uses the rotation matrix:

```
[cosA -sinA] [x] = [xcosA - ysinA]
[sinA  cosA] [y] = [xsinA + ycosA]
```

We can use these equations to calculate the new x, y coordinates after a rotation of A degrees.

Vectors

With two points with coordinates (x_1, y_1, z_1), (x_2, y_2, z_2) we will now define some useful calculations.

Dot Product

The dot product returns a scalar value by returning the sum of component-wise multiplications of two input vectors:

$$x_1{}^*x_2 + y_1{}^*y_2 + y_1{}^*z_2$$

Cross Product

The cross product (x, y, z) returns a vector perpendicular to the plane formed by two input vectors. As such, we use it to find normal vectors. The cross product is computed as follows:

```
x=  y₁*z₂ - y₂*z₁
y= -x₁*z₂ + x₂*z₁
z=  x₁*y₂ - x₂*y₁
```

Length

The length between two points can be calculated as the square root of the sum of the squares of each component difference:

$$\text{squareroot}(\ (x_1-x_2)^2 + (y_1-y_2)^2 + (z_1-z_2)^2\ )$$

WebGL Spec. Odds and Ends

This appendix contains some parts of the specification that we mentioned but did not fully cover and are listed here for reference.

WebGLContextAttributes

When we obtain our WebGL context, we can optionally pass it an object containing some or all of the following properties:

```
dictionary WebGLContextAttributes {
    boolean alpha = true;
    boolean depth = true;
    boolean stencil = false;
    boolean antialias = true;
    boolean premultipliedAlpha = true;
    boolean preserveDrawingBuffer = false;
};
```

We showed how to preserve the drawing buffer in a Chapter 5 projectile example using this:

```
gl = canvas.getContext("webgl", {preserveDrawingBuffer: true}) ||
    canvas.getContext("experimental-webgl", {preserveDrawingBuffer: true});
```

By preserving the buffer contents instead of automatically swapping buffers, we can see the trail of object movement and also produce effects such as motion blur. If performance is key and we do not need alpha or depth testing, we can disable those attributes. If we need the stencil buffer, we can enable it. We showed in Chapter 10 how to disable antialiasing. The premultipliedAlpha value affects how the alpha component of the canvas affects the overall color of the image. Setting this value to false makes the WebGL color calculation of the canvas element the same as the 2D context does.

Texture Properties

In Chapter 3, we glossed over some texture options.

Cube Map Targets

For cube mapped textures, the `target` property can be one of these:

```
TEXTURE_CUBE_MAP, TEXTURE_BINDING_CUBE_MAP,
TEXTURE_CUBE_MAP_POSITIVE_X,TEXTURE_CUBE_MAP_NEGATIVE_X,
TEXTURE_CUBE_MAP_POSITIVE_Y,TEXTURE_CUBE_MAP_NEGATIVE_Y,
TEXTURE_CUBE_MAP_POSITIVE_Z,TEXTURE_CUBE_MAP_NEGATIVE_Z,
MAX_CUBE_MAP_TEXTURE_SIZE
```

texImage2D

Formats for the texture can be as follows:

```
ALPHA:                Alpha
RGB:                  R, G, B color
RGBA:                 R, G, B color and alpha
LUMINANCE:            Luminance
LUMINANCE_ALPHA:      Luminance, alpha
```

And the types can be these:

```
UNSIGNED_BYTE
UNSIGNED_SHORT_4_4_4_4
UNSIGNED_SHORT_5_5_5_1
UNSIGNED_SHORT_5_6_5
```

With the following combinations being legal:

```
UNSIGNED_BYTE / RGBA, RGB, LUMINANCE, LUMINANCE_ALPHA
UNSIGNED_SHORT_4_4_4_4 / RGBA
UNSIGNED_SHORT_5_5_5_1 / RGBA
UNSIGNED_SHORT_5_6_5 / RGB
```

Framebuffer and RenderBuffer Targets and Attachments

In Chapter 10, we introduced framebuffers and renderbuffers. Additional legal attachment/format combinations are these:

```
DEPTH_ATTACHMENT/DEPTH_COMPONENT_16
STENCIL_ATTACHMENT/STENCIL_INDEX8
DEPTH_STENCIL_ATTACHMENT/DEPTH_STENCIL
```

Color attachment: `COLOR_ATTACHMENT0`
Addition formats: `RGBA, RGBA4, RGB5_A1, RGB565, STENCIL_INDEX`

The following concurrent attachment combinations are illegal:

```
DEPTH_ATTACHMENT / DEPTH_STENCIL_ATTACHMENT
STENCIL_ATTACHMENT / DEPTH_STENCIL_ATTACHMENT
DEPTH_ATTACHMENT / STENCIL_ATTACHMENT
```

APPENDIX D

Additional Resources

WebGL is an emerging technology with many aspects. I have done my best to compile good supplemental learning resources in this appendix.

Companion Website

You can find companion websites to this book at the following addresses:

Beginning WebGL
http://www.beginningwebgl.com/

gitHub Page
https://github.com/bdanchilla/beginningwebgl

Due to the volatile nature of the web quickly creating deadlinks, and resources that become obsolete or new resources that spring up, please refer to the companion website for up-to-date revisions of the resources listed in this appendix.

Topics

Further resources for many of the technologies mentioned in this book are listed here (alphabetically).

Ajax

XMLHttpRequest Specification
http://www.w3.org/TR/XMLHttpRequest/

Mozilla XMLHttpRequest Page
https://developer.mozilla.org/En/XMLHttpRequest/Using_XMLHttpRequest

Debugging

Khronos debugging wiki page
http://www.khronos.org/webgl/wiki/Debugging

WebGL Inspector
http://benvanik.github.com/WebGL-Inspector/

Demos

Cutting-edge Chrome WebGL experiments
`http://www.chromeexperiments.com/webgl`

Khronos demo repository
`http://www.khronos.org/webgl/wiki/Demo_Repository`

Nice water demo
`http://madebyevan.com/webgl-water/`

HTML

HTML 5 and 4 differences
`http://www.w3.org/TR/html5-diff/`

Canvas Element
`http://www.w3.org/TR/html5/the-canvas-element.html`

JavaScript

Douglas Crockford site
`http://javascript.crockford.com/`

jQuery
`http://jquery.com/`

JSON
`http://www.json.org/`

LAMP, MAMP, and WAMP

MAMP
`http://www.mamp.info/en/index.html`

XAMPP
`http://www.apachefriends.org/en/index.html`

EasyPHP
`http://www.easyphp.org/`

Bitnami
`http://bitnami.org/`

OPEW
`http://sourceforge.net/projects/opew/`

Browser Setting Adjustment
`https://github.com/mrdoob/three.js/wiki/How-to-run-things-locally`

Libraries and Frameworks

Framework listings
`http://www.khronos.org/webgl/wiki/User_Contributions`

GLGE

Project Page
http://www.glge.org

Tutorial
http://www.rozengain.com/blog/2010/06/23/hands-on-webgl-basic-glge-tutorial/

PhiloGL

Project Page
http://www.senchalabs.org/philogl/

Resources
http://www.slideshare.net/philogb/leaving-flatland-getting-started-with-webgl-sxsw-2012

Three.JS

Project page
https://mrdoob.github.com/three.js/

Documentation
http://mrdoob.github.com/three.js/docs/latest/

Wiki
https://github.com/mrdoob/three.js/wiki

Learning Resources: Paul Lewis
http://aerotwist.com/tutorials/

Learning Resources: Jerome Etienne
http://learningthreejs.com/

Nice Diagrams of Overall Objects
http://ushiroad.com/3j/
http://www.12devsofxmas.co.uk/2012/01/webgl-and-three-js/

Lighting

Direct Illumination models
http://www.lighthouse3d.com/tutorials/glsl-tutorial/directional-lights-ii/
http://www.ozone3d.net/tutorials/glsl_lighting_phong_p3.php

Phong Reflection Model
http://en.wikipedia.org/wiki/Phong_reflection_model

Figure 3-13 is a variation of http://en.wikipedia.org/wiki/File:Phong_components_version_4.png
which is Licensed under the GNU Free Documentation License

Global Illumination Models
http://http.developer.nvidia.com/GPUGems2/gpugems2_chapter38.html

Ambient Occlusion
http://http.download.nvidia.com/developer/GPU_Gems_2/GPU_Gems2_ch14.pdf
http://en.wikipedia.org/wiki/Screen_Space_Ambient_Occlusion
http://www.gamerendering.com/category/lighting/ssao-lighting/

Reflection and Refraction
http://http.developer.nvidia.com/GPUGems3/gpugems3_ch17.html
http://http.developer.nvidia.com/GPUGems2/gpugems2_chapter19.html

Shadow Mapping
http://fabiensanglard.net/shadowmapping/index.php

Mathematics

Wolfram Mathworld
http://mathworld.wolfram.com

Fractals
http://users.erols.com/ziring/mandel.html
http://66.39.71.195/Derbyshire/manguide.html
http://davis.wpi.edu/~matt/courses/fractals/index.htm
http://www.fractalforums.com/

Matrix and Vector Libraries

gl-matrix.js
https://github.com/toji/gl-matrix

sylvester
http://sylvester.jcoglan.com/

webgl-mjs
http://code.google.com/p/webgl-mjs/

Benchmarks
http://stepheneb.github.com/webgl-matrix-benchmarks/matrix_benchmark.html

Mesh File Formats

Wavefront (obj) format
http://en.wikipedia.org/wiki/Wavefront_OBJ

Collada format
http://en.wikipedia.org/wiki/COLLADA

Three.js internal JSON format
https://github.com/mrdoob/three.js/wiki/JSON-Model-format-3.0

Performance and Best Practices

Mozilla Developer Network Best Practices
`https://developer.mozilla.org/en/WebGL/WebGL_best_practices`

Gregg Tavares Google I/O 2011
`http://www.youtube.com/watch?v=rfQ8rKGTVlg`
`http://games.greggman.com/game/webgl-techniques-and-performance/`
`http://static.googleusercontent.com/external_content/untrusted_dlcp/www.google.com/en//`
`events/io/2011/static/notesfiles/WebGLTechniquesandPerformancenotes.pdf`

Profiling with about: tracing
`http://www.html5rocks.com/en/tutorials/games/abouttracing/`

Physics

Learning
`http://www.physicsclassroom.com`

WebGL Demos
`http://www.ibiblio.org/e-notes/webgl/gpu/contents.htm`

Javascript Libraries:

Box 2D Ports
`http://code.google.com/p/box2dweb/`
`https://github.com/kripken/box2d.js`

Bullet Port
`https://github.com/kripken/ammo.js/`

Cannon
`https://github.com/schteppe/cannon.js`

physi.js
`http://chandlerprall.github.com/Physijs/`

Tutorials
`http://creativejs.com/2011/09/box2d-javascript-tutorial-series-by-seth-ladd/`
`http://learningthreejs.com/blog/2012/06/05/3d-physics-with-three-js-and-physijs/`
`http://www.html5gamedevs.com/2012/01/18/webgl-bullet-js-experiences-history-programming-`
`slides/`

WebGL

Current browser support
`http://caniuse.com/#search=webgl`

Khronos group wiki
`http://www.khronos.org/webgl/wiki/Main_Page`
`http://www.khronos.org/webgl/wiki/Tutorial#Creating_the_Shaders`

WebGL Specification
`http://www.khronos.org/registry/webgl/specs/latest/`

Learning WebGL
http://learningwebgl.com/blog/

Mozilla Developer area
https://developer.mozilla.org/en/WebGL

Opera Developer area
http://dev.opera.com/articles/view/porting-3d-graphics-to-the-web-webgl-intro-part-2/

Reference Card
http://www.khronos.org/files/webgl/webgl-reference-card-1_0.pdf

Presentations
http://www.khronos.org/webgl/wiki/Presentations

Tutorials
http://www.html5rocks.com/en/features/graphics

Blending
http://mrdoob.com/lab/javascript/webgl/blending/blendfunc.html

WebGL Future

Challenges and predictions
http://www.irrlicht3d.org/pivot/entry.php?id=1255
http://codeflow.org/entries/2011/sep/11/webgl-and-html5-challenges-for-the-future/
http://www.tnl.net/blog/2011/10/23/webgl-and-the-future-of-the-web/

Support statistics
http://www.riastats.com/
http://webglstats.com/

Extension Registry
http://www.khronos.org/registry/webgl/extensions/

WebGL SL (OpenGL ES SL)

OpenGL ES 2.0 Shading Language version 1.0
http://www.khronos.org/registry/gles/specs/2.0/GLSL_ES_Specification_1.0.17.pdf

WebGL quick reference card available
http://www.khronos.org/files/webgl/webgl-reference-card-1_0.pdf

Online GLSL editors
http://webglplayground.net/
http://spidergl.org/meshade/
http://www.kickjs.org/example/shader_editor/shader_editor.html

Existing shaders
http://code.google.com/p/glslang-library/source/browse/trunk/trunk/glslang/shaders/material/

Index

■ R